bai•dar•ka bi′ darke *n -s* [Russian *baidarka,* dim. of *baidara]:* a portable boat made of skins stretched over wood frames and widely used by Alaskan coastal natives and Aleuts. Also: *baydarka, bidarka, bidarkee, bydarka,* and *bidarky.*

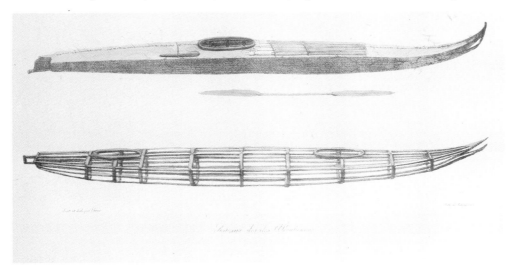

Hunting gear is lashed to the deck of this sleek one-hatch baidarka with decorated seams. Below it is the frame of a two-hatch baidarka that appears to be arbitrarily shortened at the stern.

Lithograph from Choris' Voyage, *1820-1822, after a field sketch made during the Kotzebue expedition of 1815-1818. Courtesy Pacific Northwest Collections, University of Washington Libraries.*

After two days of southeast gales, George Dyson and Kenneth Brower head south into a calm sunrise over Clarence Strait, Alaska, on August 22, 1985.

Joe Ziner

BAIDARKA

The Kayak

George Dyson

With a foreword by Kenneth Brower, author of *"The Starship and the Canoe"*

Alaska Northwest Books™
Anchorage • Seattle • Portland

First printing 1986
Fourth printing 1993

Library of Congress Cataloging-in-Publication Data

Dyson, George B. (George Bernard), 1953–
    Baidarka.

    Includes index.
    1. Bidarkas—Alaska.   2. Aleuts—Boats.   3. Indians
of North America—Boats.   I. Title.
VM357.D95   1986   623.8'29   86-10912
ISBN 0-88240-315-X

Photo credits given next to photos.
All photo descriptions written by author.

Front cover photo by Ann E. Yow. Back cover photos,
clockwise from top right: Lilly Library, Indiana University;
Ann E. Yow; Peter Thomas; George B. Dyson.

Design by Jon.Hersh

Alaska Northwest Books™
An imprint of Graphic Arts Center Publishing Company
Editorial office: 2208 NW Market Street, Suite 300
    Seattle, WA 98107
Catalog and order dept.: P.O. Box 10306, Portland, OR 97201
    800-452-3032

Printed in Singapore

Contents

ACKNOWLEDGEMENTS

The first source of inspiration regarding skin-boat building to acknowledge here is Percy W. Blandford of England. His comprehensive handbook, *Canoeing* (in America this would be termed *Kayaking)*, somehow or other fell into my hands when I was twelve. One of Percy's wooden-skeleton, canvas-skinned designs, a "P.B.K. 13," built on the diagonal in my upstairs Princeton, New Jersey bedroom, was my first boat.

Five years later in an East Pender Street bookstore in Vancouver, B.C., I found, for four dollars, a copy of Howard Chapelle's *The Skin Boats and Bark Canoes of North America,* universally acknowledged as the bible of the skin boat. While wondering in what form to put this gold mine of information to use, I took apart my brother-in-law Jason's tubular aluminum Kelty pack frame — so much lighter and less destructible than the traditional pack frame, made, like the traditional skin boat, out of wood — and discovered the following inscription stamped on the pack frame's ribs: "ALCOA - seamless - 6061-T6 - 0.375 in. O.D. x 0.049 in. wall - Lot # . . ." My first three hundred feet of ½-inch tubing cost $35 and made its way home from the Wilkinson Metals warehouse tied to Jason's bicycle. It became a sixteen-foot Nunivak Island kayak, taken directly from page 198 of Chapelle's book.

That Chapelle considered the Russian-influenced baidarka outside the scope of his work on Native American skin boats only made the baidarka more attractive as a subject for experimentation and research. The Nunivak boat was soon followed by a 31-foot three-hatch baidarka, based upon the lines of a two-hatch model on page 197. This first baidarka, and all the subsequent work represented in this book, began with that Nunivak boat. I bent the aluminum tubing over a piece of wood on my sister Katarina's back porch. Refinements like tube benders, an electric drill, and a hacksaw came later, perhaps obscuring the crude effectiveness of the skin boat's Stone-Age past that was evidenced by this first attempt, when the ends of these tubes were formed by hitting them with a rock. . . .

The next fifteen years, and 317 feet of various baidarkas, are here compressed into an alphabetical list of names. First of all, people who helped me build these boats: Jim Bates, Robert Baron, Michael Berry, John Brower, Dave Cromar, Richard Elson, Jason and Katarina Halm, Verena Huber-Dyson, Penelope Gerbode, George F. Jewett, Jr., Huey D. Johnson, Peter Johnston, Ron Keller, Lou Kelly, Jim Land, Thomas C. Macy, Will Malloff, Stewart Marshall, Jim Peters, Paul Spong, Greg Streveller, Stacy Studebaker, Harry Williams, and Joe and Donna Ziner.

And secondly, people who helped me go beyond boat building to develop the substance and structure of this book: Dr. Lydia Black, David R. Brower, Kenneth Brower, Linda Daniel, Freeman J. Dyson, Frederica de Laguna, Bob King, Jack McIntosh, Professor Richard A. Pierce,

Peter Thomas, Ulli Steltzer, and Ann E. Yow, whose eye for detail brings us the entirety of Part III.

There are many institutions and organizations without which I would not have been able to complete this work, among them: The Anchorage Historical and Fine Arts Museum; The Bancroft Library, University of California; The Beinecke Library, Yale University; The British Columbia Provincial Archives; The Canada Council, Explorations Program; Friends of the Earth, and Friends of the Earth Foundation; The George F. Jewett Foundation; The Limestone Press; The Suzzallo Library, Northwest Collections, University of Washington; The Trust for Public Land; and the Greater Vancouver Regional District, Parks Department, to whom a particular credit is due, for Belcarra Park has now been my home for almost half my life.

Finally, this book owes its existence to the aggregate of life's smaller coincidences, and to those who believed that some of my ideas might work. On a rainy day some eleven years ago, I returned to the unfinished skeleton of the *Mount Fairweather* to find the following anonymous note: "I would like to contribute to your insanity." My thanks to all who did.

George B. Dyson

September 11, 1985

—vii

Paddling toward the sunset past Porcupine Rock, Kenneth Brower and George Dyson near the entrance to Lisianski Strait on the west coast of Chichagof Island. At almost exactly the same place, 244 years earlier (July 18, 1741), the ill-fated Russian landing party from the *St. Paul* had stepped ashore.

Joe Ziner

FOREWORD

In the summer of 1974 I began work on *The Starship and the Canoe,* a double portrait of the physicist Freeman Dyson and his son George. The book was an account of the vessels the two Dysons dreamed of building: Freeman's nuclear-powered spaceship, Orion, which in its most ambitious version was to be the size of Chicago and was destined for some nearby star; and George's canoe, a resurrection of the Aleut kayak that the Russian fur hunters named *baidarka.* It was the story of two men, two arks, two views of man's destiny; and it became my most successful book.

Ten years and some months later, in the spring of 1985, I returned to the coast of British Columbia, the younger Dyson's country, and from George I rented a small cabin to which he holds the lease. I had come for a quiet place to finish a new book, arriving just as George, as chance would have it, was applying the finishing touches to this one. In the years since publication of *The Starship and the Canoe,* my interests and itinerary had wandered — a book on whales; two books on the islands of Micronesia; stories on malacologists, wood-carvers, ranchers, naturalists; sojourns in Hawaii, Quebec, The Galapagos Islands, Nepal, and other places. Freeman Dyson, too, had followed various whims — work on ice ponds as energy sources, on solar sails, on gravitation and galaxies, on underwater sound detection, on the origin of life, on two well-received and influential books, *Disturbing the Universe* and *Weapons and Hope.* George Dyson was rooted still in the fir-and-cedar forest above Indian Arm of the Strait of Georgia. George was still building canoes.

I had not speculated much about the future, in the course of writing about the Dysons in the seventies, but one thing I had known. George's attempt to revive the Aleut baidarka was admirable but quixotic, I believed, and I was certain that in ten years he would be doing something else, something more sensible. I remember trying to guess what turns his life would take, what trade the canoe-builder would be following ten years hence. All those guesses were wrong. Of the three of us, the Dysons and their biographer, George was by far the most tenacious and linear.

Everywhere in the clearing about his house, resting upside down on wooden racks, were baidarkas. Nearest the white-gravel road, bottom up, dragon-head prow down, paint somewhat duller for ten years of weather, was *Mount Fairweather,* the biggest kayak in history, a dreadnaught of baidarkas, forty-eight feet long, with manholes for six paddlers — George's one attempt at the grandiose, his equivalent to his father's starship. George, my brother John, and I had taken this super-baidarka on its maiden voyage north. I had ended my book on the Dysons with an account of that trip, and it was good to see the big kayak again. On racks downslope lay several three-man baidarkas from the six-baidarka fleet of George's 1977 expedition to Alaska.

The house itself was kayakized, baidarkafied. From the boughs of tall firs outside, wind chimes fashioned from varying lengths and diameters of aluminum pipe, the same aluminum George bends to make his baidarka skeletons, clashed in the sea breeze. Each note was as random and plangent, as bright and reverberant, as some new ideas for the improvement of baidarkas. In the basement workshop, illuminated by windows George had added in building a shedlike extension southward, rested the silvery skeleton of a baidarka in progress. At the prow, a pair of surgeon's clamps held the lashings in place, marking the point where he had left off work. Upstairs were the desks at which he sketches his baidarka plans, the drawing tables at which he lofts his baidarka lines. On the walls were photographs and drawings of baidarkas under sail or propelled by paddles. There were watercolors of the Inside Passage country George's canoes were built to navigate, fish prints of the halibut and rockfish he jigs from his canoe manholes. On his homemade light table, slides of baidarkas, the illustrations for this book, were spread out. There was a wood-burning stove. A piano. A golden retriever — Zephyr, adopted by George and Ann Yow, his photojournalist wife, at a swap meet. Ann's darkroom, in which prints for possible covers of this book had been made. Ann's two cats. Ann's garden, outside the south-facing window. Ann's sugar peas beginning their green climb of the stakes. In George's small office, an office built as tight and motion-efficient as the bridge of any ship, beneath homemade shelves lined with pilot books — volumes of Russian-American history, books on sailing, canoes, navigation — atop the desk George has customized around his typewriter, the last manuscript pages for *Baidarka* made a neat stack.

An open, paneless window above the desk looked out on a long glass window that ran the length of the room. That long window in its turn looked out at Indian Arm. The stretch of water framed doubly there was George's inspiration, lofting his canoe lines or speeding his sentences when those began wilting or dragging. That same stretch of water — I knew from having watched him work — was also his distraction, abducting him from canoe lines half-drawn and from sentences in need of finishing. The inlet gave and the inlet took, tugging tidally at George's endeavors just as it tugged at its finger of the sea. At one end of the window was the easy chair in which George sat cross-legged, drawing board in lap, to work longhand when the office grew too confining. A pair of binoculars rested on the table beside the chair. On the windowsill, within reach, were a turn-of-the-century guide to weather and Peterson's *A Field Guide to Western Birds*. The room was a pleasure to inventory. I had been there nearly an hour before I chanced to lean close to the long window, looked downward, and saw the latest canoe.

It rested, trim and white as a gull, beside the woodpile above George's small beach. It was more elegant and beautiful than anything he had built before. George's baidarkas were evolving toward simplicity. His canoes had come full circle, strangely or not, and they were converging once again with the Aleut prototype.

"What's this?" I asked, waving at the canoe. I was surprised that he had not introduced us. He smiled and led me down to it.

Ten years before, while drilling holes in the rudder plates for *Mount Fairweather*, I had found myself wondering whether this vessel might not be too big — whether at forty-eight feet George was taking the kayak idea further than it would comfortably go. George, I learned later, even then was coming to the same conclusion. Like any artist working a theme, he had felt obligated to push to his limits. Now, downscaling his craft, George was recapitulating baidarka history in reverse. He had left behind the super-baidarka of the Aleut future — a future that never was, thanks to the Russian discovery of northwestern America and of sea otters. He had experimented for most of the decade of the seventies with three-hole baidarkas, a Russian elaboration of the basic Aleut idea; then he had left that, too, behind. He had arrived now, with this new canoe below his window, at a baidarka with two manholes for paddlers, the number the Aleuts had favored in the largest of their canoes. In his three-hole days, in the absence of a brand of canvas tough enough to satisfy him, he had covered his baidarka skeletons with fiberglass. He had since found a nylon fabric he liked, and the new baidarka was covered in that — a material much closer in weight to the sea-lion skins the Aleuts had used, light yet durable, drum-tight when I thumped it with a finger. George lifted the bow, I hoisted the stern, and together we effortlessly turned the new baidarka hatch-side up. In 1974 we had made a long

Kenneth Brower (forward) and George Dyson (aft) settle in aboard a 24-foot two-hatch baidarka on the deceptively calm waters of Torch Bay, on the Gulf of Alaska coast. They are preparing to retrace their southward journey of 1974, for a Japanese television documentary based on Kenneth's book, *The Starship and the Canoe.*

Joe Ziner

Alaskan trip in his first three-hole canoe, and I remembered how, straining like Egyptian slaves, we had hauled that ponderous boat up the beach every night on log rollers or slipways of kelp. This canvas was progress. In his three-hole baidarkas, and in the six-holer, George had added a dragon-head prow, a sort of Nordic after-thought to the Aleut idea, a personal signature. With some regret he had abandoned the dragon, and the new prow was pure Aleut again. The decking of his old fiberglass canoes had been painted in Northwest Indian designs — never George's idea so much as that of artist friends who happened by his shops. I had grown accustomed to the Northwestern motifs, and the new canoe looked blank and unfinished without them. "I'm not going to paint

them anymore," George said. I realized only then that unpainted was right, perfect. It had been a mistake ever to ornament these baidarkas. A sea-bird albedo was the only color for an ocean-going kayak.

I tried to imagine some improvement in design, func-tional or artistic, and I failed. When I murmured something to this effect, George assured me there were plenty of things to refine. They all glared at him. He had already begun his list of things to fix in the next genera-tion of canoes.

Studying the latest baidarka, as it rested above its beach of shell and stone in British Columbia, I began to see the craft as an argument for place — for staying put and sticking to one thing. I thought about all the peregrinations, thematic and geographic, of my own career. In the past ten years, I asked myself, had my own style improved as much, clarified itself so? It had not.

The following pages are a history of a craft and of an obsession.

Like any good history, this one is full of surprising facts: that the Aleuts and their baidarkas traveled as far south as San Francisco Bay, where they cleaned out the sea otter, then farther still, halfway down the desert peninsula of Baja, California, a subarctic fleet venturing deep into the subtropics; that baidarkas showed up, indeed, in Micronesia, aboriginal American boats invading the atolls of the tropical Pacific, the province of the outrigger canoe. Like any good history, this one has humor. George Dyson is serious about baidarkas, and most of the old baidarka testimonials he quotes are full of sober admiration, but when a nineteenth-century traveler like Glidden jokes about the difficulty of "osculatory demonstrations" (kissing) in baidarkas, for the reason that the paddling holes were so far apart, George has the good sense to include it. (Perhaps it is a difficulty he has encountered himself.) Like most honest histories, this one has tragedy: the decimation and near extinction of the sea otter, the defeat and cultural annihilation of the Aleuts. This history is full of the small truths that make any history real and readable: Blaschke's observation, for one, that he saw amazing sights from his baidarka, sights that he would have enjoyed much more had he not been stiff with cold. (I have traveled by baidarka and I will second that.)

Yet the following history, as fine and accurate as I believe it to be, in a sense only masquerades as history. Underneath, it is a credo, a self-search and self-explanation.

I don't know why George Dyson builds baidarkas, and I wonder whether he himself knows exactly. I imagine that from time to time his own persistence dismays him.

I wrote half a book about the baidarka-builder without coming up with an answer, though I have vague ideas. How is it that a *vessel*, trim and gull-like though it be, could so take up residence in one man's dreams, in his private iconography? What is it in the baidarka's simplicity, or swiftness, or silence; in its feather-lightness or tautsidedness, or in the womblike way it embraces its paddler, that resonated so in a boy from Princeton, New Jersey? It is probably foolish to wonder. Why did Rembrandt fall in love with oils or Rutherford with electrons or Mendel with peas?

The following is a history unmarred by bias of any damaging sort, yet full of baidarka chauvinism. When George Dyson recounts the baidarka's superiority in grace and maneuverability to the *shitiki* of the Russians and other European boats that came after, it is hard to miss his satisfaction. It is apparent, between his lines, that in Davydov and other baidarka adventurers of past centuries he has found alter egos. The historian's surprise and pleasure in learning, and in passing on, the fact that John Muir once made a canoe trip against the tide in a strait where a century later the historian himself fought the tide in his baidarka, is the surprise and pleasure of someone whose search of the family tree turns up a horse thief or a queen. This book is one man's search for his antecedents, a genealogy of forebears — not blood kin but spiritual.

Ken Brower

Wasagaming, Manitoba
September, 1985

In my opinion, these baidarkas are the best means yet discovered by mankind to go from place to place...

—G.H. von Langsdorff, 1814

**Overleaf: "Natives of Oonalashka, and their Habitations,"
seen against a rugged landscape, were drawn by John
Webber in 1778. An Aleut family is atop their barabara,
while the ubiquitous baidarka is both afloat and ashore.**

*Watercolor by John Webber. Courtesy Peabody Museum, Harvard
University (photo by Hillel Burger).*

A Chain of Events

As the inhabitants of islands, the Aleuts of necessity have to have some kind of boats in order to pass from one island to another . . . But, nature failed to provide them with the material necessary for boats, that is, wood; but on the other hand, as if in compensation, she gave them greater ingenuity for the perfection of a special new kind of fleet: the baidarka.

—**Ivan Veniaminov, 1840**

Choris del.

Imp. Lith. de Bove dirigée par Noel ainé & Ce.

Vue de l'île de St Paul dans la mer de Kamtchatka (avec des lions marins)

T wo distinct groups of people made the shores of the eastern North Pacific their home: those who built dugout canoes and those who built skin boats. All the contrasts between virgin rain forest and barren island were reflected in their opposing techniques, yet the resulting vessels displayed equally sparse and graceful lines. The dugout builders took an enormous chunk of wood and eliminated everything, down to splinters, that was not essential to their definition of a boat. The skin-boat people, working in reverse, began their boats from splinters, piecing together a framework that delineated the bare minimum of their vessel. The dugout, of living cedar, was a creature of the forest. The baidarka, of driftwood, whalebone, and sea-lion skin, was entirely a creature of the sea.

The skin boat was a circumpolar concept. Along all northern coastlines, and on inland waterways as well, these craft ranged southward as far as materials, climate, and hostile forest-dwellers would permit. A hundred and fifty years ago Russian adventurers carried baidarkas with them on winter expeditions to Mexico, Hawaii, and even Micronesia, only to find the otherwise serviceable skin boats rendered useless as the equatorial sun melted the whale-fat waterproofing from their seams. Even in the refrigerated north, the skin boat's biodegradable components left archaeologists with scarcely a trace. We cannot be sure who were the first builders of these craft or when it was that the Aleuts — or pre-Aleuts — began paddling to and from their remote outposts in the sea.

Colony of sea lions separates Aleut in a baidarka, with two puffins at his side, from the *Rurik,* Kotzebue's vessel. Rig is typical of the Russian vessels of the time.

Lithograph from Choris' Vues et paysages, *1826; after field sketches made in 1816. Courtesy Beinecke Library, Yale University.*

The earliest known settlements among the Aleutian Islands date back more than eight thousand years. The skin boat might have migrated to the Aleutians from somewhere else, or it might have been invented there independently, perhaps in a period of post-glacial isolation, as the rising sea level forced land-based nomadic hunters to put their ice age-sharpened minds and tools to building boats. The kayak's ancestry can be traced to a practice evidenced among landlocked hunting cultures of both Asia and America: stuffing an animal skin with willow branches as an improvised, spur-of-the-moment boat.

"They say that their forefathers came from their original dwelling-places in the west [Asia] . . ." wrote the missionary and pioneer Alaskan ethnologist Ivan Veniaminov, concerning the origins of the Aleuts. "In that country there were no storms, no winters, but constant pleasant atmosphere, and the people lived peaceably and quietly; but in the course of time quarrels and intertribal wars compelled them to move farther and farther to the eastward, until they finally reached the sea-coast. Later they were even compelled to take to the water. But even on the coast they could not remain in peace, being pressed by other people, and therefore were compelled to seek refuge on the islands; and finally, traveling from island to island, they settled in their present villages."[1]

At the time of Vitus Bering's arrival in 1741, the Aleuts are estimated to have numbered between 10,000 and 25,000, more than the aboriginal population of the Ohio Valley, Florida, New York State, or New England. The Aleutian Islands were barren but the sea around them was rich. Until less than 250 years ago, the population existed in "pre-contact" times. Two hundred years ago, after contact had been made, the Northwest Coast of America still was shifting unpredictably from map to map. When Captain Cook arrived on the Alaskan Coast in 1778, he found that the latest maps he had brought with him from Europe showed some of the Aleutian Islands intentionally misplaced — by secretive Russian fur merchants who wished to keep the islands to themselves.

Yermak's campaign across Siberia in the 1580s had led the way for Russian fur hunters to reach the Pacific Coast. Spreading across hundreds of thousands of square miles, with less than a thousand men, Yermak's band of Cossacks succeeded in one of the greatest conquests of enemy territory the world has ever seen. Supplied with weapons, food, and encouragement by the merchants of the Stroganov family, Yermak's Cossacks were, according to an agreement paraphrased by Richard Pierce, "to pay for the supplies from their spoils, or, if they perished during the expedition, they were to redeem the expenses incurred by the Stroganovs by prayer in the next world." Within fifty years or so, Yermak's followers and their descendents — with an added measure of criminals, political exiles, and adventurous camp-followers thrown in — reached the Pacific Coast, and, under similar contracts with their merchant backers, some of them began building crudely sewn-together vessels and taking to the sea.

Sea-otter pelts, each worth a small fortune in trade with the Chinese, were what led these Russian *promyshlenniks,* or fur hunters, to willingly accept the risks. If the treacherous Pacific cast them upon some unknown — and thus otter-infested — reef, some of the crew paid with their lives while others divided an increased share of pelts.

As the Russians pushed eastward toward America along the Aleutian chain, at every inhabited island they were greeted by vessels made from skins. The word *baidara,* a term originating on the rivers of the Ukraine, was used to describe the Natives' larger, open, skin-covered craft, while the diminutive of this, *baidarka,* referred to the

distinctively hatched, smaller species of decked skin boat. The Russians commandeered all available baidarkas to hunt sea otters on their behalf, and demanded that more of them be built. The larger baidaras, too clumsy for the hunt, were confiscated to carry supplies, and to prevent the men from launching a mass attack or taking their families with them and making an escape. Armed resistance was hopeless, and any insurrection brought swift and bloodthirsty revenge. The aboriginal culture suffered wholesale upheaval and entire settlements collapsed. "God is high above, and the Czar is far away," was the unofficial motto of the campaign. Only cooperative Aleuts who served the Russian purpose were able to survive, saved by the skin of their boats.

The Russians were landsmen. Whether merchants or exiles, most arrived at Okhotsk on foot. The vessels that transfered them to Kamchatka, then along the Aleutian Islands and finally to mainland Russian America, were crude galiot-rigged craft, centuries behind their time. The Russian skippers practiced only the rudiments of navigation, blindly "following the fence" from island to island, often returning without knowing exactly where they had been. Shipwreck was all too common and near-escape the rule.

So it was that the Russians cast their lot with the Aleuts. They lived in Aleut semi-subterranean dwellings, ate Aleut food, took Aleut wives with whom they had half-Aleut children, and depended on Aleut boats. In their dependence on the baidarka, the Russians appropriated the central element in the culture of the Aleuts. In the shape of the baidarka, Aleut ethnology and technology were inseparably intertwined. The Russians could not get the one without the other; they began to see things from an Aleut frame of mind.

The Russians widened the baidarka's beam along with its use, and extended its length as well as its range. Before the traffic in skins wiped out their local sea otters, the Aleuts had had no need to forage any great distance from their homes. They had carried little with them beyond the implements of the hunt, attached securely to the baidarka's narrow deck. Their boats were not designed for the bulky spoils of Russian trade. Until Russians grew tired of paddling — making the rounds of subjugated islands collecting furs for themselves and the czar — there had been little reason to add a passenger's manhole in the center of the Aleut boats. Before their conversion to the Russian Orthodox faith, the Aleuts needed no three-hatch baidarkas to carry around the fathers of the church. Their own shamans and wizards either flew from island to island in supernatural form, or paddled their own boats.

The baidarka and its Aleut paddlers provided the Russians with a means of communication along stretches of coastline inaccessible to any other craft. The logistics defy comparison; the advance of the Russian baidarka fleets constituted as detailed a survey by a foreign power as the North Pacific has ever known. By comparison, the British and American traders merely touched the surface of the Northwest Coast. "This boat and the Aleuts who supplied its motive power were the key to Russian activity during the entire pre-1867 period," writes Richard Pierce, who has translated and edited many of the Russian sources included in this book. "Without these auxiliaries, the Russians would have had to content themselves with trading, as did the New Englanders on the coast . . . With this very adaptable form of locomotion the Russians were able to live much closer to the land and its inhabitants. Almost anywhere they went, for hunting or exploration, they depended on the baidarka."

At the turn of the nineteenth century, fleets of six and seven hundred baidarkas were sweeping annually across the Gulf of Alaska, the ranks of Koniag, Chugach, and Aleut paddlers tightened into close formation by a mutual fear of the mainland's Tlingit tribes. The journey was hard on the boats and tougher on the men. After a storm or enemy attack, crippled baidarkas were cannibalized to repair the less seriously injured craft. The survivors spent the winter building new boats in preparation for the next year's hunt. Baidarkas were being built by the thousands in the Russian-American colonies for close to one hundred years.

The design of the baidarka was never fixed. It varied according to fashion, adapted to changing function, and, above all, it searched for speed. Minute attention was paid to subtle differences in each baidarka's streamlined curves. The Gulf of Alaska, with its endless succession of storms and shallow, tide-swept seas, tank-tested the results of the baidarka's "genetic drift." Even during the final years of the sea-otter hunt, with American support vessels and repeating firearms appearing on the scene, the baidarka still earned its living through outmaneuvering one of the most evasive creatures of the sea.

The Russian hunters and explorers brought the baidarka to mainland North America more than two centuries ago, one step at a time along the Aleutian chain. When Russian America was ceded to the United States in 1867, the baidarka was thrown in as part of the deal, with fifty years or so left before the baidarka and the sea otter together grew commercially extinct. The next step in this chain of events is up to us, as heirs to a technology the Russians first learned from the Aleuts. I foresee a renaissance of the baidarka, reconstructed out of inanimate materials for purposes besides the hunt. But first we must look back, at the record left by the baidarka in the course of finding its way into our hands.

Thirty-five two-hatch baidarkas underway at Port Dick, near Cook's Inlet, comprised a small portion of the hunting party under Purtov — more than five hundred such boats.

Engraving from a sketch drawn "on the spot" (aboard the Chatham) *by Humphrys on May 16, 1794. Baidarkas to be added later, says a penciled note on the original sketch. From Vancouver's* Voyage, *1798, Vol. III. Courtesy Provincial Archives of British Columbia.*

The History of the Baidarka

It is all but impossible to find an early account of the inhabitants of Alaska that does not begin with a description of their boats, the Natives being all but inseparable from their craft. It is equally impossible to describe the baidarka without entering into a description of the Aleuts, "an integral part of the boat,"[2] as one later observer would refer to them.

Although Vitus Bering, a Dane in the service of the Russian Crown, is credited with the discovery of Alaska, he was preceded, by at least nine years, in glimpsing the American shoreline and its ubiquitous skin-covered canoes. In August of 1732, Michael Spiridovinich Gvozdev, a geodesist in command of the *St. Gabriel,* acting under the instructions first given to Bering in 1725,[3] fell in with the Alaskan coastline — a "Large Country" thought to be an island — somewhere near Cape Prince of Wales. As they passed King Island, one of the inhabitants became the first Alaskan kayaker of whom a written description has survived:

There came to us from the island a Chukchi in a leather boat which had room but for one man. He was dressed in a shirt of whale intestines which was fastened about the opening of the boat in such a manner that no water could enter even if a big wave should strike it. He told us that Chukchi lived in the Large Country, where there were forests, streams, and animals.[4]

Nine years later, Bering's second expedition, aboard the *St. Peter* and the *St. Paul,* two eighty-foot vessels built by Bering's crewmen at Okhotsk, made the first European contact with the people of the Aleutian Islands. It is from this moment that the recorded history of the Aleut baidarka begins. With Bering aboard the *St. Peter* was the German naturalist Georg Wilhelm Steller, whom Bering found to be stubborn, outspoken, and meticulous to an extreme. Steller's journals provide our most detailed account of the voyage, and shed a coldly objective light on its commander's progressively deteriorating spirits, judgment, and health. The voyage — documents from both sides having survived — takes the form of a tragic drama, with the Supreme Truth of Science, in the person of Steller, played against Bering's Absolute Law of Command.

Both were remarkable men. The navigator left his name to an island, a strait, and a sea; the naturalist left his to a sea lion, a sea cow, and a jay. It is Steller who describes the Russians' first meeting with American Natives, at the Shumagin Islands (where Nikita Shumagin had died of scurvy, the first victim of the disease that would soon decimate the crew). On September 5, 1741, while seeking shelter from a rising westerly gale and "without expectation or search," wrote Steller, "we chanced to meet with Americans. We had scarcely dropped the anchor when we heard a loud shout from the rock to the south of us, which at first, not expecting any human beings on this miserable island twenty miles away from the mainland, we held to be the roar of a sealion. A little later, however, we saw two small boats paddling towards our vessel from shore."[5]

"With the greatest eagerness and full of wonder," the Russians gazed in amazement at these amphibious strangers, while Steller proceeded to take notes:

The American boats are about two fathoms long, two feet high, and two feet wide on the deck, pointed towards the nose but truncate and smooth in the rear. To judge by appearances, the frame is of sticks fastened together at both ends and spread apart by crosspieces inside. On the outside this frame is covered with skins, perhaps of seals, and

*coloured a dark brown. With these skins the boat
is covered flat above but sloping towards the keel
on the sides; underneath there seems to be affixed
a shoe or keel which at the bow is connected with
the bow by a vertical piece of wood or bone
representing a stem piece, so that the upper surface
rests on it. About two arshins [56 inches] from the
rear on top is a circular hole, around the whole of
which is sewn whale guts having a hollow hem with
a leather string running through it, by means of
which it may be tightened or loosened like a purse.
When the American has sat down in his boat and
stretched out his legs under the deck, he draws this
hem together around his body and fastens it with
a bowknot in order to prevent any water from
getting in . . . The American puts his right hand into
the hole of the boat and, holding the paddle in the
other hand, carries it thus because of its lightness
on to the land anywhere he wants to and back from
the land into the water. The paddle consists of a
stick a fathom [six feet] long, at each end provided
with a shovel, a hand wide. With this he beats alternately to the right and to the left into the water and
thereby propels his boat with great adroitness even
among large waves.[6]*

These first two American kayakers to approach the
Russian strangers must have been fearless and brave
indeed — either the elder statesmen of their tribe, or
young men out to prove their courage in the face of the
unknown. "When yet about half a verst [⅓ mile] distant
from us," noted Steller, "both men in their boats began,
while still paddling, simultaneously to make an uninter-
rupted, long speech in a loud voice of which none of our
interpreters could understand a word. We construed it
therefore as either a formula of prayer or incantation, or
a ceremony of welcoming us as friends . . ."[7]

Steller's accurate reporting was not always matched by
subsequent journalists who relied upon his notes. In
Stepan P. Krasheninnikov's *Explorations of Kamchatka,*

**Frame of a large, open, skin boat was found by
La Pérouse at Lituya Bay in July of 1786. Evidently it was
a monument to a party of Natives recently drowned in
the entrance to the bay.**

*Engraving, after a drawing by Lieutenant Blondela, in the atlas to
La Pérouse's* Voyage, *1799. Courtesy Pacific Northwest Collection,
University of Washington Libraries.*

PIROGUE DU PORT DES FRANÇAIS.

published at St. Petersburg in 1755 (and the very first printed work to include an illustration of a baidarka), the above episode surfaced, somewhat misrepresented:

They have only one oar, several fathoms long; they use both ends of it with such agility and so successfully that head winds do not prevent them from going out, and they are not even afraid of being at sea in storms, whereas they are alarmed at the sight of our large ships tossed by the waves, and shout warnings to those who are in the ships to be careful lest they tip over, which happened to the Gabriel *[Gvozdev's vessel] several years ago when she sailed toward Cape Chukotsk.*[8]

Krasheninnikov's interpretation, for all we know, may have been partly right. If the Aleuts were not exactly shouting warnings, surely they must have been commenting under their breath concerning the top-heavy rigging of the unstable-looking Russian ships. The significance of Krasheninnikov's description, besides being the first to be published in the mass media of his day, is that we see the Russians immediately recognized the seaworthiness of the Aleut baidarka in comparison with their own cranky, outmaneuvered craft.

Among the first things the Russians learned about the baidarka was its superiority over their own boats for getting on and off the beach. "They both paddled towards shore and beckoned us to follow in order that they might give us to eat and drink," wrote Steller, who, with eleven others, climbed into the *St. Peter's* longboat to follow the Natives ashore. "The greatest misfortune was that we were not able to make a landing, because the beach was very rocky, the tide rapidly rising; wind and waves were

Tlingit dugout canoe is typical of vessels seen by La Pérouse at Lituya Bay in 1786.

Engraving after a drawing by Lieutenant Blondela, in the atlas to La Pérouse's Voyage, *1797. Courtesy Pacific Northwest Collection, University of Washington Libraries.*

likewise so high that with the greatest difficulty we kept the boat from being dashed to pieces," though this did not prevent an exchange of hospitality:

One of them got into his boat, which he had lifted with one hand and carried under his arm to the water, and came paddling up to us. He was made welcome with a cup of brandy, which, following our example he emptied quickly, but also immediately spit out again, and acted strangely, as if he did not seem to be any too well pleased with this fancied deception. Although I advised against such things as tobacco and pipes, our gentlemen opined nevertheless that the Americans had the stomachs of sailors and consequently, intending to neutralize the first displeasure with a new one, gave the stranger a lighted pipe of tobacco, which he accepted indeed, though paddling away quite disgusted.[9]

Within hours of Steller's encounter, Bering's lieutenant Alexei Chirikov and the *St. Paul* dropped anchor at Adak Island, some seven hundred miles to the west. The two vessels, having left Kamchatka in company, became separated in a gale on the twentieth of June, never to meet again. Chirikov fell in with the American Coast near 57°N, and on July 18 sent eleven men ashore in the longboat for water, near the entrance to what is now Lisianski Strait. After waiting six days in vain for their return, he sent the remaining boat ashore with four men; it, too, disappeared. With no more boats, and strong suspicions of foul play,[10] Chirikov gave up the search and headed home. He stopped at Adak Island, where the local baidarkas were the boatless Russians' only means of getting a drink. Chirikov entered his record of this first encounter in the journal of the *St. Paul:*

At the tenth hour in the morning seven small boats, one man in each, were seen rowing towards us. Each of these boats was about fifteen feet long,

Drawing of "An American in a Sealskin Boat" is a detail from a chart of the voyage of the *St. Peter* in 1741 — the Russians' first encounter with Aleuts, and the earliest illustration of a baidarka known to exist.

Original drawing by Sofron Khitrov or Sven Waxel, in the Archives of the Ministry of Marine, Leningrad. Photocopied by F.A. Golder in 1914. Courtesy Special Collections Division, University of Washington Libraries.

three feet wide, the bow very sharp, the stern somewhat rounded and blunt, and the whole covered with hair seal and sealion skins. The deck was roundish and, like the sides, was sewed with some kinds of skins except one spot between the center and the stern, where there was a round hole in which the man sat. He was dressed in a kind of shirt which covered his head and his arms and was made from the intestines of a whale or some other animal. There was something outside the hole that resembled leather breeching and which tied around the man. Some of these breechings were not tied, and we could see that there were rocks in the boats. They have light double paddles, made of birch wood, with which they paddle on both sides; and, as far as we could make out, the men were quite fearless in the water. They were not deterred by any kind of waves or seas and went through the water at a rapid rate . . .[11]

The Aleuts thought little of the Russians' first attempts at trade, opened by Chirikov's gift of a Chinese cup thrown to one of the kayakers, who "after examining it made a gesture as if to indicate that he had no use for it." The Aleuts showed equal disregard for two pieces of silk and the other Russian gifts: "small boxes, small bells, needles, Chinese tobacco, and pipes." Chirikov then appealed to the Natives on humanitarian grounds: "It was only after we made them to understand that we were out of water and had nothing to drink and that we looked to them for help that one of them dared approach us," he wrote. After further fruitless attempts to lure the Natives aboard with trinkets of dubious use, the Russians at last stumbled upon the Aleuts' preferred medium of exchange. We now know that the Aleuts had long been trading bits of iron among themselves, and, via their Bering Sea neighbors, with Asian cousins to the west:

Among them we noticed several who raised one hand to their mouth and with the other hand made a quick motion as if cutting something near the mouth. This gave us the idea that they wanted knives, because the Kamchadals and the other peoples of this region when they eat meat or anything of that kind cut it at the mouth. I ordered that a knife should be given them, and when they saw it they were overjoyed and seized it from one another and with great eagerness begged for more. We then invited as many of them as would to come aboard so that we might show them friendly attentions and persuade some of them to accompany us, as the instructions of the Captain Commander required. Not being able to understand one another, we not only failed to persuade them to go with us but even to coax one of them to come on board so that we might show them how friendly we really were. We gave them a small barrel in which to bring us water from the shore. They understood what we meant, but they would not take the barrel and showed us that they had bladders for that purpose. Three of them paddled towards the beach and returned with water. When they came alongside one of them held up a bladder and indicated that he wished to have a knife in payment. This was given to him; but, instead of handing over the bladder, he passed it to the second man, who also demanded a knife. When he got it he passed the bladder to the third man, who equally insisted on a knife. This act, as well as some other things they did, proves that their conscience is not highly developed.[12]

One wonders what the islanders had to say concerning the conscience of these foreigners, who in a few short years overran the entire Aleutian chain. "I had few men on deck but had concealed them below with their guns loaded in case of danger," says Chirikov.

The most valuable discovery of the Bering expedition was not the American continent itself, but the fur-bearing animals that abounded on the islands Bering and Chirikov had passed en route. And most valuable of all was the luxuriant pelt of the sea otter, a creature whose scarcity had rendered its fur priceless to the Chinese. According to John Meares, who later helped to open the China trade, at one time only the emperor himself could legally possess a sea-otter cloak. When Bering and his crew were shipwrecked on uninhabited Bering Island, the survivors made it through the winter by clubbing the fearless sea otters over the head and living upon their flesh. Those who made it back to Kamchatka (aboard the improvised hooker *St. Peter,* built from wreckage that had washed ashore) divided up nine hundred pelts among them and made their fortunes overnight.

Unfortunately for us, none of the freebooting hunters who explored the Aleutian Islands over the next few years had a Georg Wilhelm Steller with them to take notes. For the impressions of the Russians who followed Bering along the Aleutian chain, we are indebted in large part to William Coxe. He compiled the first English-language anthology of their accounts, transcribing source material that might not have otherwise survived.

"No sooner had Beering and Tschirikof . . . opened their way to islands abounding in valuable furs," wrote Coxe in 1780, "than private merchants immediately engaged with ardour in similar expeditions; and, within a period of ten years, more important discoveries were made by these individuals, at their own private cost, than had been hitherto effected by all the expensive efforts of the crown."[13]

Coxe describes these vessels and their crew:

Most of the vessels which are equipped for these expeditions are two-masted; are commonly built without iron, and in general so badly constructed, that it is wonderful how they can weather so stormy a sea. They are called in Russian Shitiki, or sewed vessels, because the planks are sewed together with thongs of leather. Some few are built in the river of Kamchatka; but they are for the most part constructed at the haven of Okhotsk. The largest are manned with seventy men, and the smallest with forty. The crew generally consists of an equal number of Russians and Kamtchadals. The latter occasion a considerable saving, as their pay is small; they also resist, more easily than the former, the attack of scurvy.[14]

The graceful lines of the Aleut vessels stood in dramatic contrast to these voyagers' clumsy craft, and it is no wonder the invaders took an immediate liking to the safety and convenience of the Native skin-covered boats. Even Solovief, outstanding among the outlaw hunters in his disrespect for human life, showed some respect, in Coxe's account, for the Native boats:

Their vessels consist of two sorts: the larger are leathern boats or baidars, which have oars on both sides, and are capable of holding thirty or forty people. The smaller vessels are rowed with a double paddle, and resemble the canoes of the Greenlanders, containing only one or two persons: they never weigh above thirty pounds, being nothing but a thin skeleton of a boat covered with leather. In these however they pass from one island to another, and even venture out to sea.[15]

The Aleuts had long carried on an annual sea-otter hunt sufficient to meet their own domestic needs, and it was this tradition that would be expanded upon by the Russians to become the epic hunts of later times. "In May and June they kill sea-otters in the following manner," wrote William Coxe in his description of the aboriginal Aleuts, after the account of the Cossacks Petr Wasyutinskoi and Maxim Lazarof. "When the weather is calm, they row [paddle] out to sea in several baidars: having found the animal, they strike him with harpoons, and follow him so closely, that he cannot easily escape."[16]

"The clothes of the women and children are made of sea-otter skins, in the same form as those belonging to the men," continues Coxe — before the promyshlenniks made the witholding of pelts punishable by death. From

"Man of Unalaska" wears a sea lion-whiskered hat and a waterproof kamleika (parka) of sea-mammal intestine. Headgear such as this was worn by paddlers at sea, seen only on ceremonial occasions ashore.

Engraving after a sketch made about 1790 by Luka Voronin, on the Billings-Sarycev expedition. From Sarycev's Atlas, *1802. Courtesy Pacific Northwest Collection, University of Washington Libraries.*

A Chain of Events—13

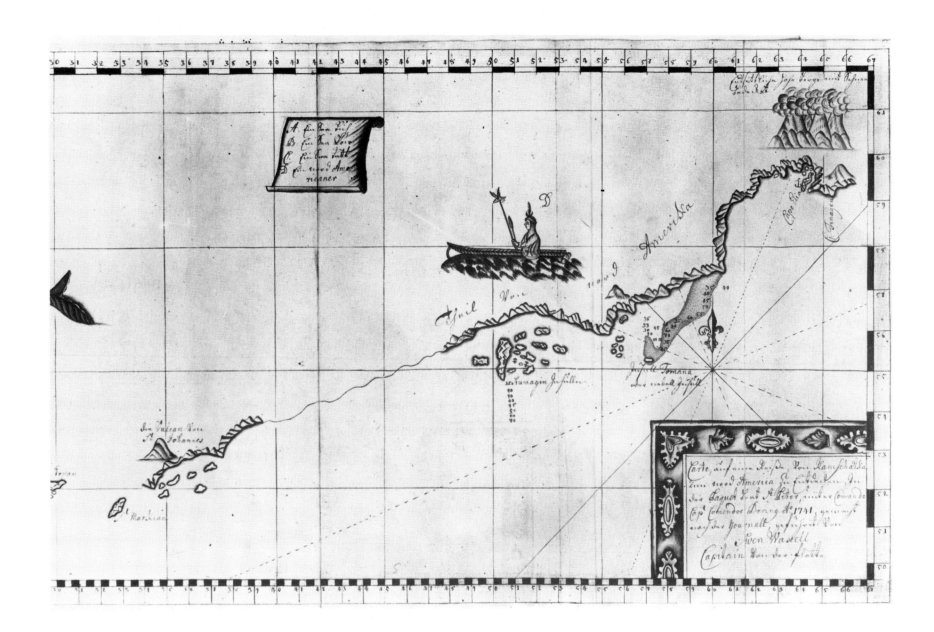

then on, their clothing would be birdskin, ground-squirrel (*evrashka,* or marmot), and hair-sealskin parkas at best, which, according to Hieromonk Father Gedeon of Kad'iak, "had formerly been what their slaves had worn."[17] By Gedeon's time, 1804, the old ways were gone but the memory survived, both in oral tradition and even in figures of speech: "They have no particular words for curses," explained Gedeon. "When he is most passionately enraged a Kadiak man will say, with an air of great importance: 'Your father did not own a baidarka and was not a hunter, and I did not wear a hair sealskin parka!'"[18]

The typical fur-hunting expedition to the Aleutian Islands, in the second half of the eighteenth century, lasted between two and six years — if all went well. Those vessels that survived their navigators' haphazard landfalls had to be laid up over the winter, and in this vulnerable state fell easy victim to the revenge of the Aleuts. It was exactly this fate that befell the *Zacharias and Elizabeth* at Unalaska during the winter of 1763-1764. The veteran hunter Stepan Korelin and three companions were the sole survivors of the well-planned Native uprising, having been away from their vessel at the time of the attack. Korelin's account, given to us by Coxe, illustrates the sorts of circumstances that forced the Russians to begin building their own skin boats:

> *Upon their [return] they found the vessel broken to pieces, and the dead bodies of their companions mangled along the beach. Having collected all the provision which had been untouched by the savages, they returned to the mountains . . . where they lived in a very wretched state from the 9th of December to the 2nd of February, 1764.*
>
> *Meanwhile they employed themselves in making a little baidar, which they covered with the leather*

This engraving of "American in his Baidar," based upon G.W. Steller's unpublished notes, was the first published illustration of an Alaskan baidarka.

From the first edition of Krasheninnikov's Opisanie, *1755, Vol. I. Courtesy Provincial Archives of British Columbia.*

The Shumagin Islands and an Aleut in a baidarka appear on a portion of an undated chart accompanying Sven Waxel's German account of Bering's voyage to America in 1741.

Courtesy Bancroft Library, University of California.

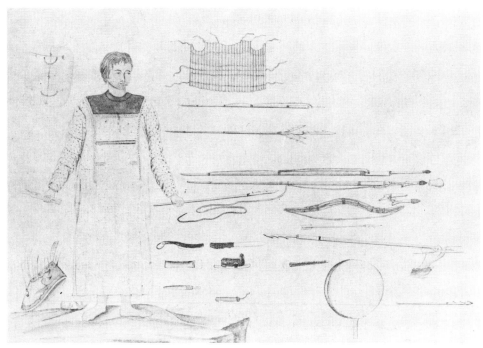

Aleut man from Unalaska appears with hunting equipment, weapons, diagram showing "how the spear is thrown by means of the throwing stick," ornamented hat, tamborine used in dancing, and tools for making baidarkas and spears.

From a portfolio of drawings by Captain-Lieutenant Mikhail Levashov in the Archives of the Ministry of Marine, Leningrad. Photocopied by F.A. Golder in 1914. Courtesy Special Collections Division, University of Washington Libraries.

of the sacks. Having drawn it at night from the mountains to the sea, they rowed without waiting for break of day along the Northern coast of Unalashka, in order to reach Trapesnikof's vessel, which, as they had reason to think, lay at anchor somewhere upon the coast. They rowed at some distance from the shore, and by that means passed three [Aleut] habitations unperceived. The following day they observed at some distance five islanders in a baidar, who upon seeing them made to Makushinsk [settlement at Makushin Bay], before which place the fugitives were obliged to pass. Darkness coming on, the Russians landed on a rock, and passed the night ashore. Early in the morning discovering the islanders advancing towards them from the bay of Makushinsk, they placed themselves in an advantageous post; and prepared for defense . . .

They were imprisoned in this cave five weeks, and kept watch by turns. During that time they seldom ventured twenty yards from the entrance; and were obliged to quench their thirst with snow-water, and with the moisture dripping from the rock. They suffered also greatly from hunger, having no sustenance but small shell-fish, which they occasionally found means to collect upon the beach. Compelled at length by extreme want, they one night ventured to draw their baidar into the sea; and were fortunate enough to get off unperceived.

They continued rowing at night, but in the day hid themselves on the shore; by this means they escaped unobserved from the bay of Makushinsk, and reached Trapesnikof's vessel the 30th of March, 1764.[19]

Later in the hunting season of 1764, another band of hunters, pressing eastward aboard the *Adrian i Nataliia* under the command of Stepan Glotov, were the first to reach Kodiak Island. This discovery was unique in that a first-person account of the Native side of the story has survived. The Danish ethnologist J.H. Holmberg, on a baidarka journey around Kodiak Island in 1856, took down the words of Arsenti Aminak, a sole surviving witness to the end of pre-contact times:

I was a boy of 9 or 10, for they already had me row in the baidarka, when the first Russian ship, a two master arrived before Aliuklik. We had never before seen a ship. To be sure we traded with the Aglegmiuts (of Nasigak Island), Tnainas (of Aliaska Peninsula) and Kolosh, and old wise men even knew of California Indians, but we did not know white men. When we saw the ship far off, we believed it was a giant whale and curiosity drove us to examine it more closely. We went out in baidarkas, but soon saw that it was not a whale, but a strange monster, never seen before, which we feared and whose stench [of tar] made us sick. The people aboard it wore buttons on their clothes, we thought they were squids [Russ. pugovichnye raki — button lobsters], but when we saw that they took fire into their mouth and blew out smoke — we knew nothing of tobacco — we could only believe that they were devils.[20]

The Kodiak Natives (termed variously *Koniags* or *Koniagas*, and lumped together generally as "Aleuts") had been hardened to the periodic attacks of western invaders over many years, and put up a harsh if hopeless fight. "The approach of day-light discovered to their view different parties of the enemy advancing under the protection of wooden screens," says Coxe of Glotov's arrival. "Of these moving breast-works they counted seven; and behind each from thirty to forty men armed with bone lances. Beside these a crowd of armed men advanced separately to the attack, some of them bearing whale jaw-bones, and others wooden shields." Glotov's gunpowder eventually won the day. He noted the screens the Natives left behind were "twelve feet broad, and above half a yard thick."[21]

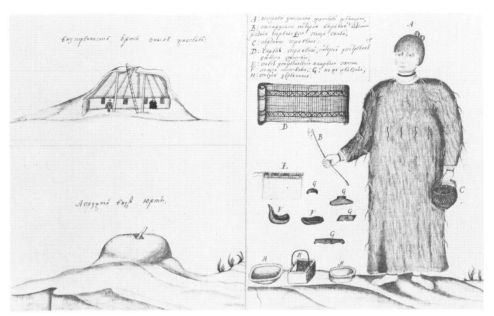

Views of dwellings and household implements are arrayed beside Aleut woman from Unalaska, about 1768.

From a portfolio of drawings by Captain-Lieutenant Mikhail Levashov in the Archives of the Ministry of Marine, Leningrad. Photocopied by F.A. Golder in 1914. Courtesy Special Collections Division, University of Washington Libraries.

Most of Europe in 1764 remained ignorant of what the Russians were up to in the North Pacific. The accounts of the Russian adventurers would have remained unpublished a good deal longer had not Captain Cook's visit, fourteen years later, brought popular attention to the scene.

Cook's third voyage remains unsurpassed among North Pacific explorations for the number of journalists aboard. Two centuries later, our best-known glimpses of the Aleut baidarka still date from that summer of 1778. In May the *Resolution* and the *Discovery* anchored at Snug Corner Cove, Prince William Sound, where they found themselves surrounded by skin canoes of both the decked and open sort, the Natives "paddling and singing with all the Jollity imaginable," says Charles Clerke, Cook's second-in-command. "We either found these good folks on one of their Jubilee days, or they are a very happy Race," he noted, perhaps because they had not yet been subjugated by the Russians and still had Prince William Sound to themselves. Entirely at home in the water, and to all appearances as waterproof as ducks, the kayakers wore feathered parkas, says Clerke, "made of water fowl skins, and exceedingly well calculated, to keep out both Wet & Cold."[22]

David Samwell, surgeon aboard the *Discovery,* was one of several who described these Chugach baidarkas in more detail:

> *The upper part on the Deck has a ridge running fore & aft, on each side of which is a gentle declivity so much as that nothing will conveniently lie upon it, & therefore there are straps fastened at each side of the Canoe & running across under which they thrust their Spears, Bows & Arrows & such things as they carry with them & are wanted ready at hand. Their furs & many other articles they keep within side the Canoe where they remain perfectly dry, the Skins being so well sewed together as not to admit of hardly any water, the small quantity that gets in they suck into a Tube & so empty it.*

> *They are transparent, most of them of a white colour but a few black, the upper part of the white had a very near resemblance to the belly of a Turtle, the Pieces of skins sewed together corresponding in some Measure with the different Shells on the belly of that Fish & and the convex form of it likewise agreeing with the Deck of the Canoe. These Canoes will not admit conveniently of any more than one person, but we have sometimes seen two make shift to thrust themselves into one Hatchway for a short Passage & have known them to stow one Person between Decks, but this is uncommon and very inconvenient.*[23]

We shall hear more of this "uncommon and very inconvenient" practice shortly. But first — from Cook's own journal for October 23, 1778, at Unalaska, a thousand miles to the west of Prince William Sound — are observations of an exceptionally swift and streamlined craft with a surface-piercing bow uncommonly similar to that developed for modern vessels in recent years:

> *The Canoes made use of by the Indians are the smallest we had anywhere seen, though built after the same manner with some little differences in the construction; the stern of these terminates a little abrumptly, the head in a forked point, the upper point projecting without the under one which is even with the Surface of the Water. Why they should construct them in this manner is difficult to conceive, as the fork is liable to catch hold of every thing that comes in the way; to prevent which they fix a piece of small stick from point to point, but I observed that this frequently got loose.*[24]

Cook's puzzlement at the bifid bow of the baidarka would be echoed by innumerable visitors to Alaska over the next two hundred years. Indeed, the first question asked about a baidarka even today is still "why the forked bow?" One answer is strictly taxonomic: The bifid bow was among the most identifiable of features that distinguished the kayaks of the Aleuts from those of other kayak builders around the world, and that all baidarkas had bifid bows, simply as an inherited, species-specific trait. But there was more to it than that. Tradition did not exist for its own sake alone.

There were two separate, diverging functions of the bow of the Aleut baidarka, and therefore the structure took a bifurcated, diverging form. The lower portion was designed to cut sharply into the water, like a knife, while the upper part was designed to present a flat, blunted, horizontal planing surface, much like a water ski both in appearance and effect. The two components of the bow were arranged in the form of the letter T. As this T-form blended aft into the rounded cross-sections of the hull,

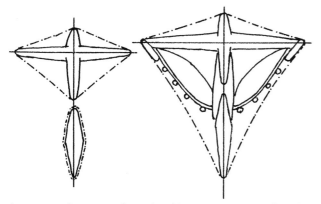

there was a key area where the skin covering was induced to take a critically flared, hollow shape: Modern yacht designers and seaplane hull engineers have universally adopted such a "hollow" form in their search for seaworthiness and speed, but it is apparent that the Aleuts were aware of the usefulness of the shape long ago.

In their case — and in the case of anyone stretching a tensile membrane over a frame — it was only by means of an open split, running the length of the bow, that the skin covering could be given this concave form. It is to be noted that the stern of the Aleut baidarka was just as

"Canoes of Oonalashka" is the title of this engraving depicting the baidarkas encountered by Cook in 1778, although the spruce-root hats, single paddles, and upswept bow of the two-hatch craft are typical of Prince William Sound (noted in faint pencil on original).

Engraving from Cook's Voyage, *1784, Vol. 3, after a wash drawing by John Webber. (Original drawing in the Dixson Library, N.S.W., Australia.) Courtesy Beinecke Library, Yale University.*

ingeniously thought out, with frame and skin forming a composite structure exquisitely suited to the function of the boat. The gunwales terminated at a T-shaped spreader, resulting in a highly flared, transomlike stern — able to slip through the water as cleanly as the tail of a fish, yet rise as buoyantly to a following sea as the well-feathered tail of a duck.

The Aleut vessels that surrounded Cook, their seams decorated with tufts of brightly colored plumage and their puffin-feathered occupants crowned with sea-lion whiskered hats, were striking in their appearance when underway. "They make use of the double paddle," noted Cook, "which they hold in both hands in the middle, stricking the water quick and regular first on one side and then on the other; thus they can go at a great rate and in a direction as streight as a line can be drawn."[25]

The Russians had been exploring Alaska for thirty-seven years when Cook's visit caught them by surprise. To the British, the first evidence of the Russian presence was an indecipherable note delivered to the *Discovery* by Native paddlers at the Shumagin Islands on June 20, 1778. "That the People who brought off this Note were no Strangers to European Ceremonies I am perfectly convinc'd," wrote Captain Charles Clerke, "for before we had any Idea of the Note, we were admiring at the strange difference in the deportment between these People and those we had hitherto met with, & wondering who the Devil cou'd have been here & taught these honest fellows to make bows."[26]

Not until October, at Unalaska, did Cook meet the Russians. (The first note, apparently, was a receipt for tribute exacted by Russians who had passed by on their annual rounds.) At Unalaska "we found them fond of tobacco, rum, and snuff, and we observed several blue linen shirts and drawers among them," noted John Ledyard of the Natives, who visited the ships in two-hatch baidarkas and presented Cook with "a cake of rye-meal newly-baked with a piece of salmon in it seasoned with pepper and salt."[27] Cook sent Ledyard, an American from Connecticut serving as corporal of the marines aboard

Native of Unalaska paddles a baidarka, with the earliest known structural diagram of a baidarka above him. Drawn about 1768.

Original drawing by Captain-Lieutenant Mikhail Levashov, in the Archives of the Ministry of Marine, Leningrad. Photocopied by F.A. Golder in 1914. Courtesy Special Collections Division, University of Washington Libraries.

the *Resolution* (and "an intelligent, decent looking man," says James King)[28] to pay a return visit to the strangers, accompanied by, according to Cook, ". . . a few bottles of Rum, Wine, and Porter which we thought would be as acceptable as any thing we had besides, and the event prove[d] we were not misstaken."[29] As James Burney, who was first lieutenant of the *Discovery*, put it, "On this occasion it was, that John Ledyard, Corporal of the Marines in the *Resolution*, first distinguished himself for enterprise, by volunteering his services to return with the messengers to gain information."[30] David Samwell, Surgeon's mate in the *Resolution*, explains:

There being only one canoe with Holes for two paddle[rs] to sit, the Corporal was obliged to suffer himself to be stowed away close in that, which had room enough barely to contain him & where he was entirely shut out from the Air, tho' he had a little Light for the Skin of the Canoe being transparent he could see the Water plain enough, in which he was in a manner buryed & only defended from it by thin Leather.[31]

We have Ledyard's own account:

It was beginning to be dark when the canoe came to us. It was a skin canoe after the Esquimaux plan with two holes to accommodate two setters. The Indians that came in the canoe talked a little with my two guides, and then came to me and desired I would get into the canoe, which I did not very readily agree to, however, as there was no other place for me but to be thrust into the space between the holes extended at length upon my back and

Local inhabitants in both baidarkas and open skin boats surround Captain Cook's two ships, the *Resolution* and the *Discovery*, as they ride at anchor in Snug corner Cove, Prince William Sound, in May of 1778.

Wash drawing by John Webber. Courtesy British Library.

wholly excluded from seeing the way I went or the power of extricating myself upon any emergency. But as there was no alternative I submitted thus to be stowed away in bulk, and went head formost very swift through the water about an hour, when I felt the canoe strike a beach, and afterwards lifted up and carried some distance, and then set down again, after which I was drawn out by the shoulders by three or four men, for it was now so dark I could not tell who they were, though I was conscious I heard a language that was new.[32]

Of these Russian hunters, Ledyard noted, as would his successors over the years, "they were very fond of the rum, which they drank without any mixture or measure."

Aftereffects were prevented by a pre-breakfast steam bath that Ledyard's hosts would not allow him to refuse: ". . . the steam which evaporated from the hot water rendered the hutt which was very tight extreemly hot and suffocating. I soon understood this was a hot bath of which I was asked to make use of in such a friendly manner, and the apparatus being a little curious so that I conceeded to it, but before I had finished undressing myself, I was overcome by the sudden transition of the air, fainted away and fell back upon the platform I was sitting on."[33]

After successfully completing his bath, Ledyard had some trouble with the Russian breakfast as well: ". . . we again dressed and returned to our lodgings, where our breakfast was smoaking on the table . . . It was mostly of whale, sea-horse and bear, which, though smoked, dried, and boiled, produced a composition of smells very offensive at nine or ten in the morning . . . the flavor of our feast as well as its appearance had nearly produced a relapse in my spirits, and no doubt would if I had not recourse to some of the brandy I had brought which happily saved me."[34]

Having accomplished his mission on Cook's behalf, Ledyard returned by way of an open skin boat, accompanied by several Russians, "better accommodated in his passage home than out,"[35] says Burney, without having

to again suffer the practice, common to most aboriginal kayak builders, of carrying supernumerary passengers stowed below.

On the fourteenth, in response to Ledyard's diplomacy, Cook and his artist John Webber witnessed the arrival of an enterprising Russian navigator who had purposefully sought out the English ships. Unfortunately, Webber's widely scattered sketches and watercolors do not seem to include a depiction of this scene:

His name was Erasim Gregorioff Sin Ismyloff, he came in a Canoe carrying three people, attended by twenty or thirty other Canoes each conducted by one man; I took notice that the first thing they did after landing was to make a small tent for Ismyloff of materials which they brought with them, and then they made others for themselves of their Canoes paddles &c which they covered with grass, so that the people of the Village were at no trouble to find them lodging. Ismyloff invited us into his tent, set before us some dryed Salmon and berries which I was satisfied was the best cheer he had; he was a very sencible intelligent man, and I felt no small mortification in not being able to converse with him in any other way than by signs assisted by figures and other Characters which however was a very great help.[36]

Cook found this Izmailov "very well acquainted with the Geography of these parts," and he invited the Russian navigator aboard the *Resolution,* where he "at once pointed out the errors in the Modern Maps."[37] Izmailov spent several days in congenial consultation with Cook, who found his knowledge invaluable, his intemperance therefore excusable, and only took note of him in praise:

This Mr Ismyloff seemed to have abilities to intitle him to a higher station in life than that in which he was employed, he was tolerably well versed in Astronomy and other necessary parts of the

Mathematicks. I complemented him with an Hadlys Octant and altho it was the first he had perhaps ever seen, yet he made himself acquainted with most of the uses that Instrument is capable of in a very short time.[38]

Thomas Edgar, master of the *Discovery*, was of the same opinion as Cook:

This said Ishmiloff is a native of Jacutz & is a very shrew'd penetrating sort of a man, his Ideas never confused & his conception vastly quick . . .[39]

This Erasim Gregorioff Sin Izmailov was one of Russian America's more remarkable men. His name appears (in various spellings) in connection with most of the adventures that highlight the establishment of the Russian presence on the North American Coast. A Gregorieff Ismailov is even listed as a soldier among the survivors of Bering's shipwreck of 1741[40] — our present character's father, perhaps.

It was Izmailov who rescued the outnumbered Baranov from a surprise attack by the Tlingit in Prince William Sound in 1792. It was Izmailov who returned to Kamchatka in 1787 with a record-breaking cargo of furs — 172,000 rubles worth. In 1788, with Bocharov, Izmailov was the first Russian to explore Yakutat harbor and Lituya Bay. He helped Shelikhov establish the settlement on Kodiak Island at Three Saints Bay in 1783, although Shelikhov would later refer to Izmailov as "an ungrateful, cowardly, feckless, and drunken man."[41] He showed little deference to any authority but his own, and caused Baranov a great deal of trouble — a near mutiny — during the winter of 1793-1794. "Ten of the veteran workers gave themselves to drink completely and corrupted others," complained Shelikhov, "Gerasim Grigor'evich [Izmailov] was responsible for this evil and was behaving the same way."[42] Among Izmailov's collection of adventures, the one that baffled Cook most was

a voyage from Kamchatka to Japan with the notorious Polish exile Count Mauritius Benyowski, who had pirated a Russian vessel from Bolcheretsk in 1771. From Japan, Izmailov claimed to have made his way to Canton, and from there, in a French ship, to France, and finally on foot to St. Petersburg, from whence he had returned to Kamchatka and the North American Coast. However, "his not being able to speak one word of French made this story a little suspicious," says Cook.[43]

The errors in Izmailov's account may well have resulted from the sign language with which he was forced to tell the English his tale. In one case, though, his intentional misinformation was transparently obvious: "Sea Otter Skins he said were Valuable at Japon but not a[t] Canton,"[44] relates Cook, a remark that suggests the astute Izmailov foresaw exactly what troubles would result for the Russians once the British discovered the market for sea-otter skins among the Chinese.

There is more to the life and times of Izmailov, but what we are concerned with here is his boat. One thing about his visit with Cook stands out above all else: This is the first instance on record of a three-seater baidarka in Russian hands. "Ismiloff was in a covered skin canoe that had three holes in it," says King, "in the middlemost of which he was seated & in the two end holes were placed the Paddlers."[45] Charles Clerke elaborates:

He enterd the Bay where the Town stands in great State, being attended by 30 or 40 Canoes, all of which however were the Single Man Canoes, excepting it with the European Cargo; it was paddled by two Men and had a third Hole, formed for the accomodation of his Russian Honour: (These small cover'd Canoes are the only Vessels we have seen among the Natives here); every Individual of this little Fleet seem'd totally devoted to the Service of this russian Gentleman, and were no sooner landed than great part of them were busied in his Employ, some building a temporary House for his Nights repose, others dressing Fish different ways

Man of Unalaska, outfitted for baidarka travel, was drawn in October of 1778.

Sepia and watercolor drawing by John Webber. Courtesy Peabody Museum, Harvard University (photo by Hillel Burger).

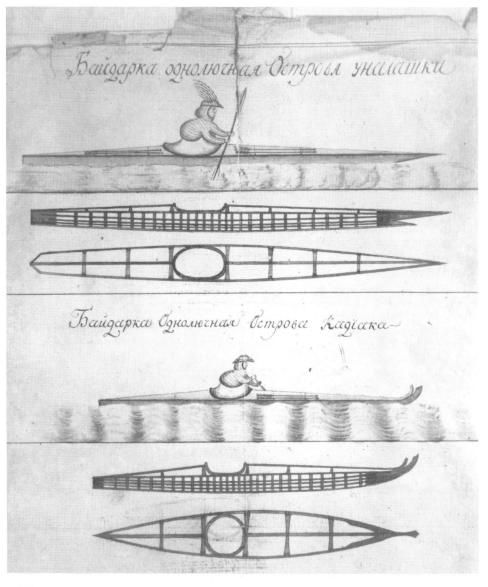

Бaйdaрka однолючная Острова Уналашки

Бaйdaрka Однолючная Острова Кадіака

for his Evening regale, and rendering various other little Services, to make matters as agreeable to him as circumstances cou'd possibly admit of.[46]

Could Izmailov have been the first to adopt the three-seater baidarka for Russian use? Although nearly all published sources credit the Russians with the invention of the three-hatch boat, there is evidence that the Aleuts of the Near Islands (near to Russia, i.e., Attu and Agattu) built three-seaters in pre-contact times — for special occasions if not for daily use.[47] The point in tracing Izmailov's movements is that if the three-hatch baidarka had existed among the Near Islands, Izmailov would certainly have been among the first to try it out. His subsequent far-flung career helps explain how the craft achieved such a widespread following over the next few years.

Izmailov's character fits our assumptions as to why the Russians began to use the three-hatch craft: He was ingenious, a shrewd trader and skilled navigator, commanded complete authority over the Natives, and enjoyed the position of leisure offered by the baidarka's center hole. If Izmailov did not himself originate the design, we must still give him credit as the first recorded proponent of the craft.

At the same time as the Russians were customizing the baidarka for themselves, they discouraged the Natives from building their own larger skin boats, for "political reasons" — as Cook himself was correct to note:

No such thing as a defensive or offensive weapon was seen among them; we cannot suppose the Russians found them in such a defenceless state,

Diagrams *(left)* show one-hatch baidarkas. Top boat is from Unalaska; bottom from Kodiak Island. A two-hatch baidarka and a three-hatch baidarka, both from Kodiak Island *(right)*, display characteristic single paddles, upswept bows, and "fish-form" hulls. (Scale is in arshins.)

Drawn by James Shields, an English shipwright and navigator in the service of the Russians, about 1798. Originals in the Holy Synod Archives, Russia. Photocopied by F.A. Golder in 1914. Courtesy Special Collections, University of Washington Libraries.

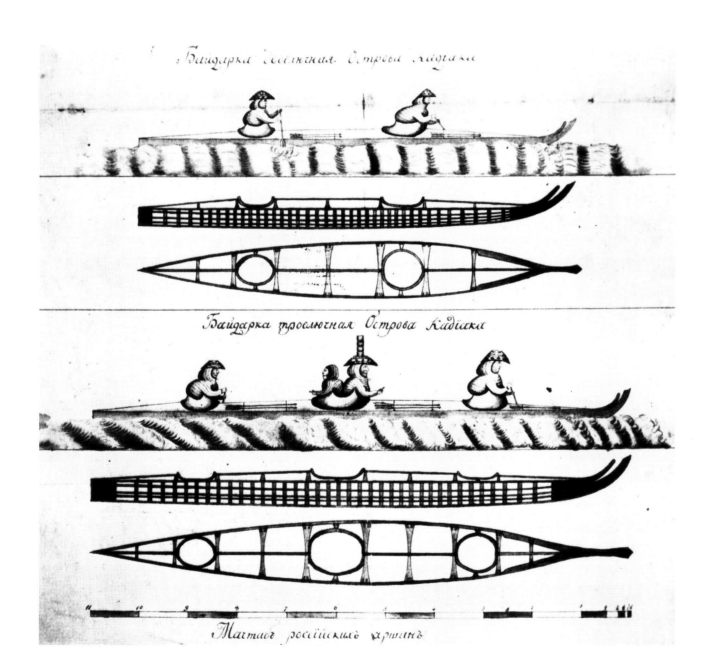

Баидарка .... Острова ....

Баидарка троемючная Острова Кадіяка

Масштаб россійскихъ аршинъ.

but rather for their own security have disarmed them. Political reasons too may have induced the Russians not to allow them to have any large Canoes, for it is difficult to believe they were original[ly] without sence all their neighbors have of them, however none were seen now except one or two belonging to the Russians.[48]

These large canoes, termed *baidaras* by the Russians (or *umiaks* by the Eskimos) were enormous, open-framed, walrus-skinned vessels that served the Natives both for long voyages and for local ferrying of passengers and freight — and for making war on enemy villages, or on foreign intruders such as they now found in their midst. "The ones that are coming to fight us come in skin boats," one of Frederica de Laguna's Yakutat informants told her of their ancient enemies to the west. "Some of them are small, and they call them 'kayak.' And the other ones . . . are big ones. They are so big that the people stay under these canoes — just like we stay under a roof."[49]

The Russians soon confiscated most of these large vessels, outlawing their unauthorized use. The decline of the baidara as a vehicle for the middle-class Aleut household emptied a functional niche that was left to a new, much larger form of kayak, the three-holer, to try and fill. How did this vessel, an isolated exception at the time of Cook's visit, manage to become the standard form of transportation in Russian America within the next few years? It was the Russian hunters who set the example, soon followed all along the coast.

Until the arrival of Russian rule there had been constant and vicious warfare between the different island groups, effectively preventing the free exchange of nautical ideas and making speed, rather than armament or carrying capacity, the measure of a boat. "The Aleuts had battles at sea . . . only when they came unexpectedly upon an enemy," wrote Veniaminov (the preferred form of warfare being the pre-dawn surprise attack). "However, having a superiority over the Kad'iak people in the speed of their baidarkas, the Aleuts sought out the latter . . . they moved in ferociously to drown him without mercy until the vanquished begged for peace."[50]

The strategic balance shifted as soon as the first armed Russian seated himself in the three-holer's center hatch. "Attended by his Indian Train, as he was going he saluted the Ships with a brace of Pistols which he carried about with him,"[51] noted David Samwell of Izmailov's departure at the head of his devoted entourage of one-hatch craft. Under Russian supervision, the Native sea-otter hunting fleet, comprised of Aleut, Koniag, and Chugach alike, transcended the traditional boundaries between neighboring populations of hunters and their distinctly autonomous models of boats. A single Russian "inventor" of the three-hatch baidarka, such as Izmailov, could have introduced the craft among most of the coastal population at once. In a few years, an essentially standardized design — a three-holer displaying hybrid lines — would be the end result. But the old feuds were not forgotten. "When they are travelling in many baidarkas and one of them capsizes," Davydov would note in 1804, "then the others will pass by unless the person in the water is from their own village."[52]

The British presence in Alaska was long preceded by that of the Russians; Spanish claims to Alaska nearly preceded Cook as well. Their third Bucareli expedition, planned in 1776 in great secret as a preemption of British claims, was delayed by bureaucratic details and did not reach the Alaskan Coast until 1779. The Spaniards were ignorant of the fact that Cook had been there first. The frigate *Virgen de los Remedios,* known as *La Favorita,* under Lieutenant Francisco de la Bodega y Cuadra, encountered a pair of baidarkas near Cape St. Elias at the southern end of Kayak Island. These were the typical Chugach variety, with gracefully upturned prow. "Their shape is exactly that of a harp," wrote Don Francisco Antonio Maurelle, describing the events of July 20, 1779, "their bow having the same curve as is made in the harp for fastening the strings."[53]

Alejandro Malaspina, the Italian commander of a later Spanish expedition in the corvettes *Atrevida* and

Descubierta, found himself surrounded by dugout canoes, and the occasional baidarka, during his stay at Port Mulgrave (Yakutat) in 1791. Yakutat, at the southern limit of the baidarka's indigenous range until the Russians began leading hunting expeditions farther to the south, was one of the few places where skin boats and dugouts had coexisted peacefully within a single tribal group. The Yakutat peoples' legends of their migration to the Yakutat area from Athabaskan territory on the Copper River, via overland glaciers to Icy Bay and then along the coast, hint at how they acquired the skin boats en route. "The Athapascans did not know about the sea, and they called one another together," dictated John Swanton's informant, Q!a'dustin, at Sitka in 1904, describing the emigrants' first view from the mountains overlooking Icy Bay. "They said, 'What is that so very blue?' They said, 'Let us go down to it. We have saved ourselves,' they said . . . When winter began to come on they built a house . . . and the settlement grew into a town . . . After they had been there ten years one person began living away from town in order to make the frame of a skin boat."[54] The man then sent his nephews out along the coast in this skin boat. This is how the K^{W}ack'wan people first arrived at Yakutat, where they made peace with the dugout builders (Teqwedi sib) who were already there.

This background is important to an understanding of how it was that the Spanish found the baidarka in use among the Yakutat Tlingit (and how it was that La Pérouse, in 1786, found the frame of a skin boat erected as a monument at Lituya Bay), several years before the Russians ventured this far eastward with the Aleuts. Tomás de Suria, official artist with Malaspina's expedition, kept a sketchbook full of notes in which we see the baidarka of a Yakutat chief serving as the flagship at the head of a small fleet of dugout craft:

The king or chief went about directing his canoes in one made of skin, shaped like a weaver's shuttle with a deck of the same material in which there were two perfectly round holes by which they enter

and leave, and which reach to their waist, where they tie them. In these canoes they pass from one island to another, and when there are bad storms and heavy seas they get inside them and leave them to the force of the waves, and are very secure as water does not enter anywhere . . .

. . . They seat themselves on their heels as is their ordinary custom, and thus they manage the canoe with the oars. They use no rudder and in order to keep going straight they paddle the same number of times first on one side and then on the other with great speed. Their oars are very curious and are painted like the canoes with various marks and masks.[55]

This is the first we hear of a paddling style that would puzzle many observers in later years. In the short, beamy, and sharply rockered single baidarkas that seem to have been the aboriginal Chugach and Yakutat craft, and to a people who preferred the single paddle — for reasons, one assumes, having something to do with the stealthy approach required to surprise the resting seals on which they preyed — the paddling style made visible sense. But when adopted later by paddlers in two-hatch and three-hatch boats, it became a curious sight.

Our most puzzling legacy of the Malaspina expedition is an ink drawing, attributed to the fieldwork of José Cardero and perhaps re-worked back in Mexico City by Fernando Brambila (students of de Suria both), depicting a lively scene among the inside waters of Vancouver Island in 1792. Unmistakable in the foreground — and surrounded by dugout canoes — is a two-hatch Alaskan baidarka, with two more baidarkas visible beyond. Was this a liberty taken in combining field sketches from opposite ends of the coast? Or did the Spanish expedition bring these skin canoes with them from their voyage to the north? The former is more likely; in either case, these are the first kayaks we see upon the Vancouver Island scene.[56]

At the same time as Malaspina's expedition but from an opposite direction, the Billings-Sarycev expedition,

commissioned by Empress Catherine the Great, carried out a four-year reconnaissance of the Siberian and Alaskan coasts. This "Northeastern Secret Geographical and Astronomical Expedition," launched in 1785, had political as well as scientific aims. Catherine realized the necessity of a complete and authoritative survey, in the style of Cook, if Russia was to support her claims to the North American Coast. The results of this expedition were to outlive the Russian possessions themselves: Sarycev's profiles of the Aleutian Islands — as engraved-for his atlas[57] — were to appear (without credit to Sarycev) in the first edition of the Admiralty's *Bering Sea and Strait Pilot*, where their presence assisted the very foreigners whose intrusions the Billings-Sarycev expedition had been intended to guard against.

Martin Sauer, the official secretary of the expedition, found himself surrounded by Aleuts "sporting about more like amphibious animals than human beings," as he noted in describing his first impression of their boats among the surf:

> *The baidars, or boats, of Oonalashka are infinitely superior to those of any other island. If perfect symmetry, smoothness, and proportion constitute beauty, they are beautiful; to me they appeared so beyond anything that I ever beheld. I have seen some of them as transparent as oiled paper, through which you could trace every formation of the inside, and the manner of the native's sitting in it; whose light dress, painted and plumed bonnet, together with his perfect ease and activity, added infinitely to its elegance. Their first appearance struck me with amazement beyond expression.[58]*

Carl Heinrich Merck (of the Merck pharmaceutical family), the expedition's naturalist, kept a journal that disappeared without a trace until discovered among some old papers at a Leipzig bookseller in 1935. Among notes made at Unalaska between June 21 and July 4, 1791, Merck recorded the Aleuts' terminology for their boats:

Ikyak, *their one seater leather boat with straight beak. Tshinatak, the same boat with bent-up beak. Alagulot, their two-seater boat. Kaukunlott, their three-seater boat.*[59]

"They know to row fast," Merck noted of some Aleut otter hunters stationed on an island of the Shumagin group, "our craft made four Italian miles per hour, and they still overtook it from far away."[60] Sarycev corroborates this instance:

He is so dextrous in the government of his bark, that the lightest sloop would certainly not be able to overtake him; for we had the experience of the Aleutians coming up with our vessel in their baidars, when it was going at the rate of four leagues an hour.[61]

Observing the Aleuts of Unalaska, Merck includes a description of the emergency procedures used at sea:

Whenever they wound a sea lion or a larger fur seal, then it sometimes happens that the animal damages the boat. For such an emergency, whether by this or by another cause, they always carry two sewn sealskins with them, which they can blow up. Or they carry two fur-seal bladders on board. Whenever their boat springs a leak, they blow these up and tie them to the boat, one in front and one in back. And in this fashion they attempt to make it to the nearest shore. If a strong storm overcomes one of these boats in the open sea, then the man is usually lost. Although the strong waves, which wash over the boat, cannot swamp it, they nevertheless tend to overthrow the boat. But if several

— five to ten — boats are out there together, then there is still hope for escape, because they tie boat to boat, one ell across [about one meter] with two straps. These are tied around each boat. And in addition each boat has an inflated sealskin tied front and back, which lies on top of the water. The outer boat, which faces the storm, may not have a bladder tied to it. But the boat at the opposite side has therefore two of them. Those who are in the middle do not row at all, but keep holding on to each other's boats. The men on the two outside boats row with care through the towering waves, in an effort to make it to the nearest land.[62]

Commander Billings was twenty-four, and the hydrographer Sarycev only twenty-two, when their undertaking, lasting a total of ten years, began. There were 141 officers, crew, and artisans involved, not to mention those hired later to assist en route. In the style of Bering, the expedition built its own ships at Okhotsk. One of them, the *Dobroe Namerenie* — or "Good Intent" — ran aground on leaving the harbor and had to be burned to recover the precious iron so the shipwrights might try again. Sarycev was a meticulous navigator who could well appreciate the craftsmanship of the Aleuts:

Nothing is more tedious and fatiguing, than their carpenter's and joiner's work, in making their baskets, their arrows, and the hulls of their baidars. One whole year and more is spent in building such a small boat, on which account they prefer purchasing it at a dear rate. The bare collecting together as much wood on the shore as is requisite for a baidar, is attended with infinite toil and trouble. The main part is the keel, 21 feet in length, which is always composed of two or three pieces. To this they fasten, by means of split whalebone, ribs of willow and alder-branches, on the upper extremities of which they place a frame with crossbars, which in the middle is a foot and a half

Facial ornamentation and elaborate garments of this woman of Unalaska were typical of the Aleuts in 1790.

Engraving from Sarycev's Atlas, *1802, after original drawings made by Luka Voronin on the Billings-Sarycev expedition. Courtesy Pacific Northwest Collection, University of Washington Libraries.*

A baidarka from Unalaska (above) and a kayak from Cape Newenham (below) — appear on one sketch from Cook's visit to Alaska in 1778.

Original watercolor by John Webber in Edward W. Allen collection. Courtesy Special Collections Division, University of Washington Libraries.

broad, and binds the whole baidar together. Over the whole they stretch the hide of a sea-lion, or a large sea-dog, leaving on the top a round but smallish opening, in which the rower sits. This baidar is so light in all its parts, that altogether it does not weigh much above thirty pounds.[63]

Billings, an assistant astronomer on Cook's third and final voyage, had taken the enterprising step of offering his services to the Russians — an offer that Catherine, concerned over Cook's intrusion into Russian waters, could not refuse. Billings' own account, unlike that of Sarycev, was never published — perhaps to keep the credit in Russian hands. The manuscript remains in the Main Archive of the Naval Fleet in Leningrad to this day.

What little we have of Billings' account comes to us via a selection of excerpts translated into Russian, and recently re-translated into English by Fritz Jaensch. Of the Unalaska, Aleuts, Billings notes:

I can say that their baidaras are very beautiful, swift in movement, made smoothly to the severest symmetry of ship construction. The frame (or skeleton of the baidara) consists of three braces of wood the entire length of the baidara . . . The upper frame with the side struts always is made shorter than the keel, and its ends are simply cut short; the bow of the baidara in its form depicts the head of a fish with opened upper and lower jaws. So that sea weeds do not become entangled in this cavity, across it is placed a thin rod. All this construction is bound very solidly [and covered] with sea lion skin. The baidara is not over 7 vershoks [12 inches] deep, and demands sometimes great balance, so as not to turn it over, keel-side up. With all that, the islanders go far out to sea in them, for several miles distance, although the wind blows fresh and presses the deep, calling forth swell after swell. In calm weather they can paddle ten sea miles an hour.[64]

Some might find it hard to believe this latter claim, given that few modern paddlers could ever attain, much less maintain, this pace. But there are many similar cases in the historical record where baidarkas exceeded the maximum theoretical paddling speed for the given length of boat.

Today's kayak designers, believing in a rigid, smooth-chined hull, call into question the evidence of the past. But we should remember that most of these instances were recorded by professional sea captains whose judgment of speed, time, and distance was of the essence to their work. They had little to gain by exaggerating the speed of the Aleut boats.

What were the secrets? Clearly, a soft, elastic skin and flexible hull had something to do with it — think of the advantage in being able to bend effortlessly over the waves rather than having to push them out of the way — as did the Aleuts' uncanny ability to gain the advantage of every wave movement heading their way. Knowledge of winds, waves, and tides was as instinctive to the Aleuts as to their amphibious prey. These exceptionally light, ingeniously flexible, seal-skinned and grease-smeared canoes were not ordinary boats, and these were no ordinary men. In the hands and biceps of the Aleuts, the baidarka was able to skim across the water with the birds.

An axiom of the marine architect's pursuit is that the limit to a displacement vessel's speed is set by its own bow wave, against which, at a speed proportional to the square root of the vessel's waterline length, the vessel expends an increasing amount of work for diminishing returns. The vessel's bow gets pushed upward by the wave it is trying to overcome, and the stern is left wallowing in the resulting trough. Only a terrific boost of horsepower and a cleanly designed "planing" hull will get the vessel over the obstacle, up on "step," and out of its own hydrodynamic way.

Did the Aleuts have these limitations figured out? Speed was their highest goal, and, if waterline length was the only answer, surely they would have built longer boats.

Yet the swiftest baidarkas, those of legendary speed, were commonly referred to as being twelve to sixteen feet in length.[65] Did the Aleuts prefer a shorter boat, that could get up on step quicker from a standing start? Look at their bow: it appears perfectly designed to cut cleanly into and through that bow wave so as to avoid an uphill fight. And the stern seems designed with particular attention to avoiding getting dragged down in its own wake. The skin covering of the hull, stretched across the deadrise between the keelson and the chines, took a concave form in the water identical to that of the fastest "cigarette boat" that any speed-seeker of our own century has been able to devise. I theorize, against prevailing opinion, that the early one-hatch baidarka could, on occasion, escape from the limits imposed on displacement craft.

The 1790s brought great changes to Alaska, due in part to the official Russian interest stirred up by the information that Billings and Sarycev brought back. And foreign vessels were flocking to the lucrative sea-otter trade, buying up furs from the Natives at prices in trade goods and firearms that the ill-equipped Russians could scarcely meet. To better counter this encroachment, and to line the pockets of those with capital and influence back home, Russian-American trade was consolidated into united companies of merchants operating under license from the Crown. Foremost of these was the Shelikhov-Golikov Company, masterminded by the Irkutsk merchant G.I. Shelikhov, a low-ranking visionary and self-declared "Columbus" of Russian expansion into the New World.

Before his premature, mysterious death in 1795,[66] Shelikhov's affairs were consolidated in the hands of his wife, Natal'ia. Her persistant lobbying — succeeding in high circles where his own attempts had failed — led to the founding of the Russian-American Company in 1799, under a charter granting her and her heirs exclusive and long-term rights to all Alaskan trade. Included was a virtual monopoly over the lives of the Aleuts. "Rumours of the effects of gunpowder and the strength of the Russians gradually inclined the others to an alliance,"[67]

are the kind words used by the author of an anonymous historical sketch, published in 1894, to describe Shelikhov's relations with the Natives upon his arrival at Kodiak Island in 1784.

Shelikhov's most brilliant — if accidental — move was the hiring of a nondescript, bankrupt merchant named Alexander Baranov, who was dispatched in 1790 to America aboard the tiny galiot *Three Saints*, to act as manager of the colonial empire Shelikhov sought to create. Shelikhov could scarcely have picked a better man. Baranov, the self-styled merchant king, was to reign singlehandedly over an empire that Shelikhov the dreamer had been able to imagine, but only Baranov was able to build.

The voyage was a difficult one, with an outbreak of yellow fever and the usual lack of fresh water wreaking havoc among the 52-man crew. With orders to head straight for Kodiak, they put into Unalaska instead. It was there, at Koshigin Bay [Kashega Bay], on September 30, that the ship was wrecked. As Kiriil Timofeevich Khlebnikov, Baranov's faithful assistant and biographer, describes it:

All through a stormy and gloomy night, heavy waves broke one after another on deck, the hatches were ripped away, and the ship began to fill with water. In the face of such destruction the only course was to save the crew. At the morning low tide they hurriedly unloaded what cargo they could onto the shore before the tide came in. The storm did not die down and on the night of October 6 the ship capsized completely. A little of the company cargo was salvaged but Baranov, the crew and the passengers were left destitute.[68]

A party of baidarkas under Alexander Molev was sent ahead to Kodiak for help, but they were attacked, with the loss of five Aleuts, by the Natives of the Alaska Peninsula, and forced to beat a retreat. With no prospect of rescue in sight, Baranov organized the construction of underground yurts for the winter. In Khlebnikov's account, they "kept alive by eating various grasses, roots, whale meat and crabs." During the later part of the winter, Baranov occupied himself with preparations for his first voyage by skin-covered boat:

With the coming of spring, measures were taken for the crossing to Kad'iak; three large leather baidaras were built and it was decided that Navigator Bocharov should take two with 26 men and set off to chart the north coast of the Alaska Peninsula. Baranov was to take 16 men with him, and five men were chosen to guard the cargo and tackle left on Unalashka.

On April 25, 1791, all the baidaras set out and on May 10th they parted in Isannakh Strait [Isanotski Strait] according to the prearranged plan. On this journey Baranov was ill with a fever for two months, but the expedition continued nevertheless. They did not want to lose the calm weather which was so suitable for crossing from island to island or going between the capes along the coast of Alaska. They reached Kad'iak on June 27th.[69]

With hindsight, we can see that it was a good thing the newly appointed manager did not reach his headquarters until after this eight-month crash course in the Alaskan way of life. "Misfortune is a great leveler of men," comments Khlebnikov, and no doubt the inexperienced Baranov learned a great deal from the seasoned hunters returning to Alaska aboard the *Three Saints.* As Baranov's genius for leadership became apparent, the previously independent hunters acknowledged a new master whose authority they might otherwise have been reluctant to accept.

Baranov, above all, was shrewd — and more than Shelikhov's equal when it came to the monopolistic game of trade. His was the enterprise and charisma that launched the great baidarka fleets, eventually numbering upward of seven hundred strong. Baranov perceived that if Russia were to compete with foreign traders for skins, the hunters would have to search further and further afield, trading where they found friends and poaching where they did not. To an end that was nothing less than securing the entire coastline of Alaska in the name of the Russian Crown, the baidarka was Baranov's most available means. The task was not an easy one, as Baranov, writing to his employer Shelikhov in 1795, explains:

Without speaking of other places the route to Yakutat alone is hard on the natives. Imagine the poor natives making this journey both ways, 2,000 versts [1300 miles] in narrow baidarkas without sails — using only paddles. They have to endure hunger on the way and often perish in stormy seas because this coast offers no adequate shelter. In places where the natives are not subjugated they are always in constant danger of attack by the bloodthirsty inhabitants of these regions. It is under these conditions that they have to hunt sea otters. For the time being they endure it, but it takes courage and supervision by the Russians, and you can judge for yourself their state of mind.[70]

Baranov was often called upon to supply the necessary courage and supervision himself. On May 2, 1799, a baidarka party was rounding Cape Suckling when thirty of the canoes and their unfortunate sixty paddlers were swallowed by a freak wave that broke over them as they were crossing the shoals. Later in the day, in Baranov's own words:

While we were still mourning the loss of our hunters, night came on, and as I saw further indications of storm, I ordered all the canoes to make for the shore, accompanying them in person in my own baidarka. In the darkness we underestimated the distance, and when at last we reached the sandy beach, exhausted from continued

A Spanish exploring party in a European boat is surrounded by dugout canoes and a baidarka in this apocryphal drawing attributed to the exploration of Vancouver Island by the *Sutil* and the *Mexicana* in 1792.

Ink drawing attributed to José Cardero or Fernando Brambila appears to be a composite. In Bauza Collection, Museo de America, Madrid. Courtesy Patronato Nacional de Museos, Ministera de Cultura, Madrid.

paddling, we threw ourselves upon the sand over-shadowed by dense forests. No sooner had we closed our eyes, than the dreaded war-cry of the Kolosh brought us again to our feet. The greatest consternation prevailed among the naturally timid Aleuts, who were filled with such dread of the well-known enemy as to think it useless to make any resistance. Many of them rushed into the forest, into the very hands of their assailants, instead of launching their canoes and putting to sea.[71]

Baranov could do nothing against the violence of the sea, but, to counter the effect of the Tlingit (or *Kolosh*, as the inhabitants of Southeast Alaska were termed collectively by the Russians), his answer was to consolidate the hunting parties into increasingly larger fleets.

One of the best documented of these annual expeditions, that organized for the season of 1794, numbered, according to its commander, Egor Purtov, "more than 500 baidarkas with two or three men in a boat."[72]

Purtov's expedition is unique in that we have a partial visual record of the scene, a glimpse of a spectacle that only a truly panoramic canvas could have conveyed. Indirectly, we owe this illustration to Cook's voyage of 1778, when young George Vancouver had been a midshipman aboard the *Discovery*. Now, sixteen years later, he was back in these same Alaskan waters in command of the *Chatham* and the *Discovery*, filling in those parts of the Admiralty's surveys left incomplete by Cook. On the morning of May 16, 1794, near Port Dick on the Kenai Peninsula, Vancouver found himself surrounded by hundreds of baidarkas belonging to Purtov's fleet:

> *. . . a sight we little expected in these seas. A numerous fleet of skin canoes, each carrying two men only, were about the* Discovery, *and, with those that at the same time visited the* Chatham, *it was computed there could not be less than four hundred Indians present.*[73]

The scene was captured by the ship's artist (minus the baidarkas, to be added later, says a penciled note on the original sketch) and was later engraved (with the addition of thirty-seven baidarkas) for the London edition of Vancouver's account of his voyage.

As Purtov's fleet swept across the gulf, life grew short for any sea otters that fell within its reach. "We arrived [at Icy Bay] on the 10th [of June] and killed about 500 sea otters," reported Purtov. "We could see more sea otters in the sea further out, but we were in a hurry to reach Yakutat Bay."[74]

At Yakutat the Natives were decidedly unfriendly and indications of hostility grew more threatening day by day. "We noticed that they had lots of guns, lead, and powder in their possession,"[75] noted Purtov, who did his best to placate the chiefs with gifts while preparing his camp for defense. Vancouver's Lieutenant Peter Puget, in command of the *Chatham*, sailed into Yakutat Bay on June 13 and offered the besieged Russians the protection of his guns. "They were in need of fresh fish," reported Purtov. "We brought them about thirty halibuts, and they gave us a fine reception, with whisky. They invited me, Purtov, to spend the night on board."[76]

One wonders — and perhaps some of the other officers' unpublished journals can tell — just how much whiskey was consumed before Purtov and his paddlers decided to tie up their baidarka for the night. This alliance between Purtov and the English — and the appearance of Purtov at the head of his baidarka fleet, in front of the Tlingit encampment, accompanied by a "whaleboat with six sailors, armed with cannons"[77] — induced the Yakutat Natives to give up the Kodiak hostages who had been the cause of the dispute. For this summer at least, the Russians were allowed to hunt in peace.

Purtov mentions presenting the *Chatham* with a three-hatch baidarka as a token of his thanks, but of this vessel, in Vancouver's narrative, we have no further trace.[78] We do have, in Vancouver's words, the details of a visit to the Russian encampment on Point Turner by Lieutenant Puget, who "found the whole party comfortably situated":

Their temporary habitations were each formed by two canoes placed edgeways, about four feet asunder, and their paddles constituted a kind of roof, over which were laid thick skins of land animals, which effectually protected them from the inclemency of the weather; and formed, though a small and low, yet a comfortable resting place; the bottom being first covered by a mat, strewed over with clean dry grass.[79]

According to Langsdorff, Purtov's fleet numbered seven hundred baidarkas and over fourteen hundred men, perhaps an exaggeration — but we have other evidence to corroborate this size fleet. "The whole party used to consist of up to 800 baidarkas,"[80] wrote Hieromonk Father Gedeon at Kodiak in 1804, and Khlebnikov, who kept Baranov's official records, agrees: "They could bring together as many as 700 baidarkas on Kodiak . . . occasionally even more could be assembled."[81]

A young Russian naval officer by the name of Gavriil Ivanovich Davydov, stationed at Kodiak over the winter of 1802-1803, outlined in his journal the logistics of one of the hunts:

The main party, consisting of around 500 baidarkas, left Kad'iak in April, followed the American coast as far, perhaps, as Bobrovaia (Sea Otter) Bay [on the west coast of Prince of Wales Island], and returned at the end of August. Although each Koniaga, when he sets off on such a lengthy journey, makes himself a new baidarka, it will hardly hold together for the return journey, especially if the summer has been wet, because this causes the skin to rot . . . In Yakutat the lakhtaks [skin coverings] are taken from the baidarkas and smeared with fat and the Americans are issued guns, which they had not been given earlier for fear that they might use them to kill the promyshlenniks in the party and then return to Kad'iak. On the return journey they also travel together as far as Yakutat and there the guns and other objects are taken away again. After this they all hurry home as fast as they can in order to catch the fish still going upstream in the rivers and to lay in stocks of them as winter food.[82]

The entire party was controlled by a single Russian *peredovshchik* who made the decisions relating to the hunt, collected the pelts from the hunters, and kept a record of their catch. The peredovshchik was also in charge of trade with the inhabitants of the regions through which they passed — "barter[ing] furs from those people from whom the Company does not dare take them," says Davydov. Attached to the peredovshchik were seven or eight promyshlenniks, and it may be seen that the ratio of Natives to Russians was nearly 100 to 1.

These annual voyages encompassed over two thousand miles, and only the toughest were able to survive the trip. "Some baidarkas, because of their state of repair, and some Americans because of their state of health are left to hunt near Nuchek [Port Etches, on Hinchinbrook Island in Prince William Sound],"[83] wrote Hieromonk Gedeon. Those who completed two or three of these expeditions across the Gulf of Alaska were rewarded by the company by being assigned to hunt somewhat closer to home. "Many such paddlers," wrote Davydov, "once they have made two such journeys, fall into a fever and are completely without strength."[84]

Davydov, eighteen years of age at the time, found in Alaska a land of rich excitement suited to his occasionally wild soul. He did well for us in recording his experiences, both on this first visit and a second one in 1805-1806. Unlike the veteran hunters he did not take the baidarka for granted, and his journals reflect his fascination with the craft:

The normal vessels for the islanders are the three-man, two-man, and one-man baidarka. These are used by the Koniagas, Aleuts, the Kinai living near the entrance to Kinai Bay, and the Chugaches. But the baidarkas vary in all the different places, and the one-man Aleut baidarka is so narrow and light that hardly anyone else would dare to put to sea in them, although the Aleuts fear no storm when in them. On the other hand the Kad'iak one-man baidarkas are shorter, broader, and easier to get used to. The two- and three-man baidarkas of the Aliaksintsy [Natives of the Alaska Peninsula] go better than the others for they are made shorter and narrower . . . Inside the baidarka the floor is laid with old skins . . . so that the rower [paddler] does not sit directly on the framework. The rower sits upright in the hole with his legs stretched forward; the Koniagas, however, for the most part, row in a kneeling position by simply placing piles of grass under their knees. The Chugaches build in small benches and instead of a litter they fit wooden knee plates . . . The Koniagas use single-bladed paddles, and the Aleuts two-bladed ones, which the former people use very rarely.[85]

Davydov claimed the baidarkas "will travel hundreds of versts from the shore," a distance that seems implausible since few of the islands were anything near this far apart. Either "from" should be read as "along," or he is referring to certain epic voyages known to have occurred. Certainly it was not unusual to cover hundreds of versts at one stretch, and given the early training of the Natives that Davydov describes, it is no surprise they made themselves completely at home at sea:

From their very early years the children begin building baidarkas and launching them; they also fashion bows and arrows, learn to shoot at birds or simply at a target. A father places his son when he is six or seven in a baidarka with him and teaches him how to paddle it. Shortly afterwards he makes him a small paddle and places the baidarka in the sea where large waves are breaking on the shore with noise and spray. To start with

the father ties a rope to the baidarka so as to draw his son in to the shore if it overturns, but later he does not even do that.[86]

As to the procedure used by grown-ups when surprised by storm, Davydov noted:

. . . if a storm breaks when they are far from shore, and they have no chance of reaching shelter, then they gather the baidarkas together in twos and threes and ride out the storm. They try to come alongside each other so that the sides of the baidarkas do not touch, for it would be easy to chafe through the leather. No more than three gather together in case there is a large wave and many of them are dashed together. If just one baidarka is caught in a storm, then two large inflated bladders are sometimes tied to its sides.[87]

Davydov was among the first foreigners able to handle a single-hatch baidarka on his own. "In my spare time on Kad'iak," he wrote, "I learnt how to paddle a one-man baidarka and grew so accustomed to it that I eventually went quite a distance out to sea. . ."[88]

For a naval officer of his day, Davydov trusted the baidarka to a special degree. On his way back to Okhotsk, his transport, the *Elisaveta,* was nearly wrecked. "If we had lost our ship," wrote Davydov, "we would have had to cross from the Aleutian Islands to Kamchatka in leather baidarkas. Then the American Company would have lost a cargo worth in the region of two million rubles."[89] No mention that they might have lost their lives. Davydov's journal while at Kodiak shows the baidarka in the hands of an adventurous young man, as on the following occasion while returning to St. Paul's Harbor (Kodiak) from a day's hunting excursion on March 20, 1803.

We were still some way from the harbour. Almost every wave broke right over us and we often got mouthfuls of sea water. But it was mostly our hands

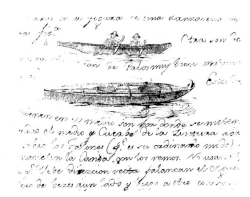

A dugout canoe and a two-hatch baidarka were sketched at Yakutat Harbor (Port Mulgrave) in July of 1791.

Ink sketch from Tomás de Suria's journal of the Malaspina expedition. Courtesy Beinecke Library, Yale University.

El Cacique de Mulgrave acompañado de otras Canoas pide la paz á las Corbetas

Stolen trousers are being offered in exchange for peace and the release of a Native hostage detained aboard the *Atrevida*. On July 5, 1791, the theft of a pair of trousers at Yakutat precipitated hostilities between the Spaniards of the Malaspina expedition and the Tlingit.

Wash drawing by José Cardero (sometimes attributed to Tomás de Suria) in Museo de America, Madrid. Courtesy Patronato Nacional de Museos, Ministera de Cultura.

Structural diagram from 1805 shows a one-hatch Unalaska baidarka. Scale is in feet.

Engraving from Langsdorff's Bemerkungen, *1812. Courtesy Bancroft Library, University of California.*

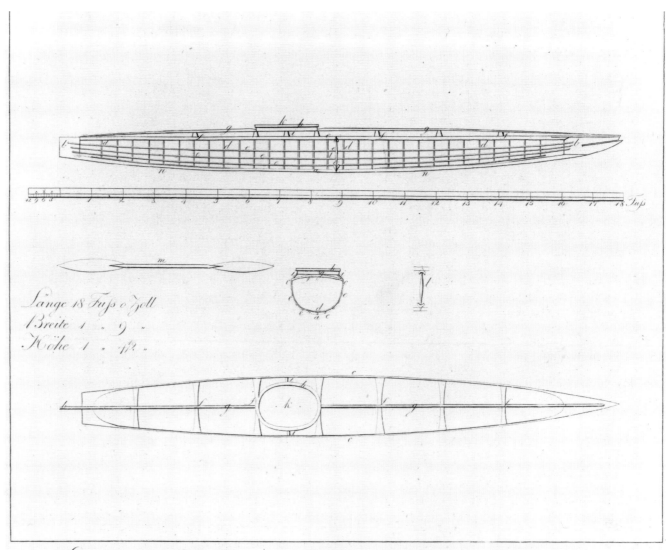

Länge 18 Fuß 0 Zoll
Breite 1 . 9 .
Höhe 1 . 4½ .

Einsitzige Baidarka von der aleutischen Insel Unalaska.

that suffered as they became numb with the wetness and intense cold. As we plunged the paddles in one side and then the other they were almost torn from our hands. Despite this the Americans in my baidarka rowed skillfully and showed no signs of fear, and as each huge wave came up they shouted: "koo, koo, koo!" in order, I think, to warn their colleagues of the coming danger. One wave tore off the covering from where I sat in the baidarka, and the boat was half filled with water, but luckily another baidarka quickly paddled over to us, and we were righted, although there was no chance to bail out the water. At last we drew near the cape in the vicinity of the harbour island, but we could not round it because of the great spray sent up by the waves breaking on the rocks. My comrades in the other baidarkas went further out into the bay, but I obstinately wanted to round the headland. My baidarka was almost dashed upon the rocks so that I too was forced out into the bay; there we portaged across a small isthmus and reached the harbour at one o'clock. We were drenched from head to foot and thoroughly frozen; it took a lot of rubbing to bring the feeling back into our arms.[90]

On March 30, Davydov was stormbound with his paddlers on Afognak Island, but nevertheless went out shooting birds from his baidarka, staying close to the shore.

An obstinate duck, winged on the first shot, led to Davydov's taking a swim:

I tried to hit it with my paddle, but I leaned over too far, lost my balance, and capsized the baidarka. For some time I hung in the water upside down until I freed my feet from the baidarka cover, kicked out, and came to the surface some way from the baidarka. The heavy clothing I had on dragged me down, added to which as I had swallowed a great deal of water I did not come round very quickly.

Two of the Americans (who were with me) caught me by the collar, and pulled me to the upturned baidarka. We all clung on to this with our right hand and paddled with our left and in this way we reached the shore. After this we did in fact catch the duck which had been the cause of our mishap.[91]

When the weather improved — calmer, yet cold enough to give Davydov a slight case of frostbite on one arm "because the waves had been breaking across the side of the baidarka and I was very lightly dressed" — he continued his tour around the northwest side of Kodiak Island, heading into Uganik Bay when the weather got too rough to continue along the outside coast. On April 4 the wind dropped and Davydov headed home, a distance of some sixty miles by sea; but Davydov was not about to lose any sleep:

Until the current changed I had to wait in Bystryi (fast) Strait [Whale Passage], so named because of the very fast currents there against which it is impossible to paddle a baidarka. When the water began to fall we set off on our way. I slumbered in the baidarka, but I was awakened by an unusual noise. This was caused by a small whirlpool at the end of Bystryi Strait. We had to paddle across it with great caution, supporting the baidarka with our paddles so that it was not capsized by the waves. The night was very calm and clear. When the baidarkas became separated I would fire a shot from my gun as a signal so they could again come together.[92]

They arrived at Pavlovsk Harbour (Kodiak) at 5 a.m., having taken eleven hours for the voyage excluding the time they were waiting for the tide to change — an average of about five knots. Davydov's confidence in the baidarka seems in no way dampened by his repeated dunkings in learning to handle the craft, such as on May 17 when he and his partner Lieutenant N.A.

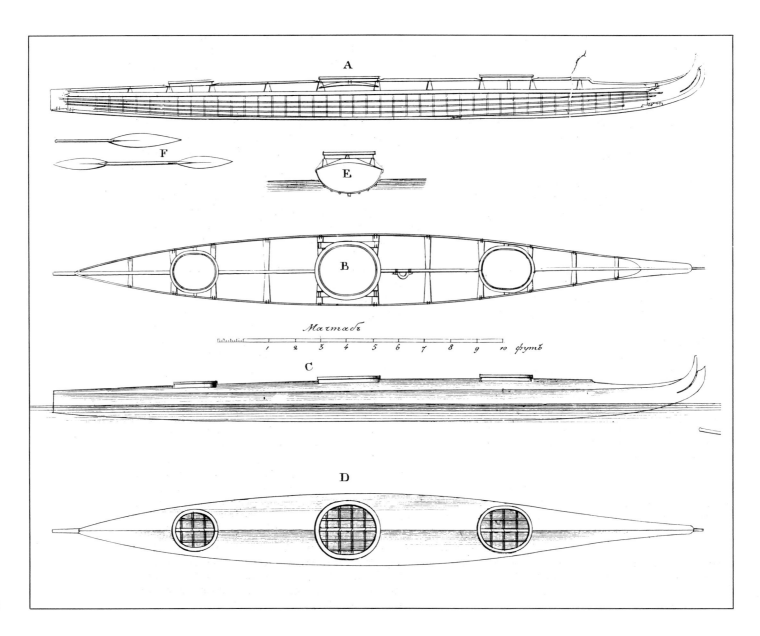

Khvostov discovered the unstable nature of an unloaded, unballasted boat:

After lunch Khvostov and I went off by three-man baidarka to the wooded island [Woody Island]. As we cast off from it we capsized, but we bailed out the water, and instead of ballast we placed another two men in the bottom of the baidarka and continued on our way.[93]

On June 17 Davydov was on another voyage to Afognak Island. In the middle of the strait and thus five miles or so from land, he found himself in a more serious mess:

Water began to appear in my baidarka, but as there was little we could do about it, we simply tried to paddle all the faster. When we arrived and dragged the baidarka out of the water, we could see three holes in the bottom, right next to the keel . . .

We were amazed that we had not sunk, for we guessed that the baidarka had been holed right back in the harbour when we had grounded on a sandbar and pushed ourselves off with our paddles. One of the wooden boards which are normally placed inside the baidarka with a bearskin over it was the only thing covering these splits. If the sea had not been so calm the whole baidarka would have come apart.[94]

Davydov took a baidarka with him back to Okhotsk. With the ship anchored off the harbor mouth to await a favorable tide and smoother sea, the impatient youth

Unusually precise drawing with scale in feet shows a three-hatch baidarka from Kodiak Island, 1805.

Engraving from the atlas to Lisiansky's Puteshestvie, *1812. Courtesy Beinecke Library, Yale University.*

managed to effect a landing in his baidarka so as to pick up his mail from home. He and his paddlers then attempted to get back out to the ship through "a terrifying surf":

. . . we got into the baidarka on dry land, put on our kamleikas, our seatcovers, and laced ourselves in. Then we waited until a very large wave came in, then we allowed ourselves to be lifted, and we began to paddle with all our might. The first wave to meet us broke only over the first paddler, the second covered his head and came up to my neck and tore off my seat cover. It was too late to turn back and it was not possible to repair the cover, thus nothing remained to us but to row for all we were worth so as to get away as quickly as possible. One more wave broke over us, but then we came out of the surf and saw so much water in the baidarka that it was hardly staying afloat. Those watching from the shore when we were in the middle of the surf could not see our baidarka and thought that we had perished, but when they finally saw us safe they began to wave their hats as a sign of their joy.[95]

"Only extreme good fortune saved me from the effects of my extraordinary foolhardiness," admitted Davydov in retrospect. "I cannot justify what I did." All too soon, the fate that Davydov had so far avoided would catch up with him. He drowned tragically, back in St. Petersburg, at the age of twenty-five, on his way back to his lodgings after a joyous evening in the Russian capital with his fellow Alaska adventurers Langsdorff, Khlebnikov, and D'Wolf. Leaping across an open drawbridge some time after 2 a.m. on October 10, 1809, he and his comrade Khvostov fell into the Neva River and were drowned. "Inseparable to the last, together they had come to a most untimely end," lamented Langsdorff, "a loss aggravated, if possible, by the recollection that the last evening of their lives was passed under my roof."[96]

Had Davydov continued with his career — and he was surely destined for a leading role either in the Russian-American Company or in the naval fleet — the Aleut baidarka might have received more of the serious attention it deserved.

There was no systematic collection or study by the Russian Navy of Native American boats. Unofficially, though, many Russian sea captains took a personal interest in the craft. Such was the case with Urey Lisiansky, in command of the *Neva* on the first Russian voyage around the world. He brought a three-hatch baidarka from Kodiak Island back with him to St. Petersburg, where it may still be seen at the Museum of Anthropology and Ethnography of the Soviet Academy of Sciences.[97]

"The baidarkas paddle very fast," noted Lisiansky, "and are safer at sea in bad weather than European boats . . . At first I disliked these leathern canoes, on account of their bending elasticity in the water, arising from their being slenderly built; but when accustomed to them, I thought it rather pleasant than otherwise."[98]

Georg Heinrich von Langsdorff, the German doctor, naturalist, adventurer, and pioneer of Alaska travel literature, grew equally fond of the baidarka during his visit to the American Coast in 1805 and 1806. He made a number of remarkable baidarka journeys, including a boldly undertaken voyage through Peril Strait from Sitka to visit the enemy Tlingit stronghold in Chatham Strait, and, later, an unprecedented exploration of southern San Francisco Bay. Langsdorff accompanied the American Captain John D'Wolf in piloting a leaky old Russian vessel, the *Rostislav,* from Sitka to Okhtosk. Perhaps for safety as well as entertainment they carried a baidarka with them on deck. "And here I feel bound to record the marvelous skill, or good luck, of the Doctor," wrote D'Wolf of a morning in August 1806 that found them becalmed and enveloped by fog somewhere along the outer Aleutian Chain, "as he killed a whole flock of four geese at one shot; and what was still better, we got out our baidarka, and took them all aboard."[99]

Langsdorff's experiences provided him with singular insight into the construction and performance of the vessel in Aleut hands:

Scarcely has a boy attained his eighth year, or even sometimes not more than his sixth, when he is instructed in the management of the canoes, and in aiming at a mark with the water-javelin. An old chief of Oonalashka, whose confidence I had gained very much, informed me that the making and managing of their baidarkas is a principal object of emulation among them. This chief made me particularly examine some of the best constructed of them, and I availed myself of the opportunity to measure them exactly, and investigate minutely the mode of their construction . . .

In some places, where the different pieces of the skeleton are fastened together, two flat bones are bound cross-ways over the joint in the inside, and this the chief assured me was of the greatest use in stormy weather. As the fastenings are apt to be loosened by the shock of the waves, these bones contribute essentially towards preventing such an inconvenience; but this art is not known to all, and is kept very much a secret by those who possess it.[100]

A well-oiled baidarka might remain in the water up to fourteen days without harm, but if the weather was rough the skin would begin to fall apart at the seams in less than a week. And accidents could happen:

If a rent be made in the leather by striking upon a rock, or any other accident, it is stopped with a piece of flesh of sea-dog, or fat of whale, of which the Aleutians always carry a provision with them, in case of such an emergency, and it is the best way of stopping the leak: it is, besides, considered as a piece of prudent foresight always to take some needles with tendon-thread upon every voyage.[101]

"I do not speak here of great voyages," adds Langsdorff, "though the Aleutians will go in them from Kodiak to Sitcha" — almost a thousand miles, not counting the detours and obstacles of the convoluted Alaskan Coast. This would be a great voyage today in any small craft, let alone a skin-covered canoe only good for a week's travel at a time. In Langsdorff's day, however, hundreds of baidarkas were making the journey, round trip, every year.

The hazards faced by these parties in crossing the Gulf of Alaska, even well into the first half of the nineteenth century, were by no means restricted to those of the elements alone: Hostile Natives made an already bad situation that much worse. Faced with a choice between death by storm or enemy attack, most Aleuts preferred taking their chances with the sea.

In August of 1805, 130 baidarkas under Dem'ianenkov, after wintering at Sitka, were returning to Kodiak when they learned the Tlingit were hoping to ambush them ashore. After a strenuous forty-mile paddle they reached Yakutat late at night and found the Russian settlement had been destroyed. There was no other shelter for hundreds of versts along this inhospitable stretch of coast, and, as Khlebnikov relates, the paddlers faced a difficult choice:

Dem'ianenkov called all the baidarkas together and asked the Aleutians to choose: either they went ashore regardless, or they cast themselves on God's mercy and made straight for Nuchek [in Prince William Sound]. The majority decided to make for Kaiak [Kayak] Island about two hundred miles distant. But the exhausted, about thirty baidarkas in all, refused, saying they could not go on. They decided to make for the shore and captivity and slavery or torture and death at the hands of the Kolosh . . . God and the Fates had decreed that those who thought they were going to certain death should be saved. They reached the shore exhausted, but rested unharmed by the Kolosh, and then

continued their journey. In the meanwhile a terrible storm had arisen, fatal for their comrades. When the storm dropped and the remaining group sailed further, they found baidarkas and the disfigured bodies of their brothers and relatives washed up on the shore. They reached Nuchek, and then Kad'iak, in safety. There they discovered that all of those who had been strong enough to set out for Kaiak Island had perished on the stormy sea.[102]

It is a wonder that any Aleuts — or sea otters — survived. In Khlebnikov's *List of Fatal Mishaps Which Befell Kodiak Aleuts in the Early Years of Baranov's Stay*, the figures for the year 1805 alone include two hundred men who "drowned enroute to Kodiak from Sitka" and one hundred who "drowned in baidarkas during storms in that same year."[103] As to the otters, official records account for at least 200,000 pelts that passed through Russian hands — a figure that does not include unreported transactions, sea otters whose skins were later lost, and the substantial numbers being taken directly by foreign trade.[104] Lisiansky describes the conduct of the hunt:

Scarcely one animal out of a hundred can save itself from its pursuers. The method is this. A number of Aleutians, more or less, go out together in separate baidarkas. As soon as any one of them perceives an otter, he throws his arrow at it, if he can, and . . . pulls to the place where it plunges. He here stations his boat, and then lifts up his oar. The rest of the hunters, on observing the signal, form a circle round it. The moment the animal appears above water, the hunter that is nearest throws his arrow, and then hastens to the spot where the animal replunges, and makes it known, as in the preceding instance, by raising his oar. A second circle is then formed; and in this manner the chase continues, till the poor beast is perfectly exhausted by the blood flowing from its wounds. I was told

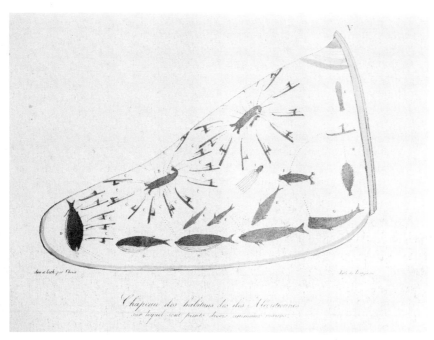

Paintings on Aleut hat depict various sea mammals (and a halibut and an octopus) with a fleet of baidarkas encircling their prey.

Lithograph from Choris' Voyage, *1820-1822. Courtesy Pacific Northwest Collection, University of Washington Libraries.*

by very expert hunters, that these animals were sometimes easily caught; whereas, at other times, twenty baidarkas would be employed half a day in taking a single otter: and that this animal has been known to tear the arrow from its body in order to escape. The first plunge of an otter exceeds a quarter of an hour; the second is of shorter duration, the third still shorter; and thus the intervals gradually diminish, till at last it can plunge no more.[105]

With the outcome of the hunt depending in large part on who saw whom first, the sea otters made themselves scarce at the first sign of an Aleut. Yet even the tip of an otter's nose, surreptitiously inhaling a breath among the kelp, was enough to give the game away. "When a Russian can just about make out something at sea," says an anonymous document from the Kadiak Mission, written in 1894, "an Aleut can say whether it is a one-man or a two-man baidarka, and when a Russian can make out a baidarka, an Aleut can recognise the faces of the men in it."[106]

To protect their remarkable eyesight, the Aleuts wore remarkable hats. We find these hats collected in as many museums as all other aspects of Aleut material culture combined. These visored helmets were integrally related to the visual nature of the hunt: They shaded the hunter's eyes from glare, spray, rain, and wind, and helped make a distant baidarka, at first glance, bear a fortuitous resemblance to a bird or two resting on a log.

Ornamented with painstaking artistry and the rarest beads, one of these hats might be worth more than the hunter's other pieces of equipment, including his boat, combined. Highly prized in this regard were bristles from the beard of the sea lion, considered as trophies of the hunt giving an indication of their bearer's rank. "Since each animal has only four bristles," notes Langsdorff, "consequently any number of them together must be a testimony of having captured a great many."[107] But the ornamentation of those hats was not designed solely to

In "the Harbour of St. Paul on the Island of Cadiack" in 1805, three baidarkas cruise near a European sailing vessel.

Lithograph, from a drawing by Lisiansky, from his Voyage, *1814. Courtesy Pacific Northwest Collection, University of Washington Libraries.*

impress other Aleuts; there were sea otters in mind. "Since the Aleuts believed the sea otters to be transformed human beings," wrote Veniaminov, "they made every effort to decorate their baidarkas, their kamleikas, and their spears as finely as possible, supposing that the sea otter, loving women's handiwork, would come of his own accord."[108]

Undertaken closer to home than the sea-otter hunt but at considerably greater risk, whale hunting had been practiced by both the Koniags and Aleuts. The traditional hunts were continued as a closely regulated industry under Russian-American Company rule.

"All that is considered best in the whale is taken by the Company," complained Hieromonk Gedeon, Alaska's first campaigner for Native American rights. "Anyone who catches more than four — the required amount — is paid by the Company in goods to the value of five rubles."[109] Small reward for an entire season's work. Gedeon describes the hunt as he witnessed it in 1804:

The harpoonists go out in their one-man baidarkas and select migrating whales whose meat and fat are softer and more tasty. When such a whale is sighted they approach it to within a distance of no more than three sazhens [twenty-one feet], trying to hit it with the harpoon below the side fin, here known as the last, and then turning away from the beast very carefully and skilfully so that they do not get crushed when the whale dives or that their baidarka does not get capsized by the disturbance. If they can not hit the side fin they try for the back fin or tail. When it is wounded the whale dives to the bottom. If the harpoon has hit home accurately then the whale is bound to come to the surface dead after three days; if the wound is away from the side fin towards the tail then the whale will take five or six days before it floats to the surface — and if the harpoon is in the tail then it will be at least eight or nine days before the whale appears.[110]

The dangers were outlined further by Ferdinand P. Wrangell, observing the hunt off Kodiak Island in 1831:

It sometimes happens that an incautious marksman is unable to put a sufficient distance between himself and the wounded whale, which throws itself from side to side in anguish, lashing its tail; this either tosses the baidar into the air like a ball or sinks it deep into the sea. The whale-hunters are regarded by the Aleuts with particular respect, and earn the esteem and admiration of all by their extraordinary daring and skill.[111]

The wounded whales were left to die by themselves at sea; the Aleuts' poison-tipped harpoons required several days to take effect. "Spear blades used in whale hunting were greased with human fat or portions of . . . [mummified] corpses . . . which are [found] in caves," wrote Veniaminov, ". . . also used were . . . some of the poisonous roots and grasses." The use of aconite poison — derived from monkshood, a weed common to the Aleutians — was well-known in Asia but a closely guarded secret among the Aleuts and Koniags, who, as Robert Heizer suggests, cooked up the human remains business as a ruse to keep the poison's true source a trade secret.

It is a tribute to the Aleut knowledge of winds, tides, and currents that they recovered as many drifting whales as they did. "Of 118 whales wounded off the island of Kadiak in 1831," reported Wrangell, "only 43 were found later." Each hunter's harpoon blades bore his own distinguishing mark; no matter where the dead whale turned up, the kill was credited to the owner's account.

The whales were hunted primarily as food, although, especially in earlier times, there had been innumerable other uses of these creatures by the Aleuts. Ales Hrdlicka, who dug around some of the abandoned village sites in the Aleutians during the late 1920s, turned up evidence concerning the former uses of the whale.

Among the many uses of the whale by Aleuts, as researched by Hrdlicka, are the following:

Hunters in a pair of baidarkas, seen from the *Seniavin* off Unalaska in 1827, demonstrate their equipment and technique. The hunter steadies his vessel by holding the paddle in the water while throwing his "javelin" or spear.

Lithograph from drawing by Friedrich H. von Kittlitz, in the atlas to Lütke's Voyage, 1835. Courtesy Beinecke Library, Yale University.

With harpoon poised, two Aleut hunters approach a whale.

Pencil sketch by Charles Scammon, from his visit to the Aleutians in 1869. Courtesy Bancroft Library, University of California.

The whale ribs and mandibles were used occasionally in construction of dwellings; the smaller vertebrae served as seats, their epiphyses for plates; from some of the whale intestines were made waterproof kamleikas and bags, from the sinews threads and cords; the shoulder-blade served for a table, desk or seat, and occasionally for a base or cover of a burial. The fat of the whale gave them light and heat, the fibres of the whalebone served for decoration of mats and baskets, the teeth of the killer whale and the compact parts of the whale lower jaw for objects of their industry. The Aleuts occasionally used chunks of ribs for coverings of the dead in a burial; and they burned the cancellous bones of whales in their cremations and on other occasions.[113]

The whales' intestines — along with those of the sea lions, the larger seals, and in some cases, bears — were processed by inflating them with air, allowing them to cure, and then splitting them lengthwise into strips of waterproof membrane as much as several hundred feet in length. This material, as waterproof yet breathable as any fabric today, was used in the manufacture of the Aleuts' *kamleikas*, or rain garments, as Langsdorff describes: "This is made of the entrails of the sea-dog, which are only three inches broad, but are sewed together with so much ingenuity, that, though ornamented with goat's hair or small feathers, the water never penetrates through the seams."[114]

"No Koniaga can travel by baidarka without one," says Davydov. "When this coat is finished then its sleeves are tied together and it is filled with water, and if there are no leaks then the kamleika is pronounced good."[115]

This sort of raingear became the standard not just for Alaskan kayakers, but for many other visitors to the coast. In some instances, foreign trading captains had their entire crew outfitted with gut-skin rainsuits for their return voyage around Cape Horn. "Thus clothed," wrote Langsdorff, "one may be out for a whole day in the heaviest rain, without finding any inconvenience, or being wetted in the slightest degree."[116]

I believe that Langsdorff (and other observers) failed to note an essential point: The regular tufts of goat's hair or small feathers, incorporated so painstakingly into each seam, served not just as ornamentation, but as a means to actively exclude all external moisture from the one place through which it might get in. This weakness is recognized today by manufacturers who include tubes of "seam sealer" with their otherwise impervious goods.

The chronology of this narrative has reached the point where particular attention should be given to the writings of Ivan Evseevich Veniaminov, although his work is of such great scope it is difficult to categorize by the period in which he wrote. He arrived as a priest at Unalaska in 1824 and remained there for ten years, during which time hardly a single detail of the surrounding landscape, natural phenomena, or human culture escaped his penetrating mind. Immediately upon landing he began to learn to speak Aleut, and, within two years, had devised an alphabet for the Aleut language, opened a school, and translated a catechism as well as the Gospel of St. Matthew into Aleut. Traveling by baidarka to reach areas where the infrequent company vessels did not call, he visited every last outpost of his vast parish — including the entire Aleutian chain, part of the Alaska Peninsula, and the Pribilof Islands.

In 1834, under Wrangell's invitation, Veniaminov was transferred to Sitka. In 1840 he was appointed Bishop of Kamchatka, the Aleutian Islands, and the Kuriles; Archbishop in 1850; and in 1868, after the sale of Alaska to the United States, he became Metropolitan of Moscow, or the head of the Russian Orthodox Church. He died in 1879, and, one hundred years later, was canonized as Saint Innocent of the Aleutians. By all accounts he was a beloved, selfless man, a true scholar, and talented with his hands. "A very powerful athletic man . . . standing in his boots about six feet three; quite Herculean, and very clever,"[117] says Captain Edward Belcher, who made his acquaintance at Sitka in 1837. Veniaminov was just

then completing his monumental *Notes on the Islands of the Unalashka District,* published at St. Petersburg in 1840. By far the most complete ethnography we have of the Aleuts, it includes the following discussion of their boats:

> *It is not known who first invented the baidarka, whether it was the Aleuts or their neighbors, that is, the Kadiaks or other North Americans. It is known only that their first baidarki were so imperfect that only with difficulty could they pass from one island to another and only in calm weather. They were wide and short, therefore very clumsy when in motion. It is beyond dispute, however, that it was the Aleuts who perfected the baidarka.*
>
> *But . . . the baidarki of the present-day Aleuts are no longer so perfect as those of the former Aleut riders. At that time . . . they were so speedy that birds could not outrun them. They were so narrow and sharp-keeled that they could not stand upright in the water without a rider, and so light that a seven year old child could easily carry them.*[118]

Veniaminov adds that the above claim is not an exaggeration, and refers to certain sea birds that "cannot rise into the air at once, but for a very long time must run over the sea, using their feet and wings, and these birds cannot escape from the best baidarka." He cites a number of quantitative references to the baidarka's maximum sustainable speed:

> *When Captain Krenitsin and Levashev were here, a certain Aleut, who was one of the best riders, was sent from Captain's Harbour [Port Levashev, in Captain's Bay] to Issanakhski Sound [Isonotski Strait, or "False Pass"] with most important news. In 25 to 30 hours he covered a distance of about 200 versts [140 miles], but upon his arrival he soon died from a flow of blood from his chest. Similarly,*

Waiting for the sea otter to rise again — the upturned paddle indicates where it submerged — Aleuts form a "surround" in the waters south of Saanak Island.

Drawing by Henry Wood Flliott, 1870s, from Our Arctic Province, *1886. Courtesy Special Collections Division, University of British Columbia Library.*

"Natives of Akoon and Akootan killing Humpback whales" shows the hunting methods of the 1870s, little changed from earlier times.

Drawing by Henry Wood Elliott, from Our Arctic Province, *1886. Courtesy Special Collections Division, University of British Columbia Library.*

many times they covered the distance from Ugamak Island [in the Krenitzin Group] to Sannakh [Island, off the Alaska Peninsula] in from 12 to 18 hours (about 120 versts) [90 miles]. The best of the present day riders can go upstream against the swiftest current in the straits, for instance that of Unalgin, [Unalga Pass, where "currents and tide rips of unusual magnitude . . . may reach 9 knots" —U.S. Coast Pilot] where at the promontory the current reaches a speed of six and one-half knots.[119]

"The greatest width of a good baidarka is not in the middle, but near the nose," says Veniaminov, who implies that the flexibility of the baidarka's skeleton might have had something to do with its speed:

In the best one-hatched baidarka, in order to give them speed, they inserted as many as 60 small bones in all the joints, the bones were used as plugs, the end of the axis, the locks, plates, etc. When such a baidarka was in motion, almost every part was in movement . . . The keel is always in three pieces in order that the baidarka may have movement when on the run or, as they say, that it may "bend" over the wave.[120]

"It is obvious that every part and even the very sheathing of the baidarka requires a skilled hand and not every Aleut can be a master," notes Veniaminov. "For this reason not every Aleut baidarka has all the good qualities." He details the construction of the framework, explaining how the structure was bound together with filaments of whalebone (baleen fibers), and noting correctly that "The principal part of every baidarka is not, as Mr. Sarychev declares, the keel, but the [gunwales] or upper frame." Of paramount importance to the skin boat, of course, was its skin:

The sheathing or covering of the baidarka is made from the esophagus of sea lions or seals. It

is placed over the baidarka and is sewn on almost completely except the upper seam from hatch to stern, and, in a two and three-hatched baidarka from the forward hatch to the stern. This last seam is sewed on the baidarka itself . . . There is no other sheathing in the interior of the baidarka, but during a trip an old esophagus is laid on the inside over the framework and then the litter and freight.

For the greater firmness of the sheathing, they smear it with fat on clear days, but no matter how much they watch over it, one covering will not last a whole year. The frame can give service for several years, if repairs are made.[121]

By "sea lion esophagus" is meant the outer hide of the sea lion's battle-toughened throat — mentioned by other sources as especially favored for long-wearing waterproof boots. As Veniaminov explains, a leather or gut-skin spray skirt was sometimes permanently attached to the hatch coaming of the Aleut boats:

The baidarka also requires a covering without which it would be impossible to ride not only on a distant voyage, but even a short distance if it is windy. The coverings are always made from the intestines or throats of sea lions. They are from one-half to three-fourths of an arshin [fourteen to twenty-one inches] in height or width. One side of the covering is put over the hatch and is fastened to the baidarka with whalebone. In cases of necessity, the rider draws the other side tight under his breast with a cord made of sinew and lashes it over his left shoulder.[122]

The Aleut paddle, according to Veniaminov, was between six and seven feet in length and "made of California *chaga* [cedar] as the lightest wood of all." On occasion, and only with their two-hatch boats, some of the Unalaska Aleuts used single-bladed paddles, as was the practice at Kodiak, Prince William Sound, and places further to the east. Stones as well as water containers were used as ballast to trim and stabilize an empty boat. And, besides a simple sea sponge such as Cook had seen in use at Unalaska in 1778, it was considered necessary to have a more effective means of bailing water out of the boat:

> *The pump is made of wood and is nothing more than a cylindrical funnel about half an arshin [13½ inches] in length. In the middle, it is no thicker than a man's arm. Its thickness gradually decreases, until, at the other end, it could be put into one's mouth. In a two-hatch baidarka the task of pouring out the water always falls to the rower in the rear, who, moreover, is always more skillful and stronger than the one in front, because it is his job to steer the course of the boat.[123]*

Potentially most valuable, among Veniaminov's notes, are the details of Aleut equipment and technique for performing unassisted self-rescue at sea (modern-day "inventors" of self-rescue systems, take note):

> *In the number of things indispensable to the baidarka, formerly belonged the bladder, i.e. the cleaned stomach of a seal or sea-lion, which was needed for the occasion when a rider overturned. In such a situation, to emerge from the baidarka and set it on its keel again without shipping water, and, even if water pours in, to bail it out, is not very difficult. But to get into the baidarka without any other point of support is completely impossible. An inflated bladder on such an occasion was extremely useful, because with its assistance the rider could maintain himself on the water and get into the baidarka. It would happen that if the sheathing of the baidarka should somehow be torn, the rider with the assistance of the bladder got out of the baidarka, turned it over, and repaired it, and then got into it again, if this took place in calm weather.*

> *In a brisk wind and under unfavourable circumstances, they placed the bladder in the baidarka, and there inflated it as much as possible. It supported the baidarka on the surface of the water, notwithstanding the fact that it was full of water.[124]*

Veniaminov gives the impression that capsizing was an unlikely if not unprecedented event:

> *All the Aleuts are able to keep their balance in every situation, and some are so agile that they can get on their feet in the baidarka, as long as they have an oar in their hands. Such actions as, for instance, the flinging of arrows, or, when setting off from shore in a small surf, to stand with one leg in the baidarka and to push off with the other, etc., are routine accomplishments . . . All that the Aleut fears and with which he cannot contend is a strong current in the straits and a strong surf at the landing place. But even with a strong surf at the landing place, a skillful and nimble rider can either make a landing or get away and thereby save himself and others. In the former case, his doom is sealed if he cannot elude the curents and pass between them.[125]*

Long, exposed crossings, demanding careful preparation and a crucial understanding of what the next day's weather might bring, were commonplace. Veniaminov went on many such journeys himself. "One can spend over 24 hours at sea," he wrote. "The Aleuts eat nothing on the morning before such journeys since, as they say, there will be no shortage of air, and they will not be tormented by thirst."[126] The Aleut sense of the elements was tuned to the extreme:

> *The most reliable indications by which they could foretell the weather for the next day, were the sunset, and the dawn, by which those who knew were able to tell without error what sort of a day was to follow.*

They observed changes in the sky with such an intensity that this, in their expression, was known as talking with the sun and sky. [127]

Veniaminov himself was of a similar heart. For seven years at Unalaska, he kept daily weather observations, the earliest Alaskan record we have. In later years, at Sitka, he became known for his skill in repairing meteorological instruments, and performed repair work for visiting ships. His understanding of the Aleutian climate was as complete as any such knowledge today.

Without compasses, and with the heavens as well as earthly bearings all too often obscured, the Aleuts developed their own navigational aids. "In going to a faraway island the Aleuts, when they lost sight of land," notes Veniaminov, "employed whitened sea-lion bladders . . . to which they tied on a long rope a stone, dropping them so far apart that they could see from one to the other." [128] The resulting reference points allowed them to keep going in a straight line. A similar device is elsewhere described as employing whitened kelp bulbs as floats. Most of the time, though, the Aleuts needed no artifice at all, finding their way by the set of an imperceptible swell or the flight of birds to and from unseen land.

"The direction, at least, of the land is indicated, which is very important in the case of small islands," wrote John Muir in 1881, in discussing this navigational system as used by the Natives of Bering Strait, "but how the birds find *their* way is a mystery." [129]

Veniaminov's opinion of sails — as "completely useless" to baidarkas — is open to some dispute. Details are scarce, even in later times when sails become a more common appurtenance to the increasingly beamy boats. The three-hatch baidarka depicted by Captain Lisiansky in his atlas of 1812 shows what appears to be a mast step installed as a permanent afterthought in the center of the boat. We hear nothing in Lisiansky's account concerning the use of sails on the baidarkas he so carefully observed, and one is left to wonder whether Lisiansky's own baidarka was one of the first experiments in this respect.

That Veniaminov, twenty years later, would be so critical of this "fanciful idea" indicates that it must have become, by then, an occasionally familiar sight.

If we hear little of sails in those days, we hear even less of certain more imaginative configurations in which the baidarka appeared. A notable exception was when Russian Fleet-Captain Feodor Lütke's naval sloop *Seniavin* hove in sight of Bering Island on September 20, 1827:

Around three o'clock we finally saw a sailing vessel advancing toward us. This was three baidarkas which had been joined together; on the middle one they had, instead of a mast, fastened a pole which supported, by way of a sail, two woolen blankets. Coming towards us on this strange vessel was the promyshlennik Senkoff.

This inventive trimaran sailor gave Lütke the required directions on where to find the company settlement, then:

After having rewarded our fellow countryman, for his trouble, with all sorts of provisions, we sent him back. He climbed, as before, onto the middle baidarka, stretched out to his full length, stoppered by the Aleut seated in the hatchway, and we continued our journey, under full sail, toward the west. [130]

Earlier, at Unalaska, Lütke had marveled at the seamanship of the Aleuts:

Seeing an Aleut bent forward with crooked legs, waddling like a duck, and then alone in his

A fleet of baidarkas, with a Russian promyshlennik sitting in the center hatchway of the lead baidarka, cradling a musket, leaves the beach after a night ashore.

Lithograph by F.A. Pettit from Harper's Magazine, *January 1906. Courtesy Special Collections Division, University of British Columbia Library.*

Among the tide flats at the mouth of the Yukon River, Natives use pairs of forked sticks to pole their baidarka through the salt marsh. The dignitary seated amidships wears a shawl as protection against the bugs.

Lithograph from Ivan Petroff's Report, 1884. Courtesy Northwest Collection, University of Washington Libraries.

baidarka . . . steering it in the middle of huge waves with extraordinary dexterity and nimbleness, one has difficulty believing it is the same man.[131]

Lütke's round-the-world commission required his filling in some of the North Pacific's hydrographic blanks, and in this he found the baidarka an indispensably versatile craft:

> *In the survey of a coastline where one often needs to land on a shore where there is surf, traverse shoals, etc., no small craft can be compared, for convenience, with the Aleut baidarka. It is safe and stable, and at the same time so light that two men can lift it without difficulty; it travels very fast, and is easily repaired. The baidarka serves, so to speak, as light cavalry at the head of our large ships.*[132]

Lütke and his crew retired for the winter to do some less-demanding survey work among the tropical lagoons of the Caroline Islands in Micronesia, where, after a few weeks, the skin boat's climatic limitations showed:

> *Upon returning to our lodging, I was embarking in the baidarka to visit the southern side of the bay; but we were hardly two hundred fathoms from the beach, when the baidarka split open, and we had a great deal of difficulty in getting back to the shore. These skin boats, in hot climates where the air and water are constantly at a temperature above 20° [C] are very unsound, and do not offer, consequently, the same advantages as where they were invented.*[133]

This was not the first time baidarkas had ventured among the islands to the south. After conquering Alaska, Baranov had sought refuge in dreams of distant conquest to fuel his belief in the eternally Russian Pacific empire that had begun slipping from his grasp. He sent an almost-successful expedition to establish a foothold on the

Hawaiian Islands — with his eyes on fresh fruit and vegetables as well as the sandalwood trade. He gave the following instructions, displaying the adaptability of the Aleuts, to Lieutenant L.A. Podushkin:

You have twenty-seven hunters with thirteen baidarkas from Kad'iak and Alaska, who can add to the appearance and increase the number of the ship's crew. They are all efficient and courageous men, hunting animals and birds. In the event that peaceful and pleasant relationships prevail, they can entertain the rulers of the islands by their dress and exploits; in case of hostilities, they will be useful with firearms, especially if it is necessary to undertake an attack at night, in fog or darkness.[134]

There was no fog, in Hawaii, under cover of which to launch a surprise attack, and the Hawaiian king was all too willing to receive the Russians as friends. But the baidarkas indeed proved useful after the dismasting of Podushkin's ship:

The ship was in such condition today that nothing else could be done for her here. It was repaired as well as possible, and supplied with provisions for a sufficient time. Entrusting it to Divine Providence and Captain Podushkin, I myself [Dr. G.A. Schaeffer] set out after dinner for Kauai in a baidarka.

I remained alive thanks only to the skill of the Aleut. A violent storm, which struck with all its horror in the channel between Niihau and Lehua [twenty miles across], threatened our lives. In the dead of night, after a sharp struggle with death, we reached the northern shores of Niihau. I spent the night in an uninhabited place, and the next day, not without danger, however, reached Kauai.[135]

Ivan Kuskov, the leading realist among Baranov's inner group, also sought to cast the Russian-American empire toward the south, in his case with a surprising degree of success. In 1808 he took the *Kadiak,* with over a hundred hunters and more than sixty baidarkas, to California, returning to Baranov in 1809 with over two thousand skins. From the Russian anchorage at Bodega, the baidarkas did their best to sneak into San Francisco Bay without drawing fire from the Spanish guns stationed at the Presidio overlooking the Golden Gate. "Marin Peninsula became a portage," writes Adele Ogden in her study of the California sea otter trade. "Landing near Point Bonita, north headland of the Golden Gate, the Aleuts shouldered their canoes and tramped across the country to the bay. In February, 1809, about fifty canoes were seen landing at the north end of the harbour [near the present Sausalito] in order to make the portage west."[136]

The *Kadiak* left Bodega on August 18th, taking a miserable forty-nine days to beat back to Sitka against adverse winds. (Five of the hunters, perhaps foreseeing this and preferring the California sun, jumped ship to pursue a more laid-back life.) In 1811 Kuskov sailed again to California, in command of the schooner *Chirikov,* returning this time with 1,160 sea otters and reports of a climate favorable to raising both livestock and grain. His contingent of 22 baidarkas was among a total of 138 such canoes hunting sea otters that summer in San Francisco Bay. The others had been brought down aboard the *Albatross* and the *Isabella* by the American skippers Nathan Winship and William Davis, hunting for shares on Baranov's account. The angry Spaniards, losing patience with this abuse, stationed armed guards at all freshwater streams where thirsty Aleuts were likely to come ashore. Many Aleuts were captured, though some voluntary desertions were probably so disguised.[137]

In 1812 Kuskov returned once again to California, this time with forty baidarkas and instructions to found and supervise a permanent Russian settlement, for which he chose a site north of Bodega Bay at Ross. But Baranov's dreams of an agricultural colony to feed the hungry Russians to the north refused to flourish; he had misjudged the effects of the cool Bodega summer fog, and

Pulled up on the beach, this three-hatch baidarka has seams that appear to have been recently smeared with grease. 1897 photo was taken at Bethel, near the mouth of the Kuskokwim River.

Photo by an unidentified Moravian missionary. Courtesy James Barker, Bethel, Alaska, and Moravian Archives, Bethlehem, Pennsylvania.

the Aleuts' unwillingness to exchange the burden of the paddle for that of the plow. When otters grew scarce the baidarkas were recalled to Sitka, and upon Baranov's death — and Kuskov's subsequent resignation, in 1821 — what remained of the settlement began to fall into the hands of neighboring American landowners through default. Had the Russians been trained to look for signs of gold instead of furs the history of California would have taken a different course.

The shallows of San Francisco Bay were close to the final limit reached by the Russians in their "following the fence" along the North American Coast. They had conquered the Aleutians, occupied the Alaskan panhandle, outhunted all competitors for the few otters that were left, and were now settled, diplomatically, on the very outskirts of the Spanish claims.

The Aleut paddles had flashed rhythmically in the sun and knifed silently through the fog as baidarkas darted in and out of the Golden Gate, dodging the Spanish soldiers stationed as lookouts around the bay. The records account for thousands of sea otters killed and skinned at familiar-sounding places like San Mateo, Yerba Buena Island, and Sonoma Creek. Was the bay originally this rich in sea otters, or did the numbers include those that had entered the shallow estuaries seeking refuge from the even larger swarm of hunters cruising the outer coast? There was no escape.

Langsdorff gives us our earliest account of a baidarka trip on San Francisco Bay. In the annals of California recreational sea kayaking, this was certainly a first. In April of 1806 the German doctor, with two Russian companions, was returning to the *Juno,* anchored at San Francisco, after a visit to the Spanish mission at San Jose:

> *The moon being very bright, we determined to return to our baidarka . . . and about three o'clock in the morning reached our boat. It was then a perfect calm, and in a very fine morning we commenced our return to St. Francisco. The channel which we followed to get into the bay was full of sea-otters and sea-dogs; many lay on the muddy shores, and others were swimming with their heads just above the water.*
>
> *. . . Our stomachs were so craving for food, that we renounced all the joys and advantages which might have been derived from the chase of these animals, and certainly a rich booty might easily have been obtained, rather than lose a moment's time in the pursuit of them.*[138]

Those were the last sea otters to be left undisturbed by a baidarka among the mudflats of San Jose. The California sea otter was soon commercially extinct: Even the Channel Islands and the lagoons of San Diego did not offer a refuge from the Aleuts. In 1839 F.P. Wrangell, after seven years as chief manager of the American

With an impressive collection of guns, Alphonse Pinart sits in front of baidarkas in 1871, with three Aleut companions in the background.

Stereophoto titled "Camping out in Ounalashka." Courtesy Bancroft Library, University of California.

colonies, would report that ". . . the animal is caught off the coasts of North and South California, as far as Seros [Cerros] Island at Latitude 27°."[139] This is halfway down the Baja Peninsula.

Understandably, the furs were not of the same thickness and quality as those found among the colder waters to the north, where, according to Wrangell, even in mid-winter the sea otter's valuable pelt was not safe:

> *During the most severe winter storms, the sea otter is accustomed to seek shelter on the shore of some uninhabited island or on outcrops of rock and, after careful examination, if he is satisfied that there are no men in the vicinity, he curls himself into a ball and sleeps. Then, while the storm persists, two Aleuts in single baidars approach from downwind. The Aleut in the foremost baidar stands upright, holding a gun or club, waiting for a wave to raise the boat and bring it nearer the top of the rock. Then he springs with lightning speed and, whilst his companion brings his baidar to safety, creeps upwind towards the sleeping otter, shoots or clubs it and regains his own baidar with the assistance of a wave and the Aleut who remained behind.[140]*

Another source supplements the handful of first-hand impressions of the baidarka supplied by Russian round-the-world voyages of the early 1800s. The clergy of the Russian Orthodox Church, like the hunters, made universal use of the baidarka in their work. But they were more likely to leave a methodical record of their day-to-day travels. And, unlike the records of the disbanded Russian-American Company, the church archives have survived largely intact.

Even though the church in the early Russian-American days was entirely dependent on the company — the company's charter requiring it to support the work of the priests, with most of the hunters paying devout attention to the rituals if not the moral principles of the faith —

the hunters and the fathers were continually at odds. Many of the conflicts, such as that which erupted into a small-scale rebellion at Kodiak during Easter of 1802, arose over differences of opinion concerning the treatment of the Aleuts. In this case, a Native chief whom Baranov suspected of inciting revolt among the Aleuts had been discovered secretly visiting the priests at night, at which point Baranov ordered his guard to capture him on his way home. "The monks found out about my intentions," reported Baranov, "and at night they dressed one of the hieromonks in chief's clothes, and put him in the chief's baidarka with the result that the hieromonk was seized by the guards instead of the rebel . . . at this point a real riot started. The fathers all ran out with the skirts of their cassocks tucked high and with their shirt sleeves rolled up as if ready for a prize fight, cursing and shouting."[141]

"I went out to them and also did some shouting," Baranov's report continues. Hieromonk Gedeon, in his account of the incident, agrees: "Baranov came running with his hunters, beside himself with rage, shouting in a disgusting manner, cursing and threatening to put the hieromonk in a baidarka and set him adrift . . ."[142]

Iakov Netsvetov was the first Native Alaskan to be ordained a priest of the Russian Orthodox Church, at the Irkutsk Theological Seminary in 1828. He presided over the remote Atkha district from 1828 until 1844. Inspired by the elder Veniaminov's example, he kept a detailed record of Alaskan life and compiled ethnographic notes.

Netsvetov, raised to the priesthood, not the hunt, asked if he could accompany the men of his parish when they went on their annual hunt. "The men of Atkha," Ivan Petroff would later write, "constitute perhaps the finest body of sea-otter hunters in the country."[143] On August 1, 1830, Netsvetov observed them at their best:

> *Immediately upon sailing out to sea, we sighted three sea otters at once, resting on a kelp bed. The hunters were ecstatic (which happens, I observed,*

Five Native hunters paddle their baidarkas past Rocky Point and Split Top Mountain at Dutch Harbor in 1892. Hunters are equipped with both spears and guns, and wear the visors and gut-skin jackets still essential to their occupation.

Photo by Samuel J. Call, from Army Signal Corps files. Courtesy U.S. National Archives.

In front of the Chignik dock on the Alaska Peninsula, a baidarka carries a passenger in the middle hatch.

Photo by J.E. Thwaites, probably 1909. Courtesy Historical Photography Collection, University of Washington Libraries.

every time they spot a sea otter, and the hunt commences with a brisk and joyous maneuvering of the baidarkas). However, in this case they could not decide on a course of action, as it was impossible to drive all three sea otters together. If they set out after one sea otter only, they would have lost the other two, and this they did not want to happen. To divide the party into three was rather hopeless: chances were that in such a case all three sea otters would escape . . . It is only when the hunting party is very large, composed of many baidarkas, that the party can be divided into two or three, according to the number of animals sighted. Our party, however, mustered only the minimal number of baidarkas. Nevertheless, the toion [chief] ordered that two sea otters be driven, and the party was divided into two, each division consisting of 5 single-hatch baidarkas and one three-hatch baidarka. Each division drove its own sea otter, guiding the animals apart, away from each other, to avoid interference between the parties, otherwise both animals might have been lost . . . In the end, each division took and killed its sea otter, and only one of the three animals sighted escaped.[144]

At Sitka, meanwhile, shipbuilding, small-scale industry, and a heavily fortified settlement had replaced the nomadic baidarka as the focus of Russian-American life. The Sitka townsite had grown rapidly to become the cultural as well as the economic center of the Northwest Coast. The establishment of Sitka (called Novo Archangel'sk or New Archangel by the Russians) created a stronghold for the baidarka deep within what had long been without question the domain of the dugout canoe.

Baranov first decided to effect a permanent settlement in Southeast Alaska in 1799, and chose Sitka Sound, which he had visited several times. "The shoreline was more densely populated than that of Yakutat and the people there had long since been visited by Europeans and Americans," wrote Khlebnikov. "They had thereby accumulated many rifles . . . and they understood the strengths and weaknesses of peoples hitherto unknown to them. Therefore more thoroughgoing measures had to be adopted. To this end a party of 550 Aleut baidarkas was fitted out."[145] This party established a fort with only relatively minor bloodshed, and the settlers managed to coexist peacefully with the Tlingit until the summer of 1802, when, in Langsdorff's account, "at a moment when all these people were dispersed, following their different occupations, such as fishing, cutting down timber, and various other things, the Kaluschians fell upon them, and almost all were killed; a very few of the Aleutians alone saved themselves by taking to their baidarkas."[146]

Back at Kodiak, Baranov's reaction to this news — and to a dispatch arriving by baidarka from Unalaska informing him that the emperor had promoted him in rank — was, according to Khlebnikov, to cry with fervor: "I have been rewarded, but Sitka is lost! No! I cannot live! I shall go — and I shall either die or make it another of the territories of my August Patron!"[147] This he eventually did, arriving at Sitka Sound in July of 1804 with a party that, in Lisiansky's account, had originally "consisted of four hundred baidarkas, and about nine hundred men; but there were now only three hundred and fifty baidarkas and eight hundred men, the rest of the men having been sent back to Yacootat from sickness, or having died on the voyage."[148]

Lisiansky's fortuitous arrival aboard the *Neva* saved the outnumbered Baranov's skin; it would have been suicidal for the baidarkas alone to attack the Tlingit fort. An impatient charge, led by Baranov himself, cost him a flesh wound in the arm and the lives of ten Aleuts.

There is disagreement between Lisiansky's and Khlebnikov's accounts over who initiated the aborted, premature attack. Khlebnikov says that "Captain Lisiansky sent an armed landing party" and "Baranov hurried to send a support party," but even Khlebnikov is forced to admit that "some of the promyshlenniks and Aleuts who were not used to battle took flight. Then it

was decided to retreat in good order and withdraw to the ships."[149] Baranov, nursing a sore arm as well as wounded pride in his Aleuts, left further strategic planning to Fleet-Captain Lisiansky, who rafted the *Neva*'s cannons within reach of the enemy fort. After a protracted bombardment — "The fort . . . was constructed of wood, so thick and strong, that the shot from my guns could not penetrate it," wrote Lisiansky — the enemy retreated under cover of darkness through Peril Strait, leaving the Russians to burn the fourteen longhouses left behind. The Russians then relocated their own settlement on high ground, with careful attention to its defense, and relations between the two nations continued in a state of uneasy truce for many years. "Kuskov's lot was not very pleasant," says Khlebnikov of Kuskov's first winter in charge of the rebuilt Sitka fort. "The number of hostile savages reached (in 400 boats) more than two thousand. The Russians, commending their souls to God, prepared to withstand the siege."[150] Artful diplomacy, rather than swift baidarkas, got Kuskov and his companions out of this mess.

As the Russians settled down to the routines of their adopted American life, the baidarka served increasingly for purposes besides the hunt. We have heard a good deal from the priests, but much less, unfortunately, from the physicians who relied equally upon the baidarka in making their rounds. In Russian America, doctors were vastly outnumbered by priests.

In 1838 there was a severe outbreak of smallpox among the Aleuts. "During the time of my service along the Northwest Coast of America, smallpox raged in the Russian colonies," wrote the physician Eduard Blaschke, charged by the Colonial Governor, Captain of the First Rank I. Ya. Kupreyanov, with the responsibility of bringing the epidemic under control. ". . . around three thousand natives perished before vaccination was introduced." [151]

Enumerating the reasons for the fatal delay, Blaschke blamed in part the difficulty of distributing the vaccine to the several dozen scattered — and in some cases nomadic — settlements in the Aleutian district. Blaschke chose the baidarka as the only possible means of reaching the fourteen hundred patients and twenty-two villages that comprised the Unalaska department. It was lucky for the Natives, and lucky for the annals of Pacific kayaking, that he did. In Blaschke's words:

One [three-hatch] baidarka was assigned to me, a second to my servant, and a third for supplies. They consisted of a small tent, a kettle for boiling water and cooking food (if the occasion presented itself), a small amount of dry bread, a sack of flour for the Aleuts (in case they had nothing else to eat), a large quantity of tobacco, tea, and sugar to present as gifts and to barter for some other supplies in the settlements, and finally, several bottles of rum.[152]

The party set out from Unalaska on June 19, and it did not take long for Dr. Blaschke to begin to appreciate the seamanship of the Aleuts:

The skill and patience of these amphibious people exceed anything that the liveliest imagination can envision. You would have to see them in their little one-hatched baidarkas during a storm and in high seas to believe it. As a guide to lead me from settlement to settlement, an Aleut in a one-hatch baidarka was provided who, knowing the area minutely, served as navigator as well. For hours on end I watched in amazement as he would disappear beneath a wave, then surface from behind it, with incredible skill avoiding the summit of the waves, which could easily have capsized his baidarka.[153]

This latter observation seems to indicate a proficiency at "Eskimo rolling" that is not often credited to the Aleuts.

Dr. Blaschke drew a plausible conclusion concerning the traditional facial painting of the Aleuts: "The decorative painting of their faces by the Aleuts, which has now gone out of fashion, without doubt served as a protective measure against the seawater, which has a most unpleasant effect on the skin." The composition of oxide pigments mixed with whale-fat ointment was almost exactly what he as a doctor would have prescribed. "In my case," he noted, "the skin entirely peeled off my face twice during the course of the journey."[154]

Blaschke found no limit to his respect for the Aleuts' intimacy with the sea:

The Aleuts know precisely the times of high and low tides . . . Such knowledge is especially important when crossing the straits against the current when the water, up to that time perfectly calm, suddenly within five or ten minutes, due to the mixing of currents, begins to boil and short waves rise so steep and high that it is impossible to cross without the baidarka capsizing or breaking up.[155]

"Every morning the old men sit on a high spot and observe the sunrise," says Blaschke, echoing the earlier observation of Veniaminov. "Their forecasts should be relied on implicitly," he warns:

If an Aleut shakes his head and says laconically "It's bad, though," this means "I think it would not be a good idea to travel today." Then one ought very quietly to remain at that place. If, on the other hand, one exhibits skepticism about his words, or accuses him of laziness, he will prepare his baidarka with the greatest indifference, invite you to sit in it, and may say "It won't be my fault."[156]

Keeping careful record of every stage of his trip, Blaschke gives the speed of his baidarka as 4½ knots on the average for lengthy passages, and up to 6 knots or more for a short stretch "when the oarsmen [paddlers] need not conserve their strength. . . . Once or twice," he says, "I have had occasion to sail 16 hours at a stretch."

Blaschke's account of one of these passages bears repeating here:

> On one such crossing, the laftak broke away from the keel of my servant's baidarka, and the water, although slowed down by the air resistance in the tightly closed baidarka, was pouring in rather quickly. My servant, who was a little behind us, let out a terrible cry — for very understandable reasons. When we got to him, he had to sit in a rather awkward position on top of my baidarka between me and the forward oarsman. Immediately, we turned over his baidarka, drew out the water with a wooden pump (an item just as essential on a baidarka as the pump on a ship), and closed up a two-inch hole with a piece of raw fish [whale blubber], which the Aleuts always carry with them for such emergencies. After doing this and having a laugh at my servant for being a coward, they continued to row in a most light-hearted frame of mind.[157]

Blaschke's mission was completed on August 25. He had thus been traveling in open sea conditions for more than nine continuous weeks. Although most impressed with the baidarka, he found the craft was not without its discomforts on such an extended voyage in these seas:

> The sight of smoking volcanoes, a sea animated with hundreds of sea lions and porpoises that at times surround the baidarka and look at it in wonderment or indifferently swim by: all this of course forms a majestic, beautiful picture, and arouses various thoughts and feelings; however, the uncomfortable position and limbs stiff with cold do not allow one to get carried away with delight.[158]

Perhaps Blaschke was at a disadvantage, seated as a dignitary in the center hatch and denied the exercise of his arms.

Forward view of a three-hatch baidarka carrying a passenger was probably taken at Cold Bay.

Photo by J.E. Thwaites, 1909. Courtesy Anchorage Historical and Fine Arts Museum.

In the tall grass, a three-hatch baidarka framework rests on storage posts. Another baidarka is barely visible behind it.

Photographer and date unknown; Clarence Andrews Photo Collection. Courtesy Special Collections Division, University of Oregon Library.

The Aleut baidarka was, by definition, not a river craft. But in the first half of the nineteenth century, as furs along the coast grew scarce, a few Russians began to venture inland to trade, taking their baidarkas places these vessels had never been before.

In 1843 L.A. Zagoskin led an expedition to explore the upper Kuskokwim River in Southcentral Alaska, using two three-hatch baidarkas that were "similar to the Kadyak ones, but somewhat shorter in order to make them easier to handle in the fast waters around headlands, or in the narrow bends of the river."[159] Zagoskin recounts his first day's introduction to the craft:

> *I cannot judge about other types, but in the so-called freight kayak which is being used by the expedition, I feel quite at home. The portable azimuth compass is fixed in front of me on a low stand; my notebook fits between the kayak's rib and its skin cover; a gun for birds on the wing is at hand, and the sack with ammunition and the daily provisions beside me. I can rest comfortably against the back of the hatch.*[160]

Zagoskin then itemizes their supplies — and it is to be noted that this was a voyage paddling upstream:

> *The two kayaks were loaded as follows: 3 puds [1 pud equals 36 pounds] of biscuits for six men; 3 pounds of tea; 12 puds of syrup made from granulated sugar; 20 sets of dried-deer rib-steak; 1 pud of dried meat; 30 pounds of astronomical instruments in a trunk; 20 pounds of tobacco; 2 fowling pieces; 1 rifle; 3 pistols; 5 pounds of shot; ½ pound of cartridges; 10 pounds of powder; a tent, a retort, a teapot, 22 pounds of various beads and other trade goods, and about ten pounds of reserve clothing for each man.*[161]

This collection of stuff totals over a thousand pounds. The reader is left to guess the purposes of the retort ("a

Bone-tipped whaling harpoons and throwing sticks poised, two Aleuts of 1909 still dress in seal-intestine raingear and wear traditional bent-wood hats.

Photo by Waldemar Jochelson, probably at Atkha, in 1909. From Jochelson's History, *1933. Courtesy Carnegie Institution of Washington.*

In a two-hatch baidarka, Aleuts demonstrate sea-otter hunting technique: The forward hunter has stowed his paddle on the foredeck and prepares to launch a spear, while his companion steers and steadies the boat.

Photo by Waldemar Jochelson, 1909. From Jochelson's History, *1933. Courtesy Carnegie Institution of Washington.*

vessel used for distilling liquids") and the nearly four hundred pounds of sugar syrup — certainly enough to sweeten their scant three pounds of tea.

In the mid-1800s the first dimensioned lumber began to enter into the construction of baidarkas, signaling the end of the many hours of beachcombing formerly an annual prerequisite to building and repairing these boats. In 1861 P.N. Golovin, sent to the colonies by the Russian Naval Ministry, gave the following report:

> *There is a sawmill for cutting lumber in New Arkhangel [Sitka]; it is powered by water as well as steam . . . Any lumber cut is nearly always used for construction of buildings either in New Arkhangel or elsewhere in the colony, or for ship repair, or for masts, or else it is sawed into boards and narrow slats. These latter are given out to the Aleuts on various islands for making baidarkas.[162]*

This sawmill was put into operation in 1833. The lumber was sold as far away as Hawaii, there being only one other sawmill (on the Columbia River) along the entire North American Pacific Coast. In reporting on the state of the sea-otter hunt during the final period of Russian rule, Golovin again mentions this lumber:

> *In order to outfit the sea otter hunting parties the Company provides the following at no cost: lumber and lavtaks for making baidarkas, whale sinews, sea lion gut and throat, cordage, two cups of rum per person for the entire period, and one and one-half pounds of tobacco. They also distribute for every 80 to 100 baidarkas a certain amount of weapons, powder and shot to kill birds that are to be used as food, and they also give out a small amount of tea, sugar, and flour for persons who become sick while they are out on the hunt.[163]*

In contrast with the 10,000 or more pelts collected annually during the heyday of the hunt, the results for the years 1842 to 1860, according to company records, averaged an annual 984 pelts.[164]

"If one compares the number of sea otters caught with the number of adult Aleuts," Golovin concluded, "it becomes apparent that each hunter does not even average one sea otter per year."[165]

The sea otter had become virtually extinct. What is less generally known is that the Russians, under Wrangell's administration, had faced up to this fact and put strict conservation measures into effect. The ritual of the hunt went on as usual, but certain key breeding areas were closed on a rotating basis, and the animals allowed to begin to reproduce. By the time Alaska was ceded to the United States there was already a slight increase in the yield. The price of otter pelts paid by the company to the Aleuts was kept artificially low, but raised one hundred percent at the very end, to fifty paper rubles per skin. This, and the Natives' isolation from any other market for their pelts kept poaching at a minimum during the period of Russian rule.

Things changed drastically for the sea otter, the baidarka, and the Aleuts when Alaska was purchased, in 1867, by the United States. Hunting restrictions were lifted and world market prices were offered for pelts. The Alaska Commercial Company took over where the Russian-American Company had left off, and private contractors moved in to expedite the hunt. An assortment of vessels, skippered by men of all description, bidded against each other for deck loads of baidarkas before racing in a free-for-all to the remote Aleutian reefs. In the words of A.C. Laut:

> No sooner has the schooner sheered off the hunting grounds, than the Aleuts are over decks with the agility of performing monkeys, the schooner captain wishing each good luck, the eager hunters leaping into their baidarkas following the lead of a chief. The schooner then returns to the home harbour, leaving the hunters on islands bare as a planed board for two, three, four months.[166]

The "outside world," to Alaskans, shifted from Kamchatka and St. Petersburg to San Francisco and the continental United States. The influx of vessels from the south brought a fresh stream of visitors to whom the baidarka presented a novel sight. Among the first Californians to spend time in Alaska was the young John Muir, attracted by mountains that exceeded his wildest imaginings, all within reach of the sea. "I am hopelessly and forever a mountaineer," he had declared. To see those mountains better, he explored the fjords of Southeast Alaska with Tlingit guides, traveling by dugout canoe. Unfortunately for us, he was too much of a walker to think of adopting kayaking as a sport, although he certainly had the opportunity. At Unalaska in 1881 he marveled at the Natives' "frail skin-covered canoes, which are so light that they may easily be carried under one's arm."[167] The Sierra Club's present interest in sea kayaking might have had a hundred years' head start.

Another visitor from San Francisco, Captain J.C. Glidden, in command of a sailing vessel on two voyages to Alaska in the years 1870 and 1871, described the construction of the Kodiak and Bristol Bay baidarkas in more detail:

> A light frame of wood is made bound together with twine. When this is ready, skins are placed around it, their edges trimmed to make good seams and fit without wrinkles as they would no sooner be tolerated by the builders, then by the belle of Saratoga or Long Branch when in the presence of the best catch of the season . . . Several kinds of skins are used; but that of the white fish [beluga whale], which abounds in the bays of the coast, is preferred, being smooth and hard when dry. After being nicely fitted they are removed and carefully sewed together by the women, using thread, made of sinews of the rein-deer . . . somewhat in the form of a long sack, having the after end open. It is then drawn over the framework from the stem to the stern, as one would draw on a stocking; the united

strength of several persons is required to perform the operation. The covering is wet when this is done, and contracting as it dries binds together the whole structure . . .[168]

Captain Glidden, with the eye of a Victorian romantic, found one deficiency in the baidarka worthy of note: "The hatches are so far apart," he observed, that "lovers cannot indulge in osculatory or other demonstrations of affection."[169] Hatches so far apart as to preclude osculatory demonstrations of affection (kissing) of course also precluded the systematic clashing of paddles of which today's kayaking couples are all too often aware; the closer cockpit spacing in modern two-seater boats precludes affection in a different way.

Along with private traders, sea captains, and assorted hangers-on, the U.S. Army, just finished with the Civil War, was sent to occupy what was classified as "Indian Country," under military jurisdiction until a territorial government could be set up.

"[The Natives'] arms and shoulders are much more muscular than those of our North American Indians," wrote Eli L. Huggins, a first lieutenant sent to Fort Kodiak from San Francisco in 1868, "owing to almost daily exercise in rowing [paddling]. They seldom walk for any considerable distance but travel in their skin boats or bydarkas."[170] In 1868 Alaska had only just left Russian hands, and the baidarka was still the workhorse of local transportation and light freight. Huggins was fascinated with the craft, whose "outward appearance in color and form is that of a mammoth cigar":

It is astonishing to see how much luggage the "bydarshiks" manage to stow into their queer little craft. The motion of the bydarka is easy and pleasant, never in the roughest seas causing any seasickness, even in the most inveterate landsman. There is no roll whatever, and scarcely any pitch. The frame is flexible, so that when the middle of the keel is on the crest of a wave, the end sags down

a little . . . From the shore or the deck of a stately ship, the bydarka looks like a very uncomfortable and risky concern, and a good deal of sympathy may be wasted on its passenger, who all the time has a feeling of perfect security, and perhaps is really safer and, except for the cramped space, more comfortable than he would be on a more pretentious vessel.[171]

Huggins reported that "the bydarka is so called from a resemblance to a shellfish of that name," but in this he appears to have his etymology reversed. The bivalve in question, an edible black mussel — or, according to some references, a chiton — was named *Kasuuqiq* in Aleut,[172] and became known as a baidarka only in later times.

Young Huggins was not long at Kodiak before falling deeply in love with Alexandra Kashevarov, a girl of twenty-two from a distinguished Alaskan family whose name still appears in many places on our charts. Under her personal instruction Huggins became fluent in Russian, thus gaining acceptance both from her family and among the Natives with whom he made several baidarka journeys during his two years' stay. To the Alaskans of 1868, English was still a foreign tongue.

On a trip to Afognak Island in 1869, Huggins' paddlers began to sing, in Russian, the ancient Cossack verses learned from Huggins' predecessors, who for generations had occupied the baidarka's center hatch:

They sing other songs, curious to hear from such people in such a place, containing allusions to war horses, battles with the Turk, nightingales, and other objects not to be found within thousands of miles, and of which they scarcely know more than the names. The channel widens until you find yourself riding upon the groundswell of the open sea. Your men bend once more to their paddles, and you are soon near the breakers which almost surround Afognak at a distance of some hundreds of yards

During the winter of 1909-1910, Aleuts of Atkha remove the skin covers from their baidarkas and put frames on stands for the winter months.

Photo by Waldemar Jochelson, from Jochelson's History, *1933. Courtesy Carnegie Institution of Washington.*

from the beach. From five to six hours is considered the right time for the trip; you look at your watch and you find you have been eight. Approaching a narrow passage between the breakers, the baidar-shiks poise the boat for a moment so near them you almost hold your breath. A few low, quick words are spoken in the native tongue, and, lifted on the crest of a wave, you dart through the opening and in a few moments are stretching your limbs on the beach.[173]

The 1870s brought the first photographers to Alaska, and the novelty of the baidarka was captured on a great number of sensitized glass plates. Few photographers, however, became as intimate with the Aleut baidarka as the French ethnologist, linguist, and adventurer Alphonse Pinart. His is the earliest photographic record represented in this book, and he was, as far as we know, the first photographer to carry his equipment — for stereophotography, no less — with him in a skin-covered canoe. In September and October of 1871 he undertook a baidarka journey from Unalaska to Kodiak, the longest of several such voyages undertaken in the course of his investigations into the culture of the Aleuts. A page from Pinart's Alaskan diary — penned in a scrawl such as only a damp baidarka or stormy campsite can produce — is excerpted here. The baidarka party was traveling eastward along the southern shore of Unimak Island — an extremely exposed stretch of coast — on September 14, 1871:

. . . the wind begins to blow strongly from the S.W. and the sea becomes very high; the wind raising a deep foam which covers all the sea and falls again in a sort of rain. The wind blows harder and harder and am obliged to tie the baidarkas two by two to keep them afloat and set only one sail, and natives giving the direction with their paddles: at last is blowing so hard that we must down all sail and were left entirely at the mercy of the wind

blowing now only on the bare pole: at last we made the N. end of Iglak Bay [Otter Cove] and then notwithstanding the terrible surf breaking on the beach we resolved to make a landing which we fortunately reached at 5 p.m. having been 11 hours in the baidarka without being able to move and all being wet around us.[174]

The distance made good that day was about thirty-five miles, and the above passage was one of the few instances where Pinart's baidarkas could use their sails. It was getting late in the season, and they were to suffer, with few exceptions, from adverse winds. We see much of the earlier Russian trade routes evidenced in the behavior of Pinart's Aleuts: Every landing place was known to them, usually associated with an anecdote from former times (carefully recorded, in either the Russian or Aleut language, by Pinart), and at points near difficult crossings there was always a Greek (Russian Orthodox) cross at which the hunting parties had prayed before setting out.

Pinart shows us a unique perspective on the past. Among the first outside the church to learn to speak Aleut, Pinart filled his notebooks with such details as the dozens of words in the Aleut language specifying different varieties of wind — information that only day after day in a baidarka with Aleut companions could bring out. We are faced with a great void in that most of the material he collected, and his stereo views of the Alaskan scene, remain unpublished to this day.[175] On the journey referred to above, he and his Aleut companions covered more than one thousand nautical miles in a total of sixty-four days, many spent immobilized by storm. Although it would be advisable to make an earlier start, few opportunities for adventure could match retracing his steps.

Posing for the photographer in 1898 or 1899, Unalaska sea-otter hunters show off their boats, gut-skin raingear, sailing rigs, paddles, spray skirts, and other equipment.

Photo by N.B. Miller. Courtesy Historical Photography Collection, University of Washington Libraries.

A decade later the freelance historian Ivan Petroff, who compiled much of H.H. Bancroft's monumental *History of Alaska* (fabricating a few choice parts of it, as we now find out — see note 137), was sent to the Alaska Territory to make an official government report, issued as part of the Tenth Census of the United States. He found the Aleutian Islands of the 1880s a swiftly changing scene, but with the baidarka as essential as ever to the Native way of life. "The mode of hunting the animal has not essentially varied since the earliest times," reported Petroff in 1881. "A few privileged white men located in the district of Ounga [Unga] employ fire-arms, but the great body of the Aleutian hunters still retain the spear."[176]

According to Petroff the sea-otter hunt was now undertaken by much smaller fleets than in times gone by — "parties of from four to twenty baidarkas" — and only by two-hatch boats. The skills required of a hunter alone in a single-hatch baidarka were now a thing of the past. "Even up to the present day, there has never been an instance of two young and healthy rowers of their own will riding out to hunt the sea otter in a two-hatch boat," Veniaminov had written forty years earlier. "This was regarded as shameful."[177]

As Petroff reports, whales were likewise now hunted only by two-hatch boats:

The two-hatch baidarkas leave the beach at early dawn for the bay where the whales have been observed. Of the two men in each baidarka only the one in front is a whaler, the other acting as his assistant or oarsman, having nothing to do but propel the canoe in accordance with the other's orders.[178]

To the very end of the nineteenth century, whale hunting from shore-based baidarkas was still being carried out. A massive New England-based whale fishery had developed in the North Pacific, yet the baidarka held onto this traditional functional niche until whales grew impossibly scarce. The reason was that the Aleut whaling industry supplied an essential part of the islanders' food, sea-mammal blubber taking the place of carbohydrate in a high-calorie diet that still included little starch.

Other new forms of hunting came to Alaska. The pelagic seal hunt — and the "fur-seal controversy" that ensued — had, by the turn of the century, eclipsed sea-otter hunting in importance to international trade. The congressional committees that were formed to draft the fur-seal treaty commissioned the first survey of the Alaskan fur industries as a whole — including the sea-otter hunt — and found them in a disastrous state.

In some places skins of any sort had become so scarce that no baidarkas at all could be built. Waldemar Jochelson, after a two years' tour of the Aleutians in 1909 and 1910, had sad news to report concerning the westernmost islands in the chain:

The Atka Aleut still use skin-boats of the one-hatched type, but the Attu Aleut have no skins to cover their boats. There are no seal rookeries at present, as the seals and other sea-mammals were exterminated by foreign hunters. I saw in Attu some small wooden boats made of planks from which they fish near the shore.[179]

The sea-otter hunt was outlawed by an act of Congress in 1911. There was debate in official circles over whether the animal had become biologically or merely commercially extinct. In the previous few years prices had skyrocketed to match the scarcity of the pelts, keeping the hunt profitable for a handful of die-hard skippers though by now a highly speculative proposition for the underpaid Aleuts. "The Aleut pursues the sea otter hunt," Veniaminov had written, "more for the sake of sport than for commercial advantage."[180] More so than ever, this was true.

In 1910, for the last sea-otter hunt in history, a handful of otters faced a handful of baidarkas — both sides fielding the remnants of their kind. It was a dim reflection of the wholesale sweep of times gone by when the visored hunters had lined up miles abreast, yet the final hunt offers us some of the best records we have of the baidarka as a hunting machine at work. A few cameras were there to record the hunters setting out, and we still have a few living eyewitnesses to the scene. Henry Swanson of Unalaska was fourteen years old in 1910 and tells the story in his own words:

There was two vessels out of here hunting sea otters on the last hunt in 1910.

The one I was on was a Jap vessel captured raiding the Pribilof Islands, the Kinsey Maru *. . . There were three ships captured and they were sold at auction. Fred Shroeder, who was the last agent at Dutch Harbor for the North American Commercial Company, bought three of them. One of them was new and the other two were pretty old. So he decided to go sea otter hunting. My stepfather, C.T. Pedersen, went as captain on this vessel [renamed the* Elvira].[181]

The *Elvira* went from village to village until it had twelve two-hatch baidarkas loaded on deck and twenty-four hunters bunked below. As Henry Swanson relates, the art of building and using the skin-covered vessels was already in decline:

They had skiffs here when I was a kid. At Unalaska here there was no baidarkies. But the villages had baidarkies. In 1910 we got most of them from Makushin and Chernofsky. There were several hunters from Unalaska that built their own baidarkies at the time for the hunt. Like, Emilian Berikoff who was chief of the hunters. Him and his partner, Peter Krukoff, they built their baidarky here and they used cow skins to cover it. And it worked fine except first time they launched the baidarkies, there at Sanak. They were the first ones to go overboard and they started to sink! The cow skins leaked, or the seams. They had to launch a couple

of baidarkies quick and go out and rescue them. But they fixed that. I guess they soaked their baidarky and oiled it.[182]

The party set out from Unalaska in March, "kind of early." On the sea-otter grounds the baidarkas would go out from the mother vessel every day. "We hunted from here to Kodiak," says Swanson, "and we got fourteen sea otters in five months." With a sole exception, firearms were used:

The hunters had rifles and shotguns and spears. The only one who knew how to use the spear was old man Berikoff. . . He would throw one of those spears out as far as he could . . . And then he'd use that first spear as a target and throw all the others in a circle around it . . . The rest of the hunters would be throwing spears in every direction!

The hunters would be out all day. When they wanted to rest and walk around they'd get the baidarkies all in one bunch and it would be like a large raft. They'd take turns walking around on top . . .

If it got foggy we had a large fog horn to use when we wanted to signal the hunters. If it got real foggy we had a little cannon, a muzzle loader. I fired it — when they let me.[183]

There was one other vessel, Samuel Applegate's *Everett Hays*, out after sea otters on the last hunt in 1910. "Applegate had nine baidarkies and he got nine sea otters," recounts Swanson. "They were almost extinct, but there was still a demand for them. The price was over two-thousand dollars for one skin — to the agent, not to the hunter. The hunters got three-hundred dollars."

The sea otters, it turns out, were scarce but not extinct, whereas of the hunters, Henry Swanson remains the sole participant alive today. The baidarka, however, was to survive among the outlying villages for a good while longer. Bill Tcheripanoff, born at Akutan in 1902, was

Passing a conspicuous headland, one three-hatch and nine two-hatch baidarkas (about the minimum number required for a successful hunt), head out from Unga.

Photo by J.E. Thwaites, probably 1910. Courtesy Anchorage Historical and Fine Arts Museum.

too young to go out on the hunts but nonetheless grew up with an intimate knowledge of the boats, as he recollected to the students of Unalaska High School in 1976:

The boat had a water container and a water pump. And spears. Both men would hunt. The back man had spears, too. If he had a chance and the head man don't see it why this one got it . . .

When the man was right-handed he had the paddle on the left side and vice versa. It steadies the boat when throwing the spear.

I heard all this from my dad. I never went on a hunt myself. My dad used to tell me stories until I fell asleep. For years and years.

If they had water in the baidarka the back man would take the pump and put it between himself and the hatch and suck the water up. This pump is made from red cedar. The frame of the boat is made from yellow cedar.

. . . The only time they used the rudder was when they went on long rides. Other than that they used the paddle to turn around quick. In sea-otter hunting they had to turn quick.

The club was used when the sea-otter or seal got tired. They hit it on the head and killed it. The man in the rear was the one who took the seal or sea-otter out and put it in the boat. The hatch covering was loosened and the seal was put in the middle of the boat. While the rear man was standing up the man in front would steady the boat so it wouldn't tip over.

Sometimes square sails would be put on the baidarkas. They used to have a sail in the middle of the boat. The man who sat in back was the one who worked the sail.[184]

According to Tcheripanoff, the characteristically upturned, bifid bow of the baidarka represented a sea otter lying on its back. The sails and rudders he mentions can be seen in photographs and in certain museum specimens collected in the first half of this century when sails and rudders had, apparently, come into more accepted use. No doubt this was a result of the baidarka serving more for general transportation and less as a specialized instrument of the hunt. There are conflicting opinions about the extent to which firearms were being adopted aboard baidarkas, and whether or not this was a central factor leading to the building of a more stable type of boat. More stable boats, in turn, favored the use of sails, though it is hard to say which came first. We have yet to locate a single early photograph showing baidarkas under sail. Surely this was a fine sight, and one hopes the image has survived somewhere.

The baidarka as all-purpose transportation in Alaska was still doing well by the time the automobile gained popularity in the Lower 48. Larry Matfay of Moser Bay, Kodiak Island, describes building a baidarka for general purposes; this was after the sea-otter hunt had ended, but before the outboard motor had come into widespread use:

Of course, I was only fourteen or fifteen years old the last time my dad and grandpa built a kayak. It was a pretty good-sized one . . . a good strong frame on top and bottom. There was a little bit of keel, not very much. Going up Olga Bay, we had to fight the ebb tide. We went just about up to Becker's cabin. The alder branches there are nice long ones and that's where we got those for the ribs of the kayak. They are about three quarters of an inch 'round, nice straight ones, not too much branch on them. You pick the right branches of alder and take them home and keep them wet and then peel the bark off them. Then whittle them down to the size you want them. Some of them are a little bit flat, some a little bit round.

Then my dad braided them with his mouth. He put them together and lashed them as close together as he could. It was certain alders that my dad used, nice straight ones with no knots on them. He shaved the knots off by biting them; then he made them round. The long ones you don't tie too tight either.

I asked my dad, "Why don't you use nails?" He said, "Nails wear out and cut the skin because nails won't ride with the sea, and they won't give when running in rough weather." My dad liked the kayaks better than the dories.[185]

Larry and his father used their baidarka to commute between their home and their seasonal place of work. Like the Chugach and Koniag for generations before them, and unlike the true Aleuts who sat with their legs stretched out, they sat kneeling in their baidarka — and probably used single-bladed paddles, though this is not specified here:

I used to ride up to Olga Bay. That is where he worked after seal hunting. We would just paddle way up there. When one of us got tired, we just fell asleep, then the other one took over. Like I said, you kneel down in the kayak; but when you kneel down too long, you get numb because you are not used to it. If you sit right down in the kayak, you can't handle the kayak very well. You have to have something to kneel on, like a blanket or something like that. Some riders can handle it, but others can't. Doing it this way (sitting), you cannot handle the kayak in rough weather. That is what my dad told me.[186]

The depression of the 1930s gave the baidarka an edge over the motorized competition for a few more years, until World War II brought gasoline in abundance and cheap outboard motors, all but eliminating the baidarka from most places along the coast.

We have a report from Kaj Birket-Smith and Frederica de Laguna who visited Prince William Sound on behalf of the Danish National Museum in 1933, where, as Birket-Smith reported, "The price of a complete baidarka was $75." Frederica de Laguna elaborates:

When I was at Chenega in 1930, and when Birket-Smith and I were there in 1933, there was still one man who made baidarkas. I was told that there had been a revival of interest in the craft due to the Depression which rendered gasboats and outboard motors beyond the means of many people. The man most skilled in this work, whose pictures Birket-Smith figured, was Black Stepan Britskalov.[187]

Birket-Smith, speaking for Britskalov, details the construction of these boats:

The frame of the baidarka was made of hemlock, whereas the stem and stern as well as the cross pieces were of spruce. The reason for the difference in material is this: that hemlock does not crack or break so easily as spruce, which is more dry. The trees were felled with a stone adze — fire was not used — and the wood was split with stone adzes and wedges of tough, young spruce wood. The fashioning of the different parts was carried out with the crooked knife, and the lashings were of spruce root. The first parts to be made were the stem and stern pieces. The former was bifurcated, forming an upper and a lower prow. After this the gunwales were fashioned, each about 10 cm wide, and the eight side streaks, four for each side, were made. The keelson was a similar, but somewhat heavier piece. No less than 45 ribs were morticed into the gunwales for a depth of 5 cm after which two prow pieces were lashed to the upper prow with spruce roots. They were thin, flat pieces of wood bent up in front in continuation of the gunwales. For a two-hole baidarka the ridge pole for the deck was made in three sections. The coaming of the man-hole was a thin board. In front, on each side of the man-hole, there was a piece made of alder wood, on which the hands were placed when getting in or out of the baidarka. Outside the coaming there was

Thirteen baidarkas, apparently part of a larger fleet, assemble side by side near Attu Island.

Photographer and date unknown. Courtesy Anchorage Historical and Fine Arts Museum.

another ring to which the sheathing of the boat was made fast with a string of whale sinews. Inside the baidarka two short vertical props were placed one in front and the other one behind the man-hole. In the same place there were also cross pieces between the gunwales. Close to the stem and the stern similar cross pieces were placed.[188]

Birket-Smith, again from data provided by Stepan Britskalov, provides details of sewing the skin coverings on these boats:

For the sheathing of a one-hole baidarka six large skins of spotted seal were necessary, for a two-hole baidarka nine, and for a three-hole twelve skins. Skins of young sea-lions might also be used. The women sewed the skins together, then the men put them on the frame, and afterwards the women sewed the longitudinal seam along the deck. The seams were all double running stitches of which the innermost was "blind" except the deck seam which was sewn with ordinary, running stitches. Every year the skin had to be smeared with lukewarm oil, the best for this purpose being shark-liver oil. The seams were not especially smeared.[189]

And the arrangement of the traditional hunting equipment upon the deck:

In front of each manhole, but rather far apart, were two cross straps under which the hunting implements were placed. On the right side, in front of the foremost hole, was the harpoon with the head pointing aft and the butt of the shaft resting in the cleft between the prow pieces. The bow was also on the right side, but inside the harpoon. On the left were the throwing board and the seal club. On the right side in front of the second hole the lance was placed with the head pointing forward, and

inside that another bow and a wooden quiver filled with arrows; the opening of the quiver was forward. On the left side was the whaling lance, also with the head pointing forward.[190]

Of particular interest is Birket-Smith's data concerning rolling and bailing the Chugach baidarkas:

Although the baidarka, as compared with the Greenland kayak, was a rather clumsy craft and the man-holes of considerable width, a skilled paddler wearing the sleeveless gutskin jacket tied around the coaming of the hole and below his armpits was nevertheless able to turn over in it. If a single man turned over in a two or three-hole baidarka, the empty holes were covered up with gutskin. The water that by and by penetrates into the interior of the boat is sucked up in a sort of siphon; then the lower hole is closed with a finger and the water drained out. The siphon is spindle-shaped and made of one piece of wood split lengthwise, hollowed out and again lashed together. A specimen from Chenega, now in the National Museum of Denmark, is 46 cm long and has a maximum diameter of 17.8 cm.[191]

Frederica de Laguna comments further concerning the paddling technique indigenous to Prince William Sound:

One peculiarity of Chugach baidarkas and related craft was that they never used the double paddle. The single bladed paddle was used by the two men: three strokes in unison on one side, then shift to three strokes on the other. This is the same way that the Yakutat sealing (split or forked-bow canoe) is paddled. I believe that the double paddle was used only for the one-man kayak among the Pacific Eskimo, and this had two paddles in the same plane, not at right angles to each other as in the White-man's paddles.[192]

Birket-Smith also recorded a useful device for predicting dangerous weather before setting out:

> Before leaving the shore an eagle feather was fastened to the prow of the baidarka, and if it trembled or shook, it was an omen of bad weather, or, as Fred Allen said: "No go — damn big storm coming."[193]

The following means of measuring when constructing a baidarka were told to Kaj Birket-Smith and Frederica de Laguna in 1933 by Black Stepan Britskalov, "the only man in Chenega who was yet able to build one without assistance":

- *Length from stem piece to the first man-hole: one arm span.*
- *Diameter of the first man-hole: one lower arm plus the hand.*
- *Distance between the rims of the first and third man-hole: one arm span plus three finger widths plus one hand with outstretched thumb.*
- *Distance from the edge of the rim of the third man-hole to stern: one arm span with the right fist closed.*
- *Length of gunwale: three arm spans plus one lower arm and hand plus one hand with outstretched fingers.*
- *Width of baidarka in the middle: one arm including the hand.*
- *Length of stem-piece: one lower arm including the hand.*
- *Width of lower prow: three to four fingers.*
- *Width of upper prow: four finger widths.*
- *Length of cleft between prows: two thumbs plus two hand widths with outstretched thumbs.*
- *Radius of curve of lower prow: one hand span (between thumb and middle finger).*
- *Height of stern below the gunwale: one hand span.*[194]

Three men in turn-of-the-century dress head upwind in a three-hatch baidarka.

Photo by P.S. Hunt, date unknown. Clarence Andrews Collection. Courtesy Special Collections, University of Oregon Library.

Baidarka frame built by Black Stepan Britskalov sits on the boardwalk in front of the chapel at Chenega, Prince William Sound.

Photo by Frederica de Laguna, 1933. Courtesy Frederica de Laguna and National Museum of Denmark, Department of Ethnography.

Upturned frame of baidarka built by Britskalov shows the construction of the hull.

Photo by Frederica de Laguna, 1933. Courtesy Frederica de Laguna and National Museum of Denmark, Department of Ethnography.

More than those of any other vessel included in this book, the dimensions of Britskalov's baidarka evidence the inseparable unity between a boat builder and his boat. Britskalov and his predecessors incorporated, literally, their own bone structure into that of their canoes. With whale-intestine kamleikas secured to sea-lion-skinned hatchways encircling their waists, the Aleuts and their close associates had become, by means of the baidarka, an amphibious species themselves.

Even in death, the two did not part: "In the Aleut oral tradition," writes the French anthropologist Jöelle Robert-Lamblin, "the kayak is not an object; it is a living being, male, a hunting partner which attempts to identify itself with its master and would like to share his married life. Their fates, indeed, are bound up together, and their lives end at the same time: they disappear at sea together or, on land, share the same grave."[195]

"The grave is covered with earth and stones are rolled over the top," Davydov, writing in 1804, had confirmed, "and the area is marked off with low boards — but there is no roof. The dead man's broken baidarka is placed over the grave."[196]

Of the fact that the earth is round they were aware as a result of the following event: their forefathers had sent out two baidarkas in which the travelers had set out young and had returned old men, and they had still not found the edge of the world. So they had concluded that there was no edge of the world and therefore it must be round.

—Hieromonk Gedeon, 1804

An Aleut harpoons a whale in this color painting by Mikhail Tikhanov, the artist with the Golovnin round-the-world expedition on the *Kamchatka* in 1818.

Original in Scientific Research Library of the Academy of Arts of the USSR, Leningrad. Courtesy Alaska and Polar Regions Department, Rasmuson Library, University of Alaska.

Paddles reflecting the
morning sun over Clarence
Strait, in August of 1985,
Kenneth Brower and I slip
easily into the long-distance
rhythm we had discovered
eleven years before. Joe Ziner

Part II
1972-1977
Frame of Mind

Inside Passage

"Even today only the chiefs have one small sail on their three-hatched baidarkas," wrote Veniaminov, the Russian priest who compiled detailed notes on the Aleuts during his stay at Unalaska between 1824 and 1834. "The fanciful idea of some Russians of equipping baidarkas with several sails is completely useless."[1]

In 1972, when I launched my first three-hatch baidarka into the waters of Indian Arm, some 1,500 miles to the southeast of Unalaska, I had not read Veniaminov, and thus did not heed his advice. I attached two small sails, and with their assistance voyaged for many thousands of miles up and down the coast. It was this fanciful idea that made me a convert to the craft. With paddles alone I might never have become a believer, and then an evangelist, of the baidarka's effortless grace. True, my sails would have been no match for the paddles of Veniaminov's Aleuts, but "completely useless" they certainly were not.

To the Russians of the nineteeth century, most of the Inside Passage — from the Strait of Juan de Fuca in the south to Cape Spencer and the landmark Mount Fairweather in the north — was off-limits to all but heavily armed hunting parties, or to low-lying baidarkas traveling surreptitiously or at night. The mainland Natives, a vengeful lot, were not hospitable to uninvited poachers in their midst. The enmity between the forest-dwellers and invading skin-boat people dated back to long before there were Russian baidarkas or a lucrative trade in sea-otter skins to fuel the feud. The otter hunters clung to fortified strongholds along the outer coast, from which they could search out their prey without falling prey themselves. The Inside Passage, its smooth waters favoring the heavily armed and at times ferociously equipped dugout canoes (the Tlingit were known to mount two-pound swivel guns at their monster-decorated bows), would have been a fine playground for the baidarka, but only recently has there been the uncontested chance to try it out.

Although an Inside Passage dweller myself, I never built a dugout canoe. I showed no hesitation about which of the two species of boat-building I was drawn toward. I once had a cedar log that would have served well as a dugout canoe, but I split it into shakes, sold the better part of them to buy aluminum tubing, and used the remainder to build a house. I lived in this cedar tree house while building some 247 feet of skin-covered boats. It would have taken a small forest to build so many dugout craft.

The tree house came about by accident. A midnight watch found me alone on deck of the forty-eight-foot auxiliary sailing vessel *D'Sonoqua* in August of 1972, motoring south toward Vancouver over a windless Georgia Strait. The coast was clear, all the headlands marked by familiar flashes of light. A single, distant tug — a triad of lights moving planetlike among the constellations of the horizon — and the hourly check on the engine gauges were the only concerns in my world. The *D'Sonoqua* wandered across the phosphorescent sea, leaving a hypnotic glow in her wake.

A terrific impact brought me back to full attention, and the captain out on deck. We had hit a huge, high-floating log. The time I took in pulling the engine out of gear suggested I had been fast asleep at the wheel. That I had been wide awake, gazing into the mountainous dawn behind us, was better left unsaid. I wished us back on course. But the captain took the wheel, threw the engine in reverse, and maneuvered us toward a second collision with the log.

This particular log, he explained, was too valuable to be left drifting haphazardly about the strait. Virgin West Coast cedar, it was thirty feet long and four feet through, without trace of damage or knots. I drove a ring-dog for a towline into a surface as stable as a government wharf. The next tide saw us through Vancouver's First and Second Narrows; evening found us anchored off Belcarra Park, near the entrance to Indian Arm. I paddled the huge log ashore and secured it at the foot of a conspicuous Douglas fir.

I soon left my berth aboard the *D'Sonoqua* to take command of my own vessel — if only a skin boat. The fir and the cedar together became my home. My first interest was in the cash that bundles of cedar shakes would represent. After making a hundred dollars in twenty-four-inch barn shakes — sold to the Log Cabin Restaurant in the nearby Vancouver suburb of Deep Cove — I began to experiment with splitting planks out of the remainder of the log. As the boards accumulated I began thinking of a house, and how a house — especially in the northern rain forest — should have an unobstructed view. The fir tree drew my imagination upward to its heights. By the end of November I was settled down — up — in that tree (ninety-five feet up, to be exact) with my first winter's fuel supplied by the trimmings from the shake-claim on the beach.

The cedar's grain was fine. For century upon century, sunlight and moisture had laid down alternate rings of growth. Some of my shakes spanned seven hundred years. The recorded history of the coastline below the tree house — the entire 194 years from Cook's landfall at Nootka Sound to the grand opening of the Log Cabin Restaurant in Deep Cove — occupied only superficial inches of the resinous heartwood paneling my walls.

Winter stormed around me. By the light of a coal-oil lamp I read volume upon volume of the journals kept by the earliest visitors to the Northwest Coast. Through the details of these outer layers I began to sense the prehistory beneath, before the years were counted and their numbers written down. The first Europeans to explore Indian Arm, I discovered, were the Spanish captains Galiano and Valdés, aboard the schooners *Sutil* and *Mexicana*, on June 24, 1792.

"It would certainly be impossible to find a more delightful view," wrote the Spaniards' anonymous journalist about the shores on which my tree house would later perch, "than that which is here presented by the diversity of trees and shrubs, by the loveliness of the flowers and the beauty of the fruit, by the variety of animals and birds . . . the observer is afforded many occasions for admiring the works of nature and for delighting his senses as he contemplates the majestic outlines of the mountains, covered with pines and capped with snow, when he sees the most glorious cascades falling from them and reaching the ground below with an awe-inspiring rapidity, breaking the silence of these lonely districts, and by their united water forming powerful rivers which serve to give life to the plants on their banks, and in which a large number of salmon are bred."[2]

My life began to follow an annual cycle in keeping with the cycle of the tree. During the rainy season I worked at building boats and immersed myself in the records of the Russian exploration of the North Pacific coast. In the summers I traveled, explored, and added rings of experience to my ideas. The tree-house winters surrounded me with wood: living wood supported me; fallen cedar sheltered me; and burning driftwood kept me warm. Yet I had not the slightest inclination to build a dugout craft. I chose, instead, the skeletal construction of the Aleuts.

The Inside Passage is a country shaped by water. Water is responsible for its character, just as wind is responsible for the butte country of the Southwest, or meteors for the surface of the moon. Water, in one form or another, did all the work.

—Kenneth Brower, 1978

In December of 1972, during the first of my three winters in the tree house, I began my research into the history and pre-history of the North Pacific coast. My library began with a first edition of the *Admiralty's Bering Sea and Strait Pilot,* found water-stained in a used-book store for two dollars, followed by a reprint of William Coxe's *Account of the Russian Discoveries between Asia and America,* a contemporary history of the first Russians to arrive on the North American coast. The adventures of these Russian fur hunters fascinated me as had nothing before or since. They were brutal men in a brutal time, yet my imagination was captured by the simplicity of their boats and the astounding magnitude of the voyages they had made.

When Coxe's account was first published in 1780, George Vancouver the explorer was a young, aspiring midshipman working his way up to his first command. The site of Vancouver the city, whose lights shone through the snowstorms swirling around the tree house, had yet to be seen by European eyes. In the life of a Douglas fir, though, this was only a short time ago.

Ann E. Yow

90—Frame of Mind

"Fog grooved the needles of the conifers and tipped the guard hairs of the wolves," wrote Kenneth Brower about the Inside Passage stretching northward from the tree house's front door *(right).* "The high annual precipitation sends the Douglas firs up two hundred feet and more, broadens their boles to seventeen, furrows their bark, and then, after a millenium or so, undermines their roots, topples them and sends them out to the Pacific, which soaks and rolls and deposits them, smooth, barkless, and colossal, in the beach windrows whose chips feed George's fire at night." When Kenneth wrote *The Starship and the Canoe,* the chapter about the tree house captured the public imagination as much as anything else. It was this chapter that *The Atlantic* excerpted in May of 1978, suitably subtitled "Upward Mobility in the Woods." "Henry Thoreau was proud of building a grounded house at Walden for $28.12½," wrote Ken. "George built higher, and for $20 less."

George B. Dyson

A tree house, in fact or fancy, has figured somehow in most people's lives. This tree house has attracted many to make the climb: The greatest number of visitors ever appearing at one time was six, three children and three adults. Here, Peter Thomas and I have pulled Oliver and Claudia Thomas up with the rope, pulley and slings used for hauling up supplies — the tree's branches being too far apart for the children to climb up on their own.

The tree house is roughly five-sided, with five windows. In winter, two large sacks of firewood — hauled up after one trip down to the ground by tying one sack to each end of a double rope running through a pulley above the tree house's front porch — would feed the Trout stove for about a week. The house, ninety-five feet up and directly at the water's edge, was exposed to both westerly and northerly winds, and the motion was occasionally extreme.   Peter Thomas

Heading north through the Inside Passage from Vancouver Island to Glacier Bay *(right)*, I am playing a flute made from a section of the *Mount Fairweather*'s tubular aluminum frame. The three-hatch baidarka we are traveling in is thirty-one feet long and thirty-one inches wide. It was built in 1972 at Belcarra Park, British Columbia, using six hundred feet of ½-inch outer diameter by .049-inch wall 6061-T6 aluminum tubing, at a cost of $112 for the tubing and another hundred dollars or so for the fiberglass-polyester skin. The frame was light — fifty pounds — but the skin was heavy, giving the complete vessel a weight of one hundred fifty pounds. Thus the anchor visible on deck: to avoid, whenever possible, having to haul the loaded craft ashore. With no Aleuts to act as Sherpas when making and breaking camp, even when ashore I found my baidarka conspicuously lacking the manpower with which its Russian predecessors had been equipped. Stacy Studebaker

Robson Bight *(left)*, on the northeast side of Vancouver Island, is now officially a sanctuary for killer whales — *Orcinus orca.* As far as anyone can remember, but as no one can yet adequately explain, killer whales have been fond of the Tsitika River's shallow, pebbled estuary.

My visit there with a three-hatch baidarka in April of 1973, with Jim O'Donnell and Paul Mockler from Toronto along to scout film locations for the CBC, was at the very beginning of an influx of whale-watchers over the next few years, unprecedented anywhere this side of Scammon's Lagoon. The seiners out of Alert Bay, to whom the bight remains a favorite place to fish, now complain that it is hard to make a set because of the number of whale-watching kayaks getting in the way of the net. James O'Donnell

Each of the baidarka's two sails *(right)* has an area of fifteen square feet, enough for the easily driven hull of this craft. Note the close-hauled cut of the sails, designed while I was experimenting with sailing-to-windward rigs — including a demountable fin-keel underneath the hull — before deciding that downwind was the only way to go when sailing kayaks, cold water, and Northwest Coast weather patterns are combined. George B. Dyson

One hundred and fifty years before us, stealthy flotillas of baidarkas had made their way along the shores of Clarence Strait, seeking new poaching grounds toward Dixon Entrance to the south. Where there had been hundreds of baidarkas, pushing south, there was now one baidarka, pushing north. The ghosts of our predecessors flickered in our imaginations around the campfire at night. The "dreaded war-cry of the Kolosh" must have been heard often in these woods. For us, the shores were deserted. We encountered not a single other paddle-powered vessel in our entire voyage up the coast.

Stacy Studebaker

The baidarka floats near glacial ice at the mouth of Tracy Arm during a layover day. I was working my way up to Juneau from Alert Bay aboard a towboat with which I had hitched a ride. This voyage with the *Widgeon* and her barge was one of the greatest adventures any of my baidarkas allowed me to undertake. Hitching such rides — much Inside Passage traffic is short-handed for the trip — is one of the finest ways to see the coast. With all my belongings aboard the baidarka, having just sailed in from Rivers Inlet the previous day, I had gone into the Bayside Inn in Alert Bay for a beer. There was the skipper of the *Widgeon* — its engine had broken down a short distance out of town. He was awaiting the afternoon plane, due to fly in with spare parts.

Skipper Carrol Martin, from Durango, Colorado, had loaded a 110-foot chip barge with the entire contents of his liquidated ranch, and was towing the whole works up to Alaska with a sadly underpowered 36-foot tugboat purchased in Tacoma, Washington, for $6,000 cash. It was an instant decision on my part to throw the baidarka aboard and sign on for the trip. The crew included Carrol's nine-year-old son (who stood a full wheel watch with the rest, and was dropped off daily onto the barge to do the barnyard chores); a British Columbian whom Carrol had picked up, like me, en route; and a sixteen-year-old hitchhiker from Tucson, Arizona. The hitchhiker fell overboard in Snow Pass, hauled himself back aboard along the towline, and could scarcely be coaxed on deck for the remainder of the trip. The cargo included four quarterhorses, three head of cattle, and twenty-five tons of eastern Washington hay. Our top speed under tow, in a dead calm, was four knots, and it took a kayaker's instincts for wind and tide to get us up the coast. George B. Dyson

The 1972 three-hatch baidarka, during her fourth season of Alaskan use, rests at anchor in Glacier Bay. Up-inlet are the great faces of the Muir and Grand Pacific glaciers, remnants of the ice sheet that extended as far as the present mouth of Glacier Bay, some sixty miles farther south, until historic times.

As recently as August of 1804, when Baranov's party of three hundred baidarkas, escorted by the *Rostislav,* entered Icy Strait en route to Sitka — taking the back route to make a circuitous circumspection of the enemy's flank — Glacier Bay as such did not yet exist. As Khlebnikov relates, "an extraordinarily thick fog, which usually remains there all year-round, hid them from the shore and the wall of ice at the entrance to the sound."[3] In Baranov's words, it was "like going into the mouth of Hell! Among icebergs which were like mountains and touched the yards."[4]

Stacy Studebaker

Here is the vista *(right)* that greeted the great baidarka fleets heading south as they turned the corner from Cross Sound and Icy Strait into Chatham Strait, entering enemy territory in which only Baranov's strongest hunting parties dared dip their paddles. What apprehensions there must have been at the prospect of meeting the fearsome Tlingit, with a daylight encounter offering no possibility of escape. Generations of enmity between the Chilkat and Sitkan tribes had put a keen edge to the Tlingit art of war, and against the foreign invaders, old feuds were put aside to present a common front. Even George Vancouver, his longboats armed with the best of 1794 British weaponry and the Royal Navy's picked few at the oars, was greeted with such a menacing collection of dugouts in Lynn Canal that he beat a retreat (thus Point Retreat of our current charts). To the Russians and the Aleuts there was no Point Retreat, but there was a Peril *(Pogibshii)* Strait (off to the right in this photograph), where toxic mussels had killed a hundred Aleuts at a single meal, a result attributed by the Tlingit to the wrath of their offended guardian spirits in the sea.

George B. Dyson

There would be no Inside Passage without the outside coast *(overleaf)*. At Cape Spencer the Inside Passage comes to an end, leaving the baidarka voyager exposed to the open Gulf of Alaska, which is indeed the North Pacific Ocean by a less-pacific name. It is then that you realize what a sheltered world you have left behind.

All evidence points to a long history of human struggle washing back and forth like the tides along these shores. The Russian baidarka fleets were certainly not the first flotillas of skin boats to make raids here. Wrote Ivan Petroff in 1882:

From a shaman of the Chilkhaat tribe, who boasted of his pure Thlinket extraction, I learned that a tradition exists among his people that in times past their ancestors held all the territory to the westward clear to the shores of "another big sea," but that the Innuits came from the north, as he expressed it, "like herrings," each in his own kayak. The sea was covered with men while women and children trudged along the shore. There was much fighting, and a final retreat of the Thlinkets, but they would one day recover their own.[5]

This tradition helps to explain — if any explanation is needed — why the Gulf Coast Tlingits (closely related to the Chilkats) were determined to destroy any Russian or Aleut baidarka travelers who fell within their reach.   Joe Ziner

The Gulf of Alaska has long been described as "Birthplace of the Winds" and "Cradle of the Storms." Here on the beach at Lituya Bay *(right)* the view is toward Mount Fairweather, but the mountain is wholly obscured. The baidarka traveler camped on the outer coast witnesses an unending succession of low-pressure disturbances rolling in across the gulf. There is a certain security in being able to see exactly what is about to hit you — as opposed to the Inside Passage, where the clouds and rain sneak up on you through the winding inlets, accompanied by often-baffling winds.

"The sky had turned gray, which would be its normal color on the voyage," wrote Kenneth Brower in 1974 as we set off together on our baidarka journey south. "The sea was gray and choppy. The near islands and the ridges of the mainland were of a grayness nearly black, and the far islands and ridges were gray in diminishing half and quarter tones. The mists that obscured some islands, and the lens clouds that capped some ridges, were of a grayness nearly white. All the grays were fluid. The clouds flowed over the landforms, the landforms flowed into the sea, the sea flowed with its tide. The baidarka, slender and blue, bisected a broad gray world."   George B. Dyson

"T he sea passed beneath in a hundred changing moods and textures," wrote Kenneth Brower of our journey in 1974, "and the sky flowed away above, forming and re-forming. I took comfort in the blonde wood of the masts, the translucent blue of the fiberglass, the holes in George's Peruvian sweater, the nap of his wool cap, the green of his eyes when he turned around. The baidarka was an island of human warmth in the midst of the elements."

Here, off the face of La Perouse Glacier, the remnants of the last ice age meet the open, pounding sea along a stretch of coastline beachcombed only by brown bears. Mount Fairweather, landmark at the Inside Passage's northern end, catches the last of the June sun as Joe Ziner and I set off from Icy Point on an all-night paddle.

Joe Ziner

Charles Clerke, Cook's second-in-command, wrote in the log of the *Discovery* for May 6, 1778, "The mountain set yesterday Noon (Whose pre-eminence above his fellows be-speaks some attention and which for distinction's sake I'll call Mount Fair Weather, having been remarkably happy in that particular since we first saw it)." It was no coincidence that the English enjoyed clear skies following their sighting of the peak *(right)*, for, as Henry W. Elliott would relate a century later in describing the whaling fleet then cruising the Fairweather Grounds, "When the whalemen saw the summit of that snow-clad peak unveiled by clouds they were sure of fair weather for several consecutive days."[6]

"Its appearance gives promise of calm seas or warns of storms," noted Frederica de Laguna another century later, in 1972, "and it is therefore called 'the paddler's mountain' by the natives."[7]

Here is a paddler's view of Mount Fairweather, as seen at sunset from the traditional Russian campsite at Lituya Bay.

George B. Dyson

A Necessary Monster

I am unable to explain the *Mount Fairweather*, a 48-foot-long baidarka, in terms of anything except the art of boat building itself. The mere possession of my newfound knowledge of Aleut boat building, it seemed, necessitated my carrying that knowledge to its extreme, whether the result served any useful purpose or not. I envisioned — and sought to demonstrate — what the Aleuts might have done with aluminum tubing and nylon twine.

"The saint both pursues and creates religion," my grandfather had written in his autobiographical *Fiddling While Rome Burns*. "The scientist both seeks and makes truth." In my historical research, I had developed such a taste for skin-boat mythology — a mythology to which I had no ancestral ties — that I inadvertently became the creator of some mythology myself.

My first glimpse of Mount Fairweather — rising to 15,300 feet within fourteen miles of the sea, guarding the Inside Passage approach to the Gulf of Alaska coast — was in late September of 1973. The summit seemed to be drawing me westward out of Icy Strait, as was an equinoctial tide dropping almost twenty feet. I spent the next summer camped directly at the mountain's fjorded base. Being near such a big mountain — "the paddler's mountain," the Tlingit had named it — had much to do with my decision to build so big a boat. The base of Mount Fairweather marked the region where the territories of the dugout canoe and the skin boat had overlapped. In my new project I sought to combine elements of both.

Why was this boat so long? At the time I began building it, the question to me was, "Why is this boat so short?"

I was twenty-one years old. The *Mount Fairweather*, as I first saw her, was to measure sixty-two feet on deck. I lofted her lines, compiled tables of offsets, plotted the body-plan sections, and drew up schedules of materials. She grew visible within paper horizons, floating upon imaginary seas. My workshop at Belcarra Park was only twenty-nine feet long; thirty-three feet of tape measure extended into the British Columbia bush. I broke ground for the shed's extension, expecting a flood of federal and corporate funds in answer to my proposals, but a 62-foot length of string is all there ever was to the keel of this far-fetched craft.

"This work consists of using aluminum alloy tubing as the basis of a simple but unique structural system enabling the building of a remarkably efficient and versatile form of watercraft . . . ," I wrote to the Aluminum Company of Canada, ". . . attached is a sketch of the 62-foot craft proposed to be built using approximately 2,400 feet of ALCAN extrusion as detailed in the enclosed estimates of materials and costs."

"This long period of a canoe-centered way of life has only recently ended . . .," I wrote to the Explorations Program of the Canada Council, ". . . and still exists in the memories and imaginations of many West Coast people. It is the objective of this project to revive this practice by further developing the design, construction, and operation of a large ocean-going canoe."

Both ALCAN and Ottawa politely refused.

My funds refused to stretch as far as the stake driven into the ground at the edge of the misted rain forest. It was time for me to scale down my plans. I calculated and recalculated how far my few hundred dollars could reach, in aluminum tubing. The final figures came to $342.39 for 984 feet of tubing, enough to build 48 feet of boat. I made out the order for the tubing and then set off north in search of spruce for the interior planking.

I paced the forests of Hanson Island, ravens screaming as I selected a windfallen Sitka spruce. Cutting it into floor-boards provided my first experience with the length of the full-size craft. It took two days to mill the planks. Will

Malloff's prototype of the 48-inch Alaska sawmill, attached to a 130 cc, 090 Stihl chain saw, had a design flaw preventing its being refueled in the cut. Sometimes a tank of gas lasted the whole trip down the log, and sometimes it did not. If not, the slab had to be wedged open and the saw backed out, uphill, almost the full length of the boat.

The *Mount Fairweather* remains an unfinished chapter in my life. I climbed only the foothills of Mount Fairweather in Alaska, and I launched but never fully completed the boat. The *Mount Fairweather* was designed for unprecedented passages among the Northwest Coast's mountain-funneled winds. She was built for sails (or rather kites) that have yet to be tried and proved, and for courses yet to be steered — perhaps a course that would take the baidarka around the world.

Once, the *Mount Fairweather* and I were balanced at a point of no return. Kenneth Brower was with me, helping to steady the all-but-flying craft. Of that moment he wrote: "The clouds thinned and the stars came out, first Venus and then Orion. There had been a light on shore, but now it was gone. I looked back for George. He was still there, sitting in silhouette against the following sea. I could not make out his face. I looked ahead. The earth had vanished in darkness. The only proof of the planet was the ghostly froth of the near waves. George's dragon prow pranced onward into a sea of stars."

We might have kept on going. We were sailing off at fifteen knots out Queen Charlotte Strait, toward our craft's distant namesake and beyond. But we turned back, drawn by tasks more down to earth — I to build a series of smaller, less interplanetary boats, and Ken to spend two years at the typewriter completing *The Starship and the Canoe.*

Was Ken Brower there to describe my boat? Or was my boat there to help express his thoughts? The *Mount Fairweather* is an incomplete chapter in my book. It is the closing chapter in Ken's. His words outdistanced the boat, conjuring images of a mythical dragon-headed craft.

"We are as ignorant of the meaning of the dragon as we are of the meaning of the universe," wrote Jorge Luis Borges in his *Book of Imaginary Beings,* ". . . but there is something in the dragon's image that appeals to the human imagination, and so we find the dragon in quite distinct places and times. It is, so to speak, a necessary monster."

We cannot explain a world created by our imagination. It may have no material counterpart in life at all.

—Sir George Dyson, 1954, in
Fiddling While Rome Burns

Sails set and plexiglas bubble hatch-covers in place, the *Mount Fairweather (left)* lies at her mooring in front of my cabin at Belcarra Park. Around each hatch coaming is stretched a narrow ten-speed bicycle inner tube, the valve stem facing inward through a hole in the hatch-coaming rim. To batten down the hatches, these inner-tube gaskets are inflated with a small bicycle pump from inside the craft, ensuring an absolutely waterproof seal as well as an air-cushioned, shockproof juncture between the bubble and the boat.

Visible along the side of the boat, on short, folding outrigger arms, are the small, parabola-shaped hydrofoil stabilizers with which I was experimenting. This type of hydrofoil — called a Bruce foil after its inventor — does not lift the boat out of the water, but merely serves to stablize a narrow craft against the heeling movement of the sails. Something along these lines would seem to be the answer to those determined to modify the kayak form of boat into an efficient sailing craft. Each of the three identical lug-rigged sails has an area of fifty square feet.   George B. Dyson

We are cutting spruce at a bay on the north side of Blackney Pass in Blackfish Sound, between Johnstone and Queen Charlotte straits.

Here, on Hanson Island, Paul Spong chose to set up an observation post for the study of wild killer whales during the summer of 1970, and he has been living here ever since. Our first paying charter with the *D'Sonoqua,* undertaken the day she was launched, was to take personnel and equipment up to Hanson Island to assist Dr. Spong with his research. During my first visit ashore I marveled at the forest that surrounded Paul Spong's camp. One cedar tree measured thirty-seven feet in circumference six feet above its base. When it was time to find inside stringers for the *Mount Fairweather,* the spruce at Spong Bay was the obvious choice.

Ron Keller and I cut up the planks and carried them down to the beach to begin a three-month saltwater cure. But how to get the unwieldly, heavy bundle of green lumber down to my workshop at Belcarra, 250 miles to the south? Two days later the fishpacker *Betty L.*, captained by David "Captain Cod" Stanhope, pulled into the bay heading for Vancouver, and the captain kindly took the planks on deck. At Belcarra I moored them out in the salt chuck for ten weeks, then brought them ashore to season for several months in the shade. Finally, after being run through a thickness planer, they were installed within the framework of the boat.

Ron Keller

When I arrived at this stage in my pursuit of canoe design I had not yet mastered the art of lofting a three-dimensional form accurately on two-dimensional paper in advance of building the boat. When I put together this canoe from the curves and patterns I had drawn, not all the lines matched up, as in the case of the gunwale stringers meeting the bow. Here I have applied a "Spanish windlass" to the obstinate stringers to try to bring them into line, but it was in the lines themselves that I had erred. The only solution was to replace the stem deadwood plates, port and starboard, as well as the stem bulkhead. Luckily this was possible without repercussions further along the boat. There is no substitute for having all the pieces fit perfectly from the start; an eighth of an inch here and there quickly adds up to trouble somewhere else. The evolution of my boat-building technique over the years was as much an evolution of my accuracy in lofting the shape of the hull and blueprinting the component parts as an evolution of the practicalities of putting these abstractions of the design into effect.
— Robert Keziere

"A seemingly disproportionate amount of the work of designing and building this vessel," I wrote in the text accompanying my exhibit of the *Mount Fairweather* at Habitat Forum in Vancouver in 1976, "went into the first few feet of the bow — a region of complex inter-related curves . . . The form taken is a result of the need to cut the water with a sharp forefoot, yet maintain flare and buoyancy in the topsides. The split in the stem resolves these two separate functions and gives rise to the figurehead . . ." In the bifurcated, differentiated function of the *Mount Fairweather*'s stem, I was of course following directly in the footsteps of the Aleuts. In the dragon-jawed figurehead, however, I was taking off on a tangent of my own. But even the figurehead could be explained in functional terms, "transmitting the strain of anchor or towline directly to the longitudinal structure without shear loading or chafe." If, in hindsight, to have designed for such strains seems to have been extreme, I should recall that my visions for this vessel included lying to a sea anchor to survive the worst imaginable of Pacific storms, and hitching long-distance rides behind deep-sea freight barges.
— Peter Thomas

With the framework nearing completion *(left)*, I am at work finishing the midships deck. At this point more than two miles of braided nylon lashings are in place, applied inch by inch over the past two months. I used a No. 21 braided nylon seine twine with a breaking strength of 220 pounds. At this stage, with floorboards in place, the structure weighs about four hundred pounds, and so could have been suspended by two single strands of the thousands of turns taken around all the seams and joints.

The primitive workshop lacks most of the woodworking machinery and paraphernalia common to most boatbuilders' yards. The tools I used were a chain saw with 48-inch bar and Alaskan mill attachment to cut the spruce interior stringers, a 6-inch thickness planer to dress the spruce, a hacksaw to cut aluminum tubing, an electric sabre saw to cut aluminum sheet and plate, a ⅜-inch electric drill to drill and countersink the uncounted thousands of holes, seven files, five clamps, three pairs of vise-grips (more would have helped), two pairs each of pliers and wire cutters, several pocketknives, a tape measure, fiberglass laminating rollers, an electric angle-grinder to trim and fair the skin, several dozen sail needles, and a half-dozen net-mender's shuttles. Perhaps most important among the hand tools was a leather sailor's glove with double palm and the fingers removed, for pulling the lashings tight.

More power tools were borrowed as needed, and other tools were improvised from things that happened to be found at hand. Boat building seems to be a scrounger's trade, and in my years around the Vancouver waterfront I had acquired scrounging skills from some true masters of the art. In mountaineering there is a proverb: "Never step on anything you can step over, and never step over anything you can step around." Rephrasing that in honor of one of my instructors, I formulated *Jim Land's Law:* "Never buy anything you can make, and never make anything you can find."   Peter Thomas

A gold sovereign *(right)*, mounted under the mast step when the *Mount Fairweather* was launched, was moved to the head of the A-frame mast with which I began experimenting in 1976. The coin shows St. George slaying the dragon, for him a symbol of evil. For me, as for many cultures before St. George and since, the dragon became a symbol of power, to be embodied for the good of life as well as art. The dragon's image has transcended the regional mythologies behind the figureheads of Aleut, Tlingit, Viking and Polynesian craft, and so I chose the dragon to serve at the head of mine. Above all, the dragon is mysterious, as was my boat. "Birds fly, fish swim, animals run," wrote Confucius. "The running animal can be caught in a trap, the swimmer in a net, and the flyer by an arrow. But there is the dragon; I don't know how it rides the wind. . ."   Peter Thomas

Viewed from the bow looking aft, the framework nears completion. Once all the lashings were complete — and any that were not tight enough, or substandard in some other way, were cut away and then replaced — all the joints and seams were impregnated with epoxy resins, thus fixing all the lashings permanently in place. An Aleut baidarka or a Polynesian sewn-plank canoe had to be taken apart and its joints re-sewn every few years at least.

The *Mount Fairweather*'s lashings could be expected to last a decade or two. Each of the many thousands of turns taken in sewing together the framework is pulled as taut as the twine's breaking strength permits; with many lashings per inch, this dynamic tension adds up. The effort exerted in sewing together the framework remains, in effect, a permanent part of the boat, recorded for years in the memory of the nylon fibers' polymeric chains. "The finished vessel is in elastic balance," I wrote in 1975, "the component parts yielding strength to each other under stress. The convenience of welding would break not only the silence but also the flexible continuity of an ultra-lightened structure. In supposedly frail and primitive watercraft, absence of rigidity, judged a weakness, is often the greatest strength."

Peter Thomas

The paintings visible here *(right)*, are the work of Stewart Marshall. After stretching the first layer of the skin over the *Mount Fairweather*'s deck I left for six weeks, awaiting warmer weather to begin laminating the rest of the skin. Stewart found this expanse of tightly stretched canvas an opportunity he could not pass up.

The skin of the *Mount Fairweather*, like that of the two aluminum-tubing-framed craft I had already built, was a thin membrane of fiberglass laminate enveloping the skeleton. It would be six years and eight boats later before I would give up the use of fiberglass for reasons transparent to me now but not then. At the time, fiberglass fabric and polyester resins seemed ideally waterproof, durable, easy to work with, available and cheap. The fiberglass laminate in the case of the *Mount Fairweather* was as follows: one layer of 24-ounce per square yard "woven roving" over the entire boat, followed by an interlayer of mat tissue (to provide optimum bonding and saturation between the layers), followed, below the hull's waterline, with a second layer of 24-ounce roving (again with a second tissue overlay), followed by a layer of 3-ounce finishing cloth overall. It took about twenty-five imperial gallons of resin to saturate this layup over the entire boat.

My application of epoxy resins to the nylon lashings along the seams in the bow appears rather crude — the excess adding little, if anything, to the vessel's strength. With much less epoxy and no fiberglass at all, I would eventually learn to build a far less toxic-skinned boat. Peter Thomas

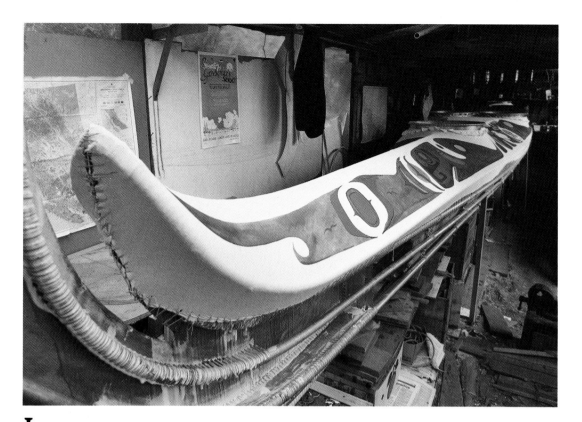

Inside the *Mount Fairweather (right)*, the forward hatchway is visible just ahead of the mast; Stewart Marshall's artwork can be seen through the translucent skin. "We make the distinction between nature and technology with our lives," I wrote in my journal while building this boat. "The future is a question of both." The inside of the *Mount Fairweather*, whether skimming over the waves, riding silent at anchor under a starry sky, or catching the tide under Vancouver's bridges and out to sea, was a grand place to think such thoughts. Upon these spruce floorboards, encircled by an aluminum rib cage, with rain falling on the drum-tight skin, it was easy to bring mythology to life. George B. Dyson

Frame of Mind—115

The interior of the *Mount Fairweather*, under construction, is viewed looking toward the bow from station No. 7.

The first step in creating the "skin" of the *Mount Fairweather* was to cover the framework with some type of tightly shrunk substrate upon which to laminate the subsequent layers. In the case of the previous 16-footer and 31-footer, and the later 28-footers, I used ordinary, untreated heavy cellophane, available in 48-inch-wide rolls. The cellophane was applied to the framework with double-stick cellophane tape and then sprayed with water. It dried in a few hours to a perfect, soap-bubble-smooth skin, immune to the effects of the styrene monomer in the resin, yet soluble in water for later removal from the inside of the hull.

Not being able to find any cellophane wide enough for the *Mount Fairweather*, I decided to try unshrunk cotton fabric instead,´shrinking it over the framework with steam. This did not work very well, and I would not advise its use. A heat-shrinking polyester fabric would have been much easier to work with and almost as cheap.

As in the case of all skin boats, the skin of the *Mount Fairweather*, except around the hatch coamings, is nowhere attached to the vessel's frame. This allows the frame and skin to flex independently and precludes the localization of stress that would result were the two in any other way attached. "This duality of frame and skin in an evolved structure is a manifesta-tion of the basic duality of the universe of physical forces it exists in," I wrote in 1975.

"With a skin under tension and a skeleton under compression, the two fundamental structural functions are separated and an ideal material may be chosen for each without compromise: the compressive strength of alloy tubing, the tensile strength of glass fibre. The two work together but independently . . ." The *I Ching* and a copy of *The Aluminum Structural Handbook* lay side by side on my workshop shelf.

"The speed, carrying capacity, and standard of living possible with this type of boat is primarily a function of its length," I had written in 1973, proposing the 62-footer that was never built, "and the limit to this is a function of the materials and methods of its construction." Certainly the forty-eight feet of the *Mount Fairweather* did not come near the limits of this construction technique, and I still find it easy to imagine craft two to three times this size crisscrossing the waters of the earth.

But the limits are set by the occupants, not by the craft. If the *Mount Fairweather* had been a Tlingit dugout, or a Chugach baidara, forty-eight feet in length, some twenty to forty warriors, trained to the paddle since birth, would have driven it through the waves. They would have carried with them only a few pieces of dried fish to chew on the way, leaving room for the booty they hoped to bring back from their raid. If the *Mount Fairweather* had been a 48-foot proa sailing among the Pacific Islands to the south, some dozen or so barefoot sailors would have scrambled upon her decks, keeping a huge sail precariously balanced to send the vessel flying through the seas. The *Mount Fairweather*, a strange hybrid of the elements of Aleut, Tlingit, and Polynesian design, was either a monument to these seafarers of the past, or is still awaiting a breed of paddlers that does not yet exist.

Peter Thomas

The *Mount Fairweather* was launched on June 21, 1975, at Belcarra Park. "As the canoe left the bridge," wrote Ken Brower, visible here in a white sweater with his reporter's notebook conspicuous in his back pocket, "the bearers began drumming on the sides. They made a savage din. The canoe broke thunderously out of the forest and onto the park lawn, where the Kingsway Frozen Food Company was in the middle of a picnic."

Of the Aleuts' canoe-launching ceremonies we know almost nothing, for their large skin vessels were of the past by the time ethnologists began taking notes, and the launching of the smaller baidarkas was by most accounts a quiet, private affair. Among the great canoe-building civilizations of the Northwest Coast and the South Pacific, however, the launching of a new vessel involved everyone in the community and sometimes even included the sacrifice of slaves. Preparations and celebrations lasted for days, and no attention to detail or tradition was spared.

We did the best we could, and toasted the health of the new canoe with champagne drunk from the Belcarra Park snack bar's styrofoam cups.   Peter Thomas

With more than a dozen people on board *(right)*, the *Mount Fairweather* leaves the beach for the first time. She weighed between eight and nine hundred pounds, and there must have been at least half again that weight in people, most of them sitting on the deck. Yet the vessel remained stable without an ounce of ballast below. What many observers of a long, narrow, unstable-looking boat do not realize is that stability is as much a function of length as it is of beam (four and a half feet in the case of the *Mount Fairweather*). One vessel, though twice as long as another and looking twice as narrow, is twice as stable.   Peter Thomas

Under Second Narrows Bridge *(left)*, the *Mount Fairweather* heads out through Vancouver Harbor. Burrard Inlet, after constricting at First Narrows alongside Stanley Park, widens to form the inner Vancouver Harbor and constricts again here some five miles to the east before dividing into two arms: Port Moody to the east and Indian Arm to the north. Belcarra Park lies at the division of these two arms, where the Natives once kept a lookout for enemy canoes sneaking in through the narrows from the west. They probably watched from almost exactly the spot where my tree house would later perch, and where the *Mount Fairweather* had been built.

On Wednesday, June 13, 1792, George Vancouver, in the *Discovery*'s yawl, accompanied by Lieutenant Peter Puget in the *Chatham*'s launch, was the first foreigner to enter Second Narrows. "The general tenor of their behaviour," noted Vancouver of the Natives, "gave us reason to conclude that we were the first people from a civilised country they had yet seen." Could Vancouver have imagined that just 184 years later these steel bridges would stand on the very spot where the villagers he encountered "shewed much understanding in preferring iron to copper," in his words? The wholesale trading in iron for furs would soon begin, and before some of the young fir trees that witnessed the event were fully grown, there would be a city of a million people bearing Vancouver's name. Peter Thomas

The *Mount Fairweather* catches the last of the ebb out of Vancouver Harbor under the Lion's Gate Bridge. We were on our way to Habitat Forum, a two-week conference hosted by the Canadian government in conjunction with the 1976 United Nations Conference on Human Settlement, where the *Mount Fairweather* was to be displayed. It was there that I first met Huey D. Johnson, who was to prove instrumental in realizing my vision of a fleet of baidarkas returning to the Northwest Coast.

At a soirée organized by Stephanie Mills, overlooking the reaches of Georgia Strait and attended by David Brower, Huey Johnson, Paulo Soleri, and the Governor of Delaware, I was delighted to discover that there was, indeed, a powerfully linked and politically gifted network of environmentalists conspiring to change the course of the world. The following morning, before catching his plane back south, Huey Johnson spent twenty minutes aboard the *Mount Fairweather*, inviting me to join the cause. In this way, in the very belly of the huge craft, the idea for the next generation of baidarkas was spawned. Peter Thomas

Frame of Mind—121

With outrigger platforms, a hexagonal tent sheltering the four central manholes from the rain, and more ground tackle than is seen on some offshore yachts, I was able to spend days in comfort without ever going ashore. The nebulous distinction between an extremely large kayak and a small cruising vessel was lost.

The *Mount Fairweather* had cost me only about $1,200 in materials to build, and with the $3,600 provided by Habitat Forum I was able to experiment widely with changes to her as well as to take the first steps — in aluminum tubing — toward building another series of boats. I took my commission to exhibit some sort of "habitat" literally, transforming the *Mount Fairweather* into a live-aboard kayak the likes of which the world had never seen.

When I had the *Mount Fairweather* surveyed for British Registry, the somewhat puzzled Queen's surveyor dutifully crawled with his tape measure from stem to stern, measured the depth of the hold, and submitted documentation that listed the vessel as three-masted, having a clipper bow, sharp stern, and schooner rig, with a registered tonnage of 1.75 — this being an estimate of how much coal the *Mount Fairweather* could carry should she be requisitioned by Her Majesty in time of war.   George B. Dyson

The *Mount Fairweather*, refitted for her second season, is passing Siwash Rock off Vancouver's Stanley Park. The outriggers are twenty-eight feet long, and built of aluminum tubing covered with a fiberglass skin. Along with the modified lateen rig they have added a distinctly Polynesian look to the craft, perhaps obscuring the simplicity of form owed to the Aleuts. "The canoe had lost its Aleut pedigree," wrote Kenneth Brower. "It was hopelessly mongrelized . . . If the Aleuts had conquered the Russians and everybody after the Russians, if the Aleutian culture had become dominant in the world, if an Aleut Pentagon had gone into building long-range strategic warships, then the warships would have looked something like this."

Peter Thomas

Frame of Mind—123

The Aleuts believed, and taught their children, that light is life and night is death; and for that reason, for health and strength of body and to live long, everyone was obliged . . . not to sleep beyond the dawn, but just as soon as the dawn began to come out, nude, face the east, and opening the mouth inhale the light and the air; and thereafter to go to the stream from which the drinking water was taken, strike it several times with the right palm, and say: I do not sleep, I am alive, I face you, the life-giving light, and will always live with you!

—Ivan Veniaminov, 1840

The *Mount Fairweather* heads south through Blackney Pass into Johnstone Strait, with a fair westerly breeze picking up from Queen Charlotte Strait. The summer westerlies here are known locally as the "Johnstone Strait express," and I would be almost a third of the way to Vancouver by dark, having left Paul Spong's place at Hanson Island about noon. These westerlies invariably bring a clearing sky; the thick morning fog usually burns off by early afternoon.

"The sea has a look of indescribable grandeur, especially when the sun falls on it," wrote Albert Einstein in 1931. "One feels as if one is dissolved and merged into Nature. Even more than usual, one feels the insignificance of the individual, and it makes one happy."[1] We need no knowledge of atomic physics to know that Einstein was right.

Paul Spong

6061-T6

The *Mount Fairweather* was a hard act to follow. I had learned that good reasons, besides the restrictions imposed by available materials, had limited the Aleuts and Russians to baidarkas of a certain length. The Russians, I realized, had based their strength on the sheer number of their baidarkas rather than on individual size. "The *Neva* could not have reached this station," wrote Urey Lisiansky in 1804, in command of the first Russian warship to visit Sitka, "but for the united assistance of upwards of a hundred baidarkas, which, though small in size, pulled with uncommon strength."[1]

For my next project I decided to build six boats. It seemed to be time for a small fleet of three-hatch baidarkas to return to the Northwest Coast. My decision became a proposal, and in January of 1977 — through the assistance of Tom Macy and Huey Johnson, gifted fund-raisers and outdoorsmen both — my proposal became a bundle of 6061-T6 alloy aluminum tubes. Some $22,000 was raised to launch us and our baidarkas on an expedition with the goal of heading toward Bering Strait.

With three assistants, the fleet rapidly took form. We laid the keels in February and launched the boats on the third of May, when we boarded an ancient halibut schooner chartered to take us north. We had to struggle only with building the first boat. Each in turn helped us to build the rest. When the tube-bending was finished we had gained proficiency at bending frames. When the lashing of the skeletons was completed we had toughened the surfaces of our hands. When the last skin was fitted we had figured out the means of doing the job right.

The laws of scale — that displacement varies as the third power of the vessel's length — rule unequivocally in favor of the economy to be found in building smaller boats. With exactly as much aluminum, spruce, and fiberglass as it had taken me to build the six hatches and forty-eight feet of the *Mount Fairweather*, we were able to build six 28-foot three-hatch boats.

Of tubing we had more than enough, but I still had to scrape around the scrapyards in search of T6 tempered aluminum sheet and plate. At North Star Salvage I found a hoard of thirty-inch aluminum STOP signs — enough 6061-T6 sheet to outfit all six boats. We designed two paddle blades and one rudder assembly to fit perfectly, like an M.C. Escher drawing, within each octagonal piece of plate.

Road signs must be resistant to corrosion and tempered to withstand projectiles directed at them from moving cars. They are North America's most widespread use for 6061-T6 alloy sheet. As we cut, filed, fitted, drilled, countersank, and sewed together our rudders and our paddles, we kept thinking of the New Jersey Turnpike with all its well-marked interchanges between Philadelphia and New York. We envisioned vast fleets of post-automobile baidarkas, their rudders and paddle blades made from road signs, their skeletons made from aluminum beer cans and magnesium hubcaps re-extruded as thin-walled aluminum tubes.

We figured it would take less than one thousand aluminum beer cans — recycled with added traces of manganese, silicon, titanium, and zinc — to build the skeleton of one of our three-hatch 28-foot boats. With Coors beer in 16-ounce push-top cans it would take 973 cans, to be exact. For Labatt's Canadian beer in 341-milliliter heavier-gauge Canadian cans, it would only take 456 to build the same boat.

We also used about thirty-five pounds of fiberglass — spun and woven from a relatively ordinary glass — and about four gallons of polyester resin, a petrochemical that could be derived, if necessary, from vegetable oil or trees. And there were, per boat, about three pounds of nylon lashings — also derived from oil — that could be made directly from renewable organic materials, polymerized into continuous high-tensile chains. As to aluminum and fiberglass, there are existing microorganisms that could be biologically re-engineered to precipitate aluminum alloys and silica fibers directly from the sea. But to use up our deposits of STOP signs, beer cans and broken glass would accomplish two things at once, and I fear the results of any biologically engineered mistakes.

These figures are for a long-distance cruiser that will carry up to a thousand pounds of passengers and freight. For a twenty-foot single touring model, cut these estimates in half. Some of us might drink that many cans of beer in the time it would take to build the boat. Meanwhile, the wood for the interior floorboards stands growing in the forest or lies seasoning upon the beach. If there is a shortage of baidarkas in North America, it is not due to a shortage of the materials to make them.

Keep in mind how long these boats will last. The skeleton has a lifetime measured in many, many years. Treated with the care given to the baidarkas of the Aleuts — shaded as much as possible from direct sunlight (an easy task in the Aleutians) and not dragged loaded over the beach — even the relatively perishable skin will last ten or twenty years. One's descendents might stretch the fourth or fifth skin over the framework their great-grandfather had made.

By building these boats in this way today, we ensure the survival of the craft — whichever way the construction techniques evolve. Perhaps future baidarka-builders will go back to using driftwood, sinews and skins, modeled after some aluminum framework found cast up on the beach. In any event, the ethnologists of the future will find our baidarka skeletons more recognizably preserved. They will not have to rely upon traces of disintegrated sinew lashings and Veniaminov's fragile notes.

It seems to me that the Aleut baidarka is so superior in its kind, that even a mathematician could not add much if anything to its further perfection.
—Ivan Veniaminov, 1840

The tubular components of three 28-foot baidarkas are laid out on the building bed. The bending was accomplished with improvised techniques, using a ½-inch RIDGID lever-action tubing bender and a ¾-inch E.M.T. electrical conduit bender as the basic tooling from which to start. No provision was made (as it has been with my more recent boats) for bending directly above a template of the part. This necessitated going back and forth between bender and pattern at every increment in the curve. One degree too much bend, and it became difficult to correct the error and get the frame or stringer back on track.

The key to productivity with free-hand bending is to duplicate the curve as soon as it is complete. With the ribs, the curves change gradually as you progress from stem to stern, and most of the stringers are required in duplicate pairs, while there are six hatch-coaming rims to be bent per boat. The sixth such duplicated part, I found as a rule, took about a quarter as much time as the first. It can be seen what a saving in time there is in bending the pieces of even three boats at once.

George B. Dyson

I am fabricating the rudder assembly knees — two per rudder, for a total of twelve — using ⅜-inch solid aluminum rod, the T6 temper being annealed slightly over a Primus stove to allow bending the rod to an angle of ninety degrees. Many parts, such as these knees, were over-built, simply to use materials we had at hand. In the case of the knees, ⅜-inch outer diameter by .065-inch wall tubing would have done the job at half the weight. Similarly over-built were our paddles, masts, and sails — again, simply because ordering lighter materials would have required time and costs we could not spare. As it was, the cost of all materials worked out to less than $500 per boat.

Peter Thomas

We are fabricating — from STOP-sign scrap — the small triangular knees (or gussets) that join each hull rib and deck beam into a complete frame along the gunwale of the boat. Each station — eleven of them per boat — requires a slightly different angle in its pair of knees, and the making and fitting of these is a time-consuming task. Repetition of the procedures vastly reduces the time spent on each individual part. There is a fine line between the satisfaction of repeating something often enough to be able to produce it accurately and fast, and the boredom of doing the same thing over and over again. Making the parts for half-a-dozen boats at once seems to be about the right compromise between the two. We built these six frameworks in two production runs of three boats each — and felt we were wasting valuable time retooling in the middle of the job.

Peter Thomas

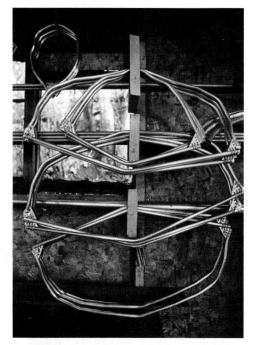

Mike Macy and Jason Halm *(right)* are polishing a pair of keel stringers (attached to the stem assemblies) before setting up the skeleton of the first boat. They are using steel wool to scour the surface of the tubing clean of oxide and grease. This is best done with the steel wool wet, to avoid raising aluminum-oxide dust. The other stringers for these three boats are visible on the rack to the left. The ¾-inch tubing — available in anything less than 2,200 pound quantities only in 12-foot lengths — was spliced by gluing internal sleeves in place with epoxy, the joints staggered at alternate intervals along the length of the boats.

Stacked to air-dry alongside the wall of the workshop are two-inch raw spruce slabs cut the previous August along Queen Charlotte Strait — enough wood for the interior stringers of the next three boats. The sawdust on the floor is from the first three boats' floorboards, which have just been cut and are drying further before being planed, sanded and installed. Any moisture in the fibrous spruce makes it all but impossible to plane without tearing the soft surface of the wood to shreds. The pickle jar to the left in this photograph holds WAX, used as a lubricant when cutting or drilling aluminum sheet.

Peter Thomas

The transverse frames for the second set of three baidarkas are hanging, prefabricated, on the workshop wall. The ends of the hollow ribs have been plugged with epoxy filler — the aluminum foil capping some of the ribs serves to hold the uncured mixture in place. I have since found it easier (and lighter) to use tightly fitting plugs cut from a sheet of closed-cell plastic foam. All the tubing in the boat is similarly sealed at every open end, giving the framework an inherent buoyancy. Sealed inside the keel tube — for future archaeologists who might closely inspect the boat — is a piece of paper stating when and where the vessel was built.

Peter Thomas

P eter Johnston — my premier boat-building assistant and a native of the Isle of Wight — is prefabricating a stern assembly, using No. 15 braided nylon twine (108-pound test) and a No. 14 sailmaker's needle to sew the vertical seam joining the stern deadwood to the bulkhead at station 1A. There is always a compromise to be made between starting with a long length of twine, and thus going farther before running out, and using shorter lengths that save tangles at the expense of more frequent splices and knots. In a situation like this, with a short, continuous seam, the best approach is to start in the center with twine long enough to do the entire job, working the halves in opposite directions.

Peter Thomas

I am lashing stringer No. 2 to the stern bulkhead at station 1A. This same fingerless, double-palmed leather glove has served me through the construction of twelve boats, through miles upon miles of twine, although the wearing surfaces have been several times replaced. The work is particularly hard on the inner skin of the finger joints of the working hand — as they take the tension when pulling the lashing tight — and on the thumb and index finger of the opposite hand, which clamp the tension in place while proceeding to the next turn.

On open stretches and exposed frame/stringer joints, the progress is surprisingly fast. It is at corners, hatch coamings and similar details that the work slows down. Careful planning is of the essence: the order in which the pieces of the boat are sewn together makes all the difference in the end. The sequence is entirely logical (or topological, rather) but the topology may only appear later as one's work gets tied up in unanticipated knots. Peter Thomas

Lou Kelly is applying the final lashings to the bow of the sixth baidarka. The five others are hanging from the workshop roof. At this point, the twelve-by-fifty-foot shed has become so crowded we will have to add a temporary annex for room to apply the skins. The anterior portion of this bifurcated bow does not flare to the same degree as that of the *Mount Fairweather*. A simpler form has been taken here, one that does not require the gunwale stringer to be bent to a compound curve, which had given me so much difficulty two years before. These baidarkas consequently do not exhibit quite the *Mount Fairweather*'s forward lift when surfing downwind at speeds exceeding that of the waves, but nonetheless their bows flare more than enough to avoid burying themselves when hitting the bottom of a steep trough.

Peter Thomas

The completed framework of one of the six baidarkas is seen looking aft from station 13. The spruce interior stringers, twenty-two feet long, weigh a total of thirty pounds per boat, and have been attached to the transverse ribs using a net-mender's shuttle to weave the lashings in between the planks. The wood will be finished to a polished surface with an epoxy sealer, sanding between the final coats. These full-length floorboards are redundant in terms of the vessel's strength, but essential in providing comfort and convenience to the occupants. The cargo slides easily along these floorboards in and out of the farthest reaches of the hull, and is kept above any water in the bilge. When it is necessary to sleep inside the boat, the two inches between the spruce floorboards' inner surface and the cold North Pacific make for a reasonably comfortable night.

Peter Thomas

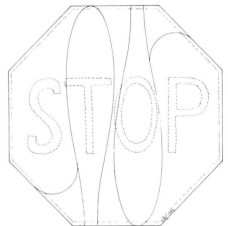

At the workshop *(right)* at the Starboard Light Lodge in Belcarra Park, three of the frameworks are completed, with the spruce interior stringers drying in the rack at the upper right. At the end of the workshop are some of the STOP signs we were using as raw material; we peeled off the reflective coating after the components were cut to shape.   George B. Dyson

The mast partner is fitted to the deck stringer just aft of the forward hatchway at station 9. Details such as this produce the most time-consuming work. The hatchways are elliptical, eighteen inches wide and twenty-two inches long. The hatch-coaming rims are the most difficult tubular parts to bend, their form requiring incremental bending throughout their length. Any deviance from symmetry is visible in the finished boat. There are six of these rims per boat, and to bend thirty-six of them would have been an unrewarding task except for the satisfaction of completing the later ones in a fraction of the time it took to bend the first — from an hour and a half at the beginning to twelve minutes at the end.   Peter Thomas

We were able to derive two paddle blades and two rudder blades out of one thirty-inch 6061-T6 aluminum STOP sign, with almost nothing going to waste.

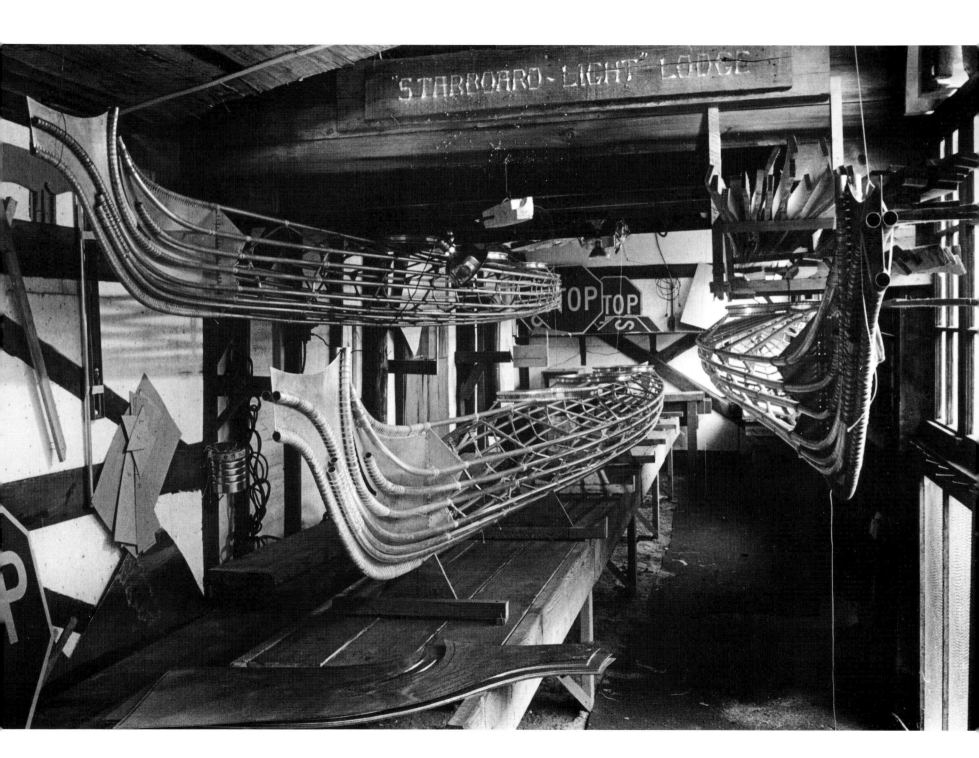

Joe Ziner is trimming the cellophane around the center hatch, exercising surgical precision with his knife. The roll of cellophane is visible at the end of the workshop, where it can be unrolled to apply a boat-length at a time. Such a roll of true cellophane is becoming increasingly hard to get, these days. It has been replaced in packaging and "cellophane" tape with plastic films that do not have the properties (moisture-shrinking, yet solvent-resistant) that we need.

The bow structure of these baidarkas has been covered with a four-ounce polyester fabric, sewn into the form of a "sock" that is applied to the boat and then shrunk tight with heat. This works more securely than cellophane on the intricacies of the bow, where much pushing and prodding will be done in applying the reinforcement to the skin. To shrink the fabric, a domestic iron set just a bit above "polyester" is about right. Peter Thomas

On May 3, 1977, the six 28-foot three-hatch baidarkas, their fresh skins not yet fully cured, lie on the beach at Belcarra Park on the eve of their voyage north to Chichagof Island aboard the *Betty L.*

Verena Huber-Dyson

Off the face of the La Perouse Glacier *(above)*, we head south, in the wake of our Aleut predecessors who paddled along the Gulf of Alaska coast. And Baranov's huge baidarka fleets of 170 years ago were almost certainly not the first waves of skin boats to migrate southward along these shores. "Out of the foam," is how the Tlingit legends tell it, referring to almost-forgotten ancestors who skirted the ice-bound coast. George B. Dyson

In the glow of sunset *(right)*, Mike Macy and one of the local inhabitants are securing the baidarka for the night. Mike and Tom Macy have just landed at Port Alexander, Baranof Island, in baidarka No. 6. The name of this bay, at the southwest extremity of Chatham Strait, first appeared on Teben'kov's maps issued in 1849. The town of Port Alexander had an official population in 1960 of eighteen. Like other small outposts on the Southeast Alaska coast, the sleepy winter village awakens each summer with the influx of the fishing fleet. The boom years, though — first for sea otters and then for salmon — are a thing of the past. One would like to know how long it had been since the last three-hatch baidarka visited this bay. Tom Macy

The Path of Least Resistance

Nature, so far, has neglected the development of sails. So did the Aleuts, whose paddles were busy keeping their families clothed and fed, since sea otters invariably swim upwind when wounded in the hunt. Not until the early 1900s — after their Russian taskmasters had left — were the Aleuts free except on rare occasions to make life easier by adding sails and rudders to their craft.

We were not the first, in 1977, to hoist small sails from our baidarkas, except in one respect: Where the sails of the Aleuts and Russians had been triangular or square, ours were semicircular. The idea behind these fan-shaped sails was simply to catch as much wind as possible, as close as we could to the center of gravity of the boat. Within this radius the sail's shape is defined, and any resemblance to other creatures is purely coincidental.

The winds of our atmosphere — and, as some theorists would have it, the electromagnetic winds of space — have shaped the very origins of life. Yet the winds' course is followed only by spiders, certain coelenterates, and by the plant kingdom's drifting, expendable seeds. No creature with more intelligence than a jellyfish has demonstrated much interest in exploring the use of sails. As one opinion has it, these jellyfish choose either the port or the starboard tack and stick to it for life — reasonable strategy for a jellyfish, less suitable for a boat.

Are the leisures of sailing, for most higher creatures, incompatible with evolution's rules? Imagine a school of filter-feeding aquatic animals, tacking back and forth through the plankton-blooming meadows of the open sea. The translucent, cartilage-ribbed membranes of their dorsal sails would be perfectly trimmed, their pectoral fins adjusting for a minimum of lateral slip as a rich pelagic diet fattens their underwater bellies to suit the hydrodynamics of laminar flow. But there is only a moment to imagine these peaceful creatures before picturing the predators whose carnivorous appetites would spell their end. Sailing, I believe, is a development that evolution has saved for us.

Is this presumptuous on my part? Can drifting along in these boats, as irretrievably windblown as a school of jellyfish, be anything but a back eddy in the sweep of evolution's flow? Or is the gift of our intelligence an ability to learn things from other forms of life? Where does technology fit in? Is it at odds with biology itself? Or is our technology the flowering of life's mandate from the universe at large, the imperative not only to reproduce one's kind, but to spawn those forms that do not yet exist?

"I make a sharp distinction between intelligence and technology," my father, Freeman J. Dyson, once wrote concerning what might be taking place on other worlds. "It is easy to imagine a highly intelligent society with no particular interest in technology," he added, addressing the question of why such societies might not make themselves visible to us. Our own whales and dolphins, for instance, could be argued as examples of this type.

It is equally fascinating to speculate on the reverse: highly intelligent technologies with no particular interest in the society from whence they sprang. The far reaches of space, light-years beyond our grasp, can be envisioned as belonging to technology alone.

Closer to earth, and within our own lifetimes, we may see "space-baidarkas" unfold. The name is not so absurd as it sounds: If the massive chemical rockets with multiton payloads that we have been building are called spacecraft and spaceships, sure the smaller, more manageable, and perhaps even self-propelled space vehicles I am thinking of might be termed space-kayaks (or space-baidarkas if the Russians should once again be first). Even the most speculative of spacecraft is, for sure, denied the use of paddles. But space-baidarkas will be able to make up for this deficiency with their sails — navigating by means of electromagnetic keels and rudders, their sails filled with a constant solar wind as they take advantage of gravitational acceleration to move themselves slingshot-style about the solar system in whatever direction they wish.

"The second of my technological initiatives is a serious effort to exploit solar sails as a cheap and convenient means of transportation around the solar system, at least in the zone of the inner planets and the asteroid belt," proposed Freeman Dyson in 1982, speaking on the occasion of the twenty-fifth anniversary of the United States' first venture into space. "The main reason why solar sailing has never seemed practical to the managers of NASA is that the sails required to carry out interesting missions were too big. Roughly speaking, a one-ton payload requires a square kilometer of sail to drive it, and a square kilometer is an uncomfortably large size for the first experiments in packaging and deploying sails. Nobody wants to be the first astronaut to get tangled up in a square kilometer of sail. But the development of solar sails would be a far more manageable proposition if it went hand-in-hand with the development of microspacecraft . . . The idea of the microspacecraft is to miniaturize space sensors and navigation and communication systems so the whole apparatus is reduced in scale like a modern pocket calculator . . . A one-kilogram microspacecraft would go nicely with a thirty-meter-square sail, and a thirty-meter-square is a reasonable size."

We have only begun to explore the configurations that will make such vessels work. One thing is certain, though: the ancestry of these skeletal spacecraft will not be traced to the dugout canoe; it will belong to the skin boat.

Besides taking us forward along evolution's path, the baidarka allows us to slide backward into our past. We are told — by our biologists if not by our own desire to lie motionless in the sun — of the existence within all of us of the vestiges of a reptilian brain. Within these skin craft, we take on their outer reptilian form: We snake our way by day across the sea and crawl upon the sand at night to rest.

From the reptilian perspective of the baidarka, we gain a fresh appreciation for the lowliest of living things. Take kelp, for example. A kelp bed is just the place for a baidarka to rest when faced with adverse wind and tide. Securely tied to a kelp anchor, we catch some sleep if the surf is running too high to attempt a landing on the beach. When the surf subsides, we head for a mat of kelp that has been washed up by the storm — a frictionless slipway under the loaded belly of the boat.

On our baidarka voyages we used kelp siphons to drain the water from our boats. My friend Joe Ziner carved delicate and unpredictably tuned kelp flutes. We once made an elaborate kelp lasagne.

The sweep of the salmon's tail is felt in paddling from side to side with our arms; the wings of the gull are folded up at night within our sails. Galaxies of phosphorescent plankton blink back at the stars. Conversations of whales can be overheard through the crude eardrum of the baidarka's outer skin. Day after day, drawn by liquid currents reflecting both sun and moon, we journey in company with all of Creation's forms.

In Aleut times, it took at least one baidarka to gather the materials to build the next. This regenerative cycle, repeated from year to year, carried the craft toward perfection of design.

I built these six boats intending them to reproduce, too. It is too early yet to tell. Whether they disappear to gather driftwood and walrus hides along an unnamed northern coast, or form a tax deductible "School of Baidarkas" to win the support of ALCOA in the form of miles of aluminum tubes, the important thing is that the craft be kept alive. The design of these boats will adapt from generation to generation to meet the unforeseen, and to venture where no such craft has ever been.

The universe is an archipelago, with small islands of habitable ground separated by vast seas of space.

—Freeman J. Dyson, 1978

Under sail in baidarka No. 4, Paul Barnes traverses Dixon Entrance, with Dundas Island barely visible against the horizon. The afternoon's northwesterly has dropped with the setting sun, yet we are still making about five knots toward Prince Rupert. Another hour of sailing lies ahead of us before we will have to paddle in toward land and look for a place to camp.

Our fan-shaped sails have an area of forty square feet each, and are strictly for downwind use. On the glacier-fjorded Northwest Coast, headwinds or tailwinds are the rule. The mountainous landforms funnel the overall pressure gradient into one of two directions — "up" or "down" the coast — with occasional calm periods between. These craft are designed for paddling directly into the wind and waves, and for running downwind at high speed under sail, rather than compromising these qualities in favor of all-around performance under sail. Among the Pacific Islands to the south, with steady trade winds prevailing across vast stretches of open sea, windward sailing ability was a necessity and elaborate outrigger canoes the result. Baidarkas, however, usually can tuck in somewhere to await an inevitable change in the direction of the wind or, if progress is necessary, paddle in stages along the shore. In these cold waters, at any event, sailing is most comfortable with the wind directly at your back. George B. Dyson

It is twelve minutes past slack water — a few more minutes and the channel out of Lituya Bay, Gulf of Alaska, will be impassable to any kind of boat. This was the last frame of film I exposed before Joe Ziner, seated in the cockpit behind me, persuaded me to put down the camera and help paddle for our lives. "The sea breaks entirely across the entrance, except with a smooth sea," says the *U.S. Coast Pilot* of 1908. "Sailing directions of practical value cannot be given for entering Lituya Bay." The sixth edition of the *U.S. Coast Pilot* (No. 9), issued in 1954, is somewhat more specific as to the dangers: "Ebb currents, running against a southwest swell, cause bad topping seas or combers in which no small boat can live. Small-powered vessels in the bay should stay away from the entrance on the ebb to avoid being swept through." Such was the fate that befell "twenty-one brave seamen" who assisted the French navigator Jean F.G. de La Pérouse with his discovery of the bay in 1786. At exactly this spot, on July 13, while on a surveying excursion inside the bay in the ships' boats, they were swept to their deaths.

Ten years later, Baranov's talented shipwright and navigator, James Shields, would report to his commander on the dangers of entering the bay: "The mouth of L'tua Bay is very dangerous: the current is fast and beats against underwater rocks, making it like rapids; the rocks therefore are not seen; in bad weather the entrance to it is still more frightening. I prefer to enter in calm weather, towed. Believe me when I say that the tide in the sea was a sazhen and a half [one sazhen equals seven feet] more than in the bay, and we rolled as if under a mountain, with incredible quickness and indescribable danger. Once beyond the capes it was safe."[1]

From Lituya we returned south.

George B. Dyson

Two per baidarka *(above)*, Mike Macy, Tom Macy, Donna Holyoke, and Joe Ziner paddle north along the Gulf of Alaska coast, off Cape Spencer, in baidarkas No. 6 and 3. The Macys are sitting in their aft and center hatches, Joe and Donna fore and aft. None of the six baidarkas was occupied by three passengers at a time except for short jaunts — day trips, fishing expeditions and, on July 4th at Gustavus, a race out into Icy Strait.

"On the whole, that third, middle hole seems to be a nuisance," wrote Frederica de Laguna in 1981 in answer to my inquiry about her personal experience. Although still enamored of the three-hatch for its versatility and capacity for gear, I have found Professor de Laguna's observation to be often-times correct. Certainly that third hole when taken up by the dead weight of a Russian official — "who could ride in state without doing anything," says de Laguna — was a nuisance to the Aleuts. But only a three-hatch baidarka can be used by one, two or three persons interchangeably, remaining in all instances a balanced craft without need of ballast to trim the boat. George B. Dyson

Cape Ommaney *(right)*, the southern extremity of Baranof Island, appeared to Tom Macy, Mike Macy, and Paul Barnes in baidarkas No. 4 and 6 exactly as it must have looked 150 years ago to the much larger baidarka parties that rounded this imposing headland every year. To our baidarkas, the outer coast represented the dangers of the open sea, in contrast to the more sheltered waters inside the cape. To the baidarkas of the early nineteenth century, the hazard was exactly the reverse. Those who ventured past the cape risked massacre at the hands of the enemy Tlingit, more life-threatening than the familiar perils of the outer coast. Among the instructions given to an Inside Passage hunting party in 1818 were the following: "1) no one separates from the party; 2) guards are to be kept very alert both day and night; 3) campsites are to be selected which are not surrounded by forests; 4) you are to change sites as often as possible . . . Do not offend the Koloshi and in no way trust them."[2] Tom Macy

Tiny by comparison, Tom and Mike Macy, in baidarka No. 6, paddle through the sixty-foot-high natural arch at Boussole Head on the Gulf of Alaska coast between Cape Spencer and Lituya Bay. Baidarka travel is a series of lengthy intervals spent watching distant headlands, islands or landmarks grow slowly closer by degree, the intervals punctuated by those moments when you actually round the headland, pass the island, or reach the distant shore. And then the next objective comes into equally distant view. Few such turning points are as satisfying as paddling through this arch at Boussole Head, with Icy Point and the empty Gulf of Alaska stretching into the distance. At times like this, one looks back at the following baidarka and finds it easy to imagine having been one among a party of three hundred or more baidarkas paddling along this coast, the line of paddlers stretching out for miles, the beaches wall-to-wall baidarkas every night. George B. Dyson

Foothills of Mount Fairweather *(right)* rise beyond Tom and Mike Macy, in baidarka No. 6, as they head past Cenotaph Island, Lituya Bay. The island, an anomalous outcropping in the middle of the bay, received its name for the cenotaph erected there in July of 1786 by the French explorer La Pérouse, in memory of those who drowned when their boats were swept away by the tide. "AT THE ENTRANCE OF THIS HARBOUR PERISHED TWENTY-ONE BRAVE SEAMEN. READER, WHOEVER THOU ART, MINGLE THY TEARS WITH OURS," reads the message deposited in a bottle at the base of the cenotaph. No trace of either the message or the monument has ever been found. In La Pérouse's account — based on dispatches that survived the expedition's subsequent tragic fate in the South Seas — the head of Lituya Bay "is perhaps the most extraordinary place in the world."

Directly above the left extremity of Cenotaph Island can be seen what resembles a clearcut in the forest reaching a height of 1,740 feet up the northern shore of Lituya Bay. This marks the height reached by the great wave of July 9, 1958, the result of ninety million tons of rock falling into the head of the bay during an earthquake along the Fairweather fault. Huge logs were swept as far as five miles out to sea, and the beaches are still littered with remnants of the debris. George B. Dyson

Under a reefed sail in a strong north-westerly breeze, the Macy brothers head south off Icy Point in the Gulf of Alaska. The four of us — Joe Ziner and I in baidarka No. 3 and the Macys in No. 6 — were heading back to Icy Strait after finding out that the other two baidarkas had turned back from Torch Bay. On our way north we had camped for several days at Icy Point, which we now sailed by without stopping. It is a fine campsite, although the landing at Kaknau Creek can be accomplished safely only at high water and with a smooth sea in Palma Bay. Hot springs have been reported here. Those we could find were lukewarm, though we did not make a thorough search. Captain James Colnett, aboard the *Prince of Wales,* anchored off here on June 12, 1788. The second mate, sent in the ship's boat to investigate, reported, "At this place was a house & garden neatly fenced in, & Euro-pean plants growing, but only saw 8 women, a lad & a boy."[3]

Other sources indicate there used to be a settlement of Hoonah Tlingit somewhere near this spot, and, as to the garden, native tobacco — already in cultivation at certain other places along the coast — would seem the likely crop, though a fenced-in cemetery could be another interpretation of the account.

Our greatest inconvenience at Icy Point was the large number of brown bears wandering around the beach itself and using the well-trod "bear expressway" that closely parallels the shoreline along this entire stretch of coast. We yielded the best campsites to them and kept a sharp look-out when following their pathways through the bush. Our expedition was unarmed, though not from any notion that the danger of attack was not ever-present and real.
George B. Dyson

Paddlers in baidarka No. 6 *(right)* inspect the kittiwake colony among the cliffs on the south side of Cenotaph Island, Lituya Bay. "Because they are accustomed to these inaccessible places, kittiwakes have developed little of the aggressive nest-defending behaviour of other gulls," wrote Kenneth Brower in 1974 of a kitti-wake colony some thirty miles to the south, "and because they are not aggressive, they like inaccessible places. It's hard to know which came first, the kittiwake or the cliff."
George B. Dyson

The seas in the open gulf seemed smooth after the breakers we had brushed up against off La Chaussee Spit. Baidarka No. 6 is heading south just after we made our exit from Lituya Bay. "The Indians seemed to have considerable dread of the passage," wrote La Pérouse in 1786, "and never ventured to approach it, unless at the slack water of flood or ebb. By the help of our glasses we distinctly perceived that, when they were between the two points, the chief, or at least the principal Indian, arose, stretched out his arms toward the sun, to which he appeared to address a prayer, while the rest paddled away with all their strength."[4]

We raised our sails, reefed to a third of their full extent, to a freshening north-westerly. The ground swell was building along the shallow coastal shelf. There is nothing in my experience to compare with the exhilaration of surfing at breakneck speeds along the icebound coast in seas such as this, although Tom Macy, speaking from experience, compared the sensation to that of "being catapulted in a Phantom jet off the deck of a carrier in the Tonkin Gulf."

George B. Dyson

Later the same day, off Dixon Harbor, the wind has died down and we have put up full sail as we head in toward the shore. With a fair wind, one is better off staying farther out where the wind is steadier and the sea less confused by wave reflection from the rocks. When paddling, especially against the wind or tide, one is better off hugging the shoreline, finding smoother water inside the kelp beds. Darkness overtook us before we reached a place where we could land, and we threaded our way through the luminous breakers to a small

bight at the entrance to Torch Bay, where we spent a mosquito-ridden night. To find campsites that are not overrun with bugs, bears or both, yet have a suitably sheltered beach, is not easy.

Without the local knowledge that baidarkas shared in the past, we are at a disadvantage despite having better charts. Note the anchor carried conspicuously on the Macy baidarka's afterdeck. Made of aluminum and weighing only three pounds, it offers a campsite of last resort.

A chief virtue — or disadvantage — of

a multivessel expedition such as ours is that the people can split up as they wish and go separate ways. At this time, five of our baidarkas, in three separate camps, were within a few miles of each other on the Gulf of Alaska coast, yet for communication purposes they might as well have been oceans apart. What we lacked — and among the first things to provide if we do this again — was radio contact between the various baidarkas. It was all too easy for us to separate, and all but impossible to rendezvous later.

The different detachments of our fleet crossed paths a number of times and at others came tantalizingly close, as we heard from locals and transient fishermen that "one of those things just came through here yesterday," or other comments to that effect. But for us to locate one moving baidarka from another, even if only a few miles apart, was beyond our means.

How the Russians managed to maintain communication with their scattered hunters remains a mystery. I suspect that lack of communications when in enemy territory cost many hunters their lives.

George B. Dyson

At anchor in the mist, baidarka No. 1 — in which I was now traveling — lies among the Finlayson Islands, Chatham Sound, British Columbia. Upon our return in boats No. 3 and 6 from Lituya Bay to the village of Gustavus in Icy Strait, we found the disposition of the other four baidarkas as follows: No. 1 lay stored in Bartlett Cove; No. 2, under the command of Harry Williams, had headed south; No. 4, under Donna Holyoke, had headed to Elfin Cove on Chichagof Island, and thence, under Paul Barnes, for Sitka and points south along the outer coast; and No. 5 lay stored in Gustavus, where Peter Johnston would later return to sail it back to British Columbia. With the collapse of our united effort toward the north, the six baidarkas were literally scattered to the winds.

"Peter & Lou felt inclined to go south on account of the prevailing wind being NW," wrote Harry Williams in the journal of baidarka No. 2 for June 9, 1977, while they were weatherbound behind Sugarloaf Island on the outer coast, " . . . so after several hours of discussion we decided to pull out and go whichever way the wind blew." The Macys, in baidarka No. 6, stayed in Gustavus for a few days to resupply and then headed back out to the west coast of Chichagof Island — where they were to meet up with baidarka No. 4 and travel as far as Ketchikan, where the two boats again went separate ways. Baidarka No. 2 was out on the west coast of Chichagof as well, but heading in a beeline south, and the vessels missed crossing paths. Meanwhile, back at Gustavus, Joe Ziner stayed with baidarka No. 3 while we organized the expedition's loose ends, outfitted No. 1, and then, each alone in a 28-foot baidarka, paddled out of the Good River and headed south. To us, our anchors were more than just conveniences — they were a necessity to single-handed management of our heavily laden boats.

George B. Dyson

Becalmed in the middle of Chatham Strait *(left)*, Joe Ziner leans over to stretch his legs. Our two baidarkas were so heavily loaded that we could safely stand up in them while underway, or climb out on deck to get at something that was stowed in the forward or after hatch. We avoided, whenever possible, having to unload the boats and bring everything ashore. Nevertheless, curiosity and a slight saving in distance led us to try taking a shortcut via the Hoonah-Tenakee portage, cutting through the center of Chichagof Island — "a real easy carry," our local informant, Jeff Scafflestead of Hoonah, had understated. It was a long wait for the flood tide to allow us to inch our craft up into the last in a series of saltwater lakes. The portage itself was dreadfully overgrown and apparently long out of use. The only trace of recent activity, and the only reward for the trouble to which we went, was my finding a two-man tent fly that some previous party, equally impatient to escape the merciless bugs, must have dropped while beating through the bush.

George B. Dyson

A fillet of salmon is about to be grilled to Tom Macy's taste, his preferred method being to lay the fish, skin side down, directly on a perfectly prepared bed of coals — a sort of fire-walking ceremony that does not burn the fish. Our baidarkas shared a motley collection of discarded pots and pans, with many meals cooked and eaten with no utensils at all.

Our expedition subsisted largely on what we could forage en route: on the Pacific Northwest coast, neither a difficult nor a monotonous task. A list of local items that were on our menu would include: halibut, caught most easily with a set-line left out overnight; salmon (five species were captured by hook or by crook); rockfish, a loose generic term including rock cod, red snapper, kelp greenling and an assortment of similar species; lingcod (a single individual often providing food for days); shellfish, a staple item including mussels, clams, cockles, abalone, limpets, sea urchins and crabs; Dolly Varden (Tom Macy, an artist with his spinning rod, was able to catch all we could eat); seaweed, predominately kelp; goose tongue, a beach vegetable growing just below extreme high tide; plantain, sorrel, and various other leafy greens; beach grass, the succulent stems an ever-present treat; mushrooms, often but not always plentiful; and berries — salmonberries, huckleberries, and blueberries, for which we competed with the bears.

We were constantly drinking spruce tea (rich in vitamin C) and we used sea water in cooking much of our food. We carried at most a gallon or two of fresh water per boat, stored in such bottles as we happened to find on the way. There were other articles of diet I have not mentioned here, such as birds' eggs and, in Harry Williams' case, a deer appropriated from a pair of wolves who had just killed it on the beach. We did no hunting, although after so much seafood we were tempted to go after birds — except that by most accounts they would have tasted strongly of fish.

Tom Macy

S hrouded by Dixon Entrance fog,
baidarkas No. 3 and 4 head south with a
light westerly in their sails. At the mercy
of an unpredictable current sweeping in
and out from the open sea, we are about
six miles from shore. Our invisible landfall will be decided by a consensus of blind
luck: each of us has a different opinion
about the right direction to head.

George B. Dyson

Baidarka No. 3 (right) heads south under sail in the Gulf of Alaska off Cape Spencer, with George Dyson in the center cockpit and Joe Ziner seated aft. To travel safely along such an exposed and storm-swept coast requires navigational skills more akin to instinct than science — both a sense of where you are and a sense of what the constantly changing tides and weather will bring.

The long hours of Alaskan summer daylight are greatly to our advantage — there are several hours of twilight to search for shelter and it is not disastrous if one ends up having to paddle all night.

How the Russians managed to cross the Gulf of Alaska in winter remains beyond belief. On an afternoon like this, though, with a steady breeze in our sails, a 35-mile day's run behind us, and a secure camp-site up ahead, we feel as carefree and at home as the birds keeping us company among the waves.

"But don't they tip over?" asked a local inhabitant as Peter Johnston once sailed up to a dock in Elfin Cove on Icy Strait. "Do birds tip over?" Peter replied. Tom Macy

Sleeping bags hanging from our masts in the morning sun *(overleaf)*, we head out of Tenakee Inlet, Chichagof Island, after a damp night. With even a slight breath of fair wind such as this, it was a delight to throw our gear into the boats, drink up the last warm tea or coffee as we put the fire out, and cast off from the beach. Within a few hundred yards the insects would be left behind and we could safely take off our shirts as we rarely could ashore. We did a lot of actual living in the boats: eating, sleeping, reading, writing, drawing, talking, and the like — not just while at anchor, but also when underway in benign conditions such as this. We found we could adopt a sailing-induced semi-hypnotic state, catnapping ten minutes or so at a time, the tracking ability of our craft requiring us to surface from sleep only occasionally to correct the course of our boats. When the wind died away completely after such a lazy after-noon we were able to summon the strength to paddle many more miles before making camp. Sleep was something to be gathered in quantity when available, like dry firewood or clams. George B. Dyson

Transformed into a tent *(above)*, the sail of baidarka No. 3 gives shelter to Joe Ziner. The small tent is my own barely one-man affair, made of cotton and weighing only two and a half pounds, a welcome refuge from the bugs. We also carried a much larger three-man, double-walled, pyramid tent. But for rugged camp life on the beach, such lightweight nylon back-packing gear generally is out of place. Our driftwood campfires were large and often burned all night, keeping insects and bears at a distance — but nylon sleeping bags, rain-gear, and tent flies have to be kept at a distance as well. "I'll take canvas soaked in equal parts of beeswax, pine tar, and linseed oil over any of this new-fangled stuff," scoffed Lou Kelly, our senior marlinspike sailor, upon inspection of the bolt of bright green, newly invented fabric with which we experimented in outfitting the six boats. A wool blanket, a two-and-half-pound axe, and a cast-iron skillet were parts of our outfit as valued as any of the more modern gear.   George B. Dyson

Among the groundswells of Dixon Entrance *(right)*, fan-shaped sails of baidarkas No. 3 and 4 are seen from the cockpit of baidarka No. 1, about midway between Ketchikan, Alaska and Prince Rupert, British Columbia. When Joe Ziner and I, in boats No. 1 and 3, sailing south down Clarence Strait, ran into Paul Barnes, in boat No. 4, paddling north, each of us alone represented nothing more than an infinitesimal point. Together, as a triangle of boats, we at least defined our own dimensions among the utter vastness that surrounded us in every direction. With a lone baidarka there exists the germ of an idea: the baidarka the center of one's universe, and empty wilderness all around. With two baidarkas, one sees a mirror image of one's self: the two vessels joined in a direct, reciprocal bond. With three baidarkas, however, a completely new situation evolves: the potential for survival of a skin-boat culture — in all its human complexities — becomes three-dimensional and real.   George B. Dyson

In the morning fog, a completed two-hatch baidarka rests on Burrard Inlet at Belcarra Park. The vessel's length overall is 24 feet (737 centimeters), the beam is 29½ inches (75 centimeters); the depth amidships is 15½ inches (39 centimeters), and the total displacement is 85 pounds (38.5 kilograms).   Ann E. Yow

In Alliance With The Past

Reconstructing the Craft

"Some people live a two-dimensional life, just for the present. Others look into the past," says historian Richard Pierce, my mentor with regard to the Russian era on the North American coast. "It enriches the present . . . and gives things more scope and greater depth." As a would-be baidarka builder fifteen years ago, I was forced to look into the past — and to correspond with historians like Professor Pierce — because such vessels were no longer being built. I looked back a hundred years and more because that was when the development of the baidarka had stopped. Modern kayak design paled in comparison with the designs of the Aleuts, whose vessels had evolved in imitation of the sea mammals out of whose skins and skeletons they were made.

The shape of things to come, whether in biology or in boat building, lies in the past. The pinnacles of evolutionary design result from a species looking back and remembering, genetically, those things that worked. The 25-knot speed of a killer whale, the delicate form of an Arctic tern in transoceanic flight, and the seaworthiness of an Aleut baidarka are not the result of visionary insight, but of the increment of trial and error over the years. Careful record-keeping is what makes the system of development work.

The Aleuts were disciplined record-keepers. For untold generations it was a matter of life and death to take immediate note of even the slightest improvement to their craft. In museum specimens, and in the measurements derived from them, the results of this collation have survived. In building further upon the Aleuts' designs, we become the curators of the data they collected and embodied for us in the form of their boats. As we handle this information, rearranging things here and there, the process of evolution proceeds from where the baidarkas of the last century left off. But evolution is as much the product of failure as it is of success. The 24-foot two-hatch baidarka depicted here may or may not be a step forward in the evolution of the craft. Time alone will tell.

The lines of this vessel are based upon — but do not faithfully replicate — those of the baidarkas built at Unalaska a century ago. This example is not a thoroughbred of the type, but its lineage is secure. It is designed as a general-purpose boat, reasonably swift of paddle, yet stable enough to safely carry some sail. I have compromised, with many second thoughts, the traditional five-stringered arrangement of the Aleut baidarka in favor of the reduced weight and simpler construction of this three-stringered form. Economy of design, in this example, means being simple and affordable to build without sparing strength, safety, or speed. The materials for this boat as constructed here cost about $350; less if you scrounge around.

I have defined the shape of this boat precisely — and built this example out of aluminum tubing covered with a nylon skin — without intending to limit the materials from which it could be made. Split cedar or unsplit bamboo might serve in place of tubing. Bamboo? "I cannot help thinking we shall soon be able to use our kayaks in open water," wrote Fridtjof Nansen in 1895, referring to a pair of bamboo-and-sailcloth kayaks that weighed forty-one pounds each. "Life would be another thing then! Fancy, to get clear for good of this ice and these lanes, this toil with the sledges, and endless trouble with the dogs, only oneself in a light craft dancing over the waves at play!"[1]

Fridtjof Nansen and Hjalmar Johansen were making one of the epic kayak journeys of all time, in boats they had lashed together themselves. They had set off northward in March of 1895 in an attempt toward the pole, leaving their ship, the *Fram*, held fast in the Arctic ice. Out of sight of the *Fram* and her crew, they were taking their chances at finding their way back to Norway on their own. They reached a high northing of 86°13′N on April 7, then turned and headed south, wintering in Franz Joseph Land (at 82°N) in a crude hut, subsisting on the meat of polar bears and walrus, having long since consumed the last of their twenty-eight dogs. It was July of the following year before their bamboo kayaks — still waterproof, thanks to a coating of polar bear fat and walrus-part repairs — brought their journey safely to an end.

Consider the bamboo baidarka. We have seen what might have happened to aluminum tubing in the hands of the Aleuts, but what if Aleut civilization had spread to the bamboo-covered islands to the south? Bamboo, if not as familiar to our machinists as aluminum, has a remarkable advantage: It grows. Bamboo tubing, equipped with strategically placed watertight bulkheads, is extruded from the ground at the rate of a foot or two per day. Could young bamboo shoots, I wonder, be guided into individual jigs through which bamboo frames and stringers would grow to exactly the required curves?

Woven nylon, sea-lion skins, split walrus hide, or a filament-wound silk cocoon might serve as this hypothetical baidarka's skin. The skin-boat builders of our imagination will use the materials at hand, and use the lines of this baidarka as I, and many others, have used Howard Chapelle's draft of the United States National Museum's one-hatch Aleut baidarka, collected at Unalaska by Ivan Petroff in 1894. From it the lines of this vessel are derived.

Let us imagine where the baidarkas of the future might go. The geographic limitations of materials are now relegated to the past, and the baidarka, perhaps with a solar-reflective skin, can safely roam the world. A reverse-osmotic hand pump allows the paddler of the baidarka to drink sea water and thus avoid the most disagreeable of fates: to be saved from drowning only to die of thirst.

Without a water supply to weigh these baidarkas down, surprisingly long voyages become commonplace. Even the most polluted waterways can be safely traversed. Cruise-missile guidance technology reaches the surplus markets, and we see baidarkas develop microchip instincts for finding their way home. Kite-sails bring trans-oceanic passages within reach.

"Kites, however, will occasionally perform things which neither horses nor steam have ever done, or can do," wrote the English schoolmaster George Pocock in 1827, in his visionary treatise *The Aeropleustic Art, or, Navigation in the Air, by the use of Kites, or Buoyant Sails.* But Pocock's brilliant experiments with kite-powered vehicles came to naught because he did not foresee either the stringing of telegraph wires across open country roads nor the automobiles that would make his kite-drawn carriages obsolete. Besides facing hills, trees, winding roads, intersections and toll gates, the greatest obstacle, Pocock found, was "waggoners, people with carts, foot passengers, &c . . . standing directly in the way and gaping upwards" as the "undreamt-of-equipage" made its approach.

The baidarka is a vehicle far better suited to the application of Pocock's Aeropleustic Art.

"Does it follow that a thing which cannot always be used should never be used?" replies Pocock to his critics' objections (with the same argument I have made in favor of downwind-only sails). "Surely that would be an absurd conclusion . . . That kites cannot be employed at all times, just at a person's will and pleasure, is certainly little objection as it respects their application for recreative excursions; for surely there will be a sufficient number of windy days in the course of a year for the purpose of amusement. The exercise of patience is occasionally very wholesome, and the withholding of indulgences for a season, frequently serves to give greater zest to enjoy-

. . . Then Raven went to a river beyond Copper River called Laxayi'k and told the people that they were to make canoes out of skins. . .

—Tlingit legend

ment." A Pocket Pocock, including his "Travelling Song for High Winds," will be a requisite accessory for those pursuing this avenue of research.

The North Pacific wilderness — much of it now more sparsely populated than at any time in the past few thousand years — is likely to remain among the baidarka voyager's favored haunts, both for part-time recreational adventurers and for individuals seeking to adopt a semi-nomadic life. The success of the whole Russian-American experiment was based on the baidarka, and in our own explorations of this coastline we can hardly do better than to pattern our vessels upon those the Russians used. Perhaps it is wrong to admire the Russians' having taken such advantage of the Aleuts. But one reason the Aleuts survived their period of Russian subjugation as well as they did was that no matter how totalitarian the rule, the individual Aleut still remained the master of his own vessel. "He who has a baidarka is rich," wrote Gavriil Davydov in 1804. "Such a person is even now regarded with respect by the Russians." The independent self-sufficiency of the baidarka deserves the same respect today.

But are these boats suitable for those of us without obscure skills to build? Yes and no. There are secrets even the most detailed blueprints never will reveal, and techniques that pass best from hand to hand. The craft of boat-building, to the early Aleuts, was the domain of a secret society organized along religious lines. Yet the layman, when necessity arose, was expected to be able to build a serviceable boat. Anyone could apprentice to the trade. The best approach is still that of learning from someone else's mistakes.

It is roughly as difficult to build one of these baidarkas as it is to build a flying model airplane without a kit. Such models — the old-fashioned, skeleton-and-skin, balsa-wood sort — are time-consuming to build and no small challenge to fly. The ones I completed used to crash as often as not. You can buy ready-made plastic models, unbreakable ones, that fly surprisingly well. Yet a thriving subculture continues to build the more fragile craft in the traditional, painstaking way. In a similar direction lies the future of the skin boat. Be circumspect of any and all commercialization of the design. The true baidarka is one you build yourself. Here is the outline of the design, the table of offsets, the genetic code at the nucleus of the craft. It is your turn.

A stockpile of future baidarkas *(right)*, in the form of perfectly straight aluminum tubes, sits outside the workshop at Belcarra Park. No matter how many of these vessels are built, and no matter how far we go with the evolution of their design, their form will bear a resemblance to the past because the laws of the ocean have not changed. The shape of a vessel is drawn from experience, and many thousands of years contribute to the bending of these tubes.

The tubing seen here in 25-foot lengths is ¾-inch OD (outside diameter) by .049-inch wall, used for the gunwales, deck stringers, hatch coaming frames, and keels; ½-inch OD by .049-inch wall is used for the remaining stringers and the ribs. The tubing is cold-drawn 6061-T6, the highest-strength alloy that can be commercially produced as thin-walled tubes. Ann E. Yow

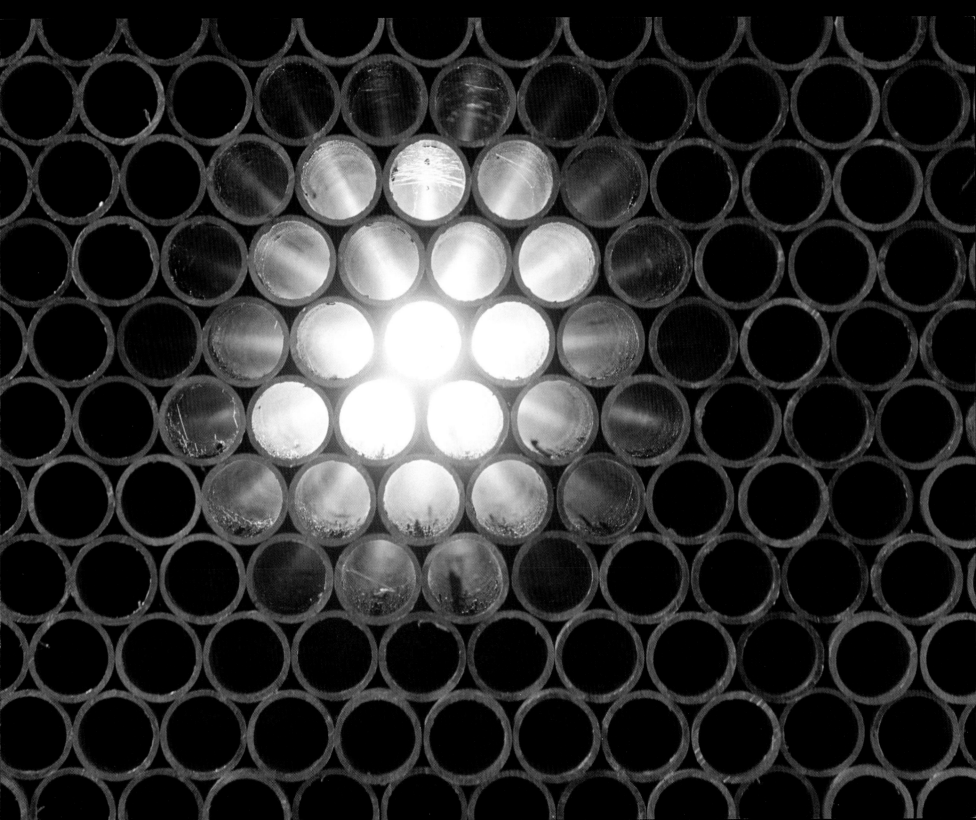

A bandsaw *(left)* is used in cutting the outlines of the sheet aluminum components, such as the stem plate and the stern deadwood visible in the foreground here. The cockpit coaming knees — one of which is being trimmed — are being made from the scrap removed in lightening the deadwood at the stern. The internal lightening holes are cut out with a reciprocating sabre saw. Small pieces are drilled before being cut out; larger pieces are cut into shape before being drilled.

Sawing aluminum is noisy, and ear protection is a must. Also, no machine tools should ever be used without first protecting one's eyes.

Aluminum can be cut and drilled easily with ordinary woodworking tools and techniques, and causes less wear and tear on the tools' edges than does wood. For this reason, newly purchased saw blades, drill bits and files are designated "aluminum only" in my shop. Steel tools actually become sharper when first used upon aluminum, as was known to surgeons who used to draw their scalpels across a small block of aluminum as the final step in preparing for the cut. The microscopic scratches in the steel's surface are filled by the softer metal, and a near-perfect edge is thus obtained. Many of the used cutting tools that find their way into Boeing's South Seattle disposal yard are still perfectly sharp though sold as scrap.

Ann E. Yow

More than 1,600 holes *(above)* must be drilled to produce the skeleton of this boat, and each hole has to be countersunk from both sides. A drill press — even a cheap one — is one of the best investments the workshop can make.

Most of the holes are $\frac{1}{8}$-inch diameter, with some of them $\frac{9}{64}$-inch. High-speed twist drills are used at between 1,000 and 1,500 rpm. With such small-diameter bits, torque is minimal if the work piece should get jammed. This is not so when drilling larger-diameter holes in aluminum, when it is essential to clamp the work.

For smooth countersinking, a sharp bit at low speed — about 250 rpm — is the key. Careful countersinking saves trouble later on, when even a slight imperfection may cut the twine being pulled tight across the edge of the hole.

Neither the bandsaw nor the drill press requires much power to do the job, and a pedal-powered version would suffice.

Ann E. Yow

With the sheet components completed (the stem plate is hanging on the wall), the bending of the baidarka's tubular components begins *(above)*. The longitudinal stringers (this is stringer No. 1, starting from the keel) are bent following individual templates secured to a bed that incorporates a hollowed-out pair of vise jaws to hold the tube *(right)*.

Five different stringer-bending templates are required to build this boat: three for the ½-inch-diameter stringers and two for the ¾-inch-diameter tubing of the gunwales and keel. The templates, made of laminated plywood, are drilled to accept ¼-inch-diameter registration pins that keep the stringer exactly "on track" while it is being bent. The actual bending is done with an ingenious patented device manufactured by the Holsclaw Brothers of Evansville, Indiana — a hand-operated, gear-driven rotary draw-bender that is ideally suited to the job.

In bending tempered aluminum tubing, true draw-bending is the key; it is essential to avoid any compression of the tubing at the bend. The draw-bender actually stretches the tubing by means of a moving bending-shoe — well-lubricated — around a hollow die. The tubing is work-hardened through being stretched, and becomes slightly stronger, if slightly thinner, at the bend.

Ann E. Yow

The Holsclaw tube bender *(above)* truly comes into its own when bending frames. Because the bender operates by counter-rotation around a central axis fitted with a removable shaft, it is possible to construct a simple bending jig for each individual frame, allowing a systematic production of the baidarka's ribs. Each of the boat's nine frame stations is represented by a jig-board (made of 2-inch laminated plywood) with bushings positioned at the centers of the various bending radii so the Holsclaw benders are exactly situated to produce the particular frame.
Ann E. Yow

Hand-operated benders *(above)* allow just the right degree of "feel" for accurate results; tempered tubing has a "springback factor" that requires a delicate hand and empirical experience to control. There is no reason, of course, that all of these jigs could not be nested together on one board. It is easy to envision a universal jig incorporating these ideas. The jig's input would be the offsets for any baidarka's frame stations and its output would be a set of ribs.
Ann E. Yow

Ann E. Yow

Anyone with a love of boat building is also a lover of tools, and the Holsclaw bender deserves the affection reserved for the best. Of simple, rugged cast-iron, with no unnecessary finish or frills and a minimum of moving parts, the Holsclaw bender bends tubing — and that's it. Few other bender configurations will allow precise bending directly above a template, as is required here. In preparing to set up production of these boats, I wrote to more than thirty manufacturers of tube-bending equipment, and was looking at thousands of dollars' worth of equipment to do the job. I found that the shoes and dies alone for most bending machines cost as much as several Holsclaw benders, complete.

Ann E. Yow

Since bending *(below)* a perfect ellipse in ¾-inch-diameter tubing is no simple task, the most difficult pieces of tubing to bend for the baidarka are the hatch-coaming frames. Any irregularities in their symmetrical shape will stand out, especially in this visible part of the boat. Few benders will allow a length of tubing to be bent back upon itself like this; again the Holsclaw bender proves its worth. The heavy-duty ¾-inch model is required because the tensile yield strength of drawn 6061-T6 tubing is above 35,000 pounds per square inch.

Here, the bending operation is at an end. As the curve around the template has progressed, the registration pins have kept the coaming in place and the bender will now be removed. The ends of the tubing are then trimmed to a butt joint with a single bandsaw cut, and a tubular internal sleeve is inserted to complete the splice.

Ann E. Yow

Stem and stern assemblies are prefabricated next. The thin, flimsy pieces of aluminum sheet, when joined into three-dimensional form, become a rigid structure that assumes a life of its own. When the longitudinal stringers are sewn in place, the bow of the baidarka becomes nearly as strong as if it were carved from a solid aluminum block — yet the structure weighs ounces, not pounds.

The first step in prefabricating these assemblies is to tie-wire everything in place — twisting the wires tight with a pair of end-cutters and removing the wire as the permanent nylon lashing takes its place. The lengths of twine *(left)* are measured in fathoms: the reach of one's outstretched arms, exactly six feet in my case. One fathom to me may not be one fathom to you, but the difference is immaterial here because two fathoms, yours or mine, is the upper limit of the length of string with which it is practical to proceed. It is less trouble to put in another knot than to deal with more string than can be pulled taut within arm's reach.

There are few knots visible in these photographs because the knots have been concealed along the inside edge of the seam. The knot used is a simple sheet bend, or weaver's knot, tied in both strands at once — and it is here that hemostats *(right)* are essential, to maintain tension while the knot is put in place. The nylon twine I am using has a phenolic resin coating that ensures any knots tied in it will hold. With plain uncoated nylon, knots invariably slip and lashing becomes a nightmare of loose ends. Ann E. Yow

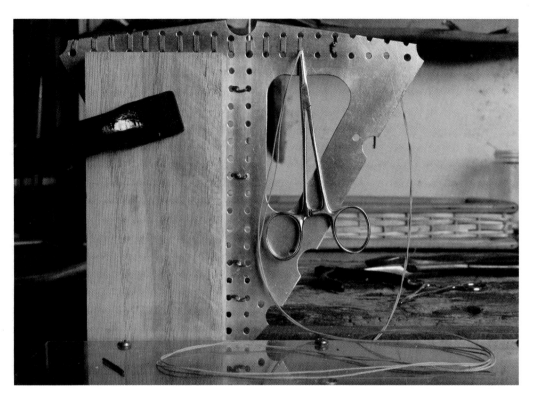

Among the first components to be prefabricated are the frames, each composed of an upper and lower rib joined at the gunwale with sewn knees. As much as possible of the baidarka's skeleton is prefabricated at the workbench before assembling the boat itself.

In sewing aluminum-to-aluminum seams, I work with a double length of twine, threaded through a sailmaker's needle (a No. 15 or No. 16 needle with the sharp triangular edges filed dull), pulling the two strands taut at one time. A glove on the right hand (I am right-handed) is essential to pull the lashings tight — above 40 pounds of tension is maintained while working with doubled twine. The holes are on one centimeter centers with each hole receiving either four or six strands of twine, depending upon the type of seam. The twine tests at about 50 pounds, with the result that the tensile strength of these seams is between 1,000 and 1,500 pounds per inch.

The ends of the tubular ribs are left unfinished at this stage; when the frames are complete the intersections will be beveled out with a ¾-inch rotary file to receive the gunwale stringers, for which a thinly scribed guideline, engraved while the rib was in place on the bending-jig, is visible here. Before the gunwales are fitted to the frames, the ends of the tubes will be filled with waterproof foam rubber plugs, elastomerically sealed in place.

Ann E. Yow

Nothing compares with a plain old rat-tail file when it comes time to bevel tubing-to-tubing joints. Here, the end of stringer No. 3 is being filed to fit fairly against the gunwale stringer (No. 4) at the baidarka's bow.

A complex juncture such as this deserves a page of detailed notes to itself. There is a right-handed and a left-handed bevel to be filed because the two stringers are not interchangeable between port and starboard.

A tubing cutter is visible here, at the lower left, as are five short lengths of ½-inch-diameter tubing used as stringer spreaders at bow and stern. All these bits and pieces appear in detail on the blueprints and require the same attention to close tolerances as the major components of the boat. Errors have a tendency to accumulate, throwing things out of line somewhere else. In the long run, it is easiest to ensure that everything is equally precise. Ann E. Yow

Stringer No. 3 is wired in place, starting at the bow, after the end of the stringer has been filed to a close fit. (The value of an accurate diagram of the bevel is that the stringer fits into place on the first try.) The stringer will be trimmed later to exact length at the stern.

The seam joining stem plate and keel, visible here, has been sewn up in advance as the final step in the prefabrication of the bow. Five holes to the left of my thumb is one of the knots joining one length of twine to the next. In this type of seam, two fathoms of twine produce only ten centimeters of progress along the keel. All exposed ends of twine, at knots or elsewhere in sewing the boat, are melted flush with a cigarette lighter — one of the essential tools of the trade. Ann E. Yow

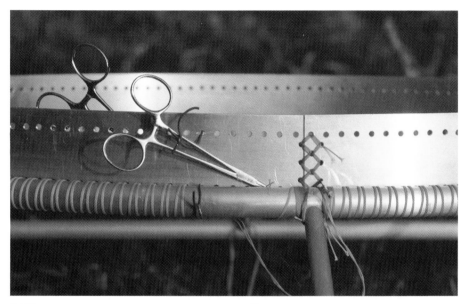

The skeleton of the baidarka *(left)* makes its full-length appearance overnight, as the assortment of prefabricated pieces are tie-wired into place. An accurate, secure building bed assists in setting up the frames. The jigs seen here at every station are made of STOP-sign scrap and old hockey-stick handles, two ubiquitous byproducts of modern Canadian life. Lag bolts through the hockey sticks into the work table allow precise alignment of the jigs. A center line stretched from stem to stern serves as a base line for the initial setup, and ensures that everything remains exactly in place during the building of the boat. Ann E. Yow

A hemostat *(above)* secures one of the more tedious seams in the almost complete boat. The cockpit coaming, close to six feet in circumference, requires more than twenty fathoms of twine in this lower seam, even with only four strands per centimeter joining the coaming to the frame. The final length of twine has run out within inches of reaching the end. I will have to put in another knot.

The upper line of holes is for the attachment of the cockpit coaming rim, a procedure left until after the baidarka has been fitted with its skin. On previous baidarkas I sewed on aluminum tubing rims; on this baidarka I will sew coaming rims made of nylon rope; on my next baidarka I plan to experiment with a coaming rim made of wood. Ann E. Yow

The lashings *(above)* that join the stringers to the frames are the mainstay of the baidarka's rib cage. There are eighty-four of these tubing-to-tubing intersections, yet these all-important structural elements are probably the easiest to complete — no needles to thread, no doubled twine to keep from getting tangled, and no knots to splice. A simple Boy Scout lashing is used, applied with a single strand of twine unwound from a net-mender's shuttle. The shuttle serves as a convenient handle to pull the lashing tight. Eight complete turns are taken, finished with a clove hitch around the lashing's core. The completed joint has a tensile strength of more than 1,400 pounds. Ann E. Yow

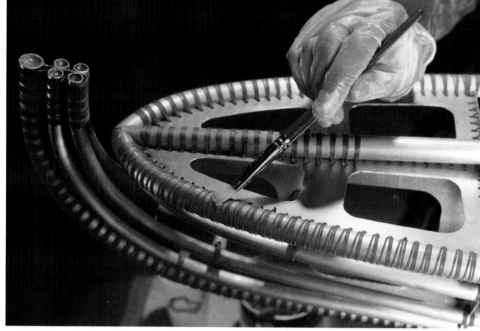

The seam *(left)* joining the stern deadwood to the deck stringer is being finished at the bulkhead at station 1A. The keel stringer has yet to be trimmed to its finished length at the stern, and the tail ends of the nylon lashings have not yet been melted flush.

The origins, pedigree, or provenance of any baidarka can be distinguished almost as readily by its stern as by its bow — and the tail end of this example is unmistakably Fox Island (Unalaska) Aleut. We can only guess, but it would seem that the inspiration for this form of flared transom derived from the buoyant stern and flared tail feathers of a bird.   Ann E. Yow

After the completed framework *(above)* has been checked over for loose ends and final alignment, the lashings are given a coating of epoxy varnish to set them permanently in place. A solvent-carried penetrating resin is applied for two or three coats over a 48-hour period to saturate the twine. The framework remains attached to the building bed until the first coat of epoxy has cured, at which time it can be rotated to reach the areas underneath. The skeleton gains considerable rigidity in the process: the added stiffness in each individual stand of twine adds up to a noticeable change in the character of the boat.   Ann E. Yow

Floorboards *(right)* transform the bare skeleton of the canoe into a furnished home. Full-length floorboards such as ours were unheard of in the past. In this example, five 16-foot-long split-cedar planks, about ½-inch by 3-inches amidships, are lashed individually to the baidarka's ribs, becoming an integral part of the boat. The planks weigh less than three pounds each, and are finished with four coats of the same epoxy varnish as is used to seal the lashings elsewhere in the hull. There is no structural necessity for these floorboards, but they add immeasurable comfort and convenience and are well worth the extra weight. With them you can stretch out, dry and securely cradled, with the warmth of wood sheltering you and your gear from the cold sea against the baidarka's skin. When loading and unloading the canoe, the floorboards allow stuff to slide in and out, and keep your belongings out of the bilge.

The yellow cedar mast step is seen here lashed to the central floorboard, with the mast partners, of aluminum tubing around a central sleeve, linking the hatch coaming frame to the deck stringer at station No. 5.

Ann E. Yow

Ann E. Yow

W ith its frame — its skeleton — complete, the rest of a skin boat is its skin *(right)*. After the dust had settled from my boat-building campaign in 1977, I resolved to put an end to using fiberglass in my boats before glass fibers put an end to me. I set out to find something resembling sea-lion skin or split walrus-hide — the *lavtak* of Russian times, rationed out annually to everyone building or repairing a boat. This new kind of *lavtak* needed to be currently available, and cheap. I knew that if I chose something produced for purposes having anything to do with boats, it would surely be far from inexpensive. In the end it was the pulp-and-paper industry — where costs are shaved to the fraction of a cent — that helped me out.

I searched for a fabric base for the skin, something with high elasticity, great tenacity, and as much abrasion resistance as could be found. Also required was some means of joining this covering at the seams — sewing, of course — and then the means of shrinking this covering tightly over the frame. Nylon fiber appeared to most closely fill the bill, with a tenacity approaching 9 grams/denier (well above 50,000 psi), an elongation of more than thirty percent and a tendency, in its greige state, to shrink up to ten percent with heat. (Nylon's polyaramid cousin, *Kevlar,* though providing somewhat higher tensile strengths, would be of little use because of its inability to stretch. For similar reasons, the various polyesters were also a second choice.) It remained to find a

E asy to lift *(above)*, the complete skeleton of this 24-foot baidarka weighs about fifty pounds (twenty-two kilograms). This is a spacious boat for its length, yet with refined waterlines underneath. The complexities of this hull form reflect the uncompromising genius of the Aleut designers who first developed this craft: An unparalleled mastery of the canoe designer's art graced the compound nature of the baidarka's bow and stern. A hunting machine with the tools of the trade laid out upon its decks, the baidarka's need for orderly equipment and reserve buoyancy defined the broad surfaces above. Speed under paddle, not carrying capacity, defined the shape of the hull below.

nylon fabric thick enough, closely woven from continuous-filament yarns, produced on a wide enough loom. I envisioned a rhinoceroslike skin, and the twelve-ounce "ballistic nylon" commonly sold as "bullet-proof" was not even half equal to the task.

As in the case of the tube benders, it took a lengthy search (including statements by a number of qualified sales agents that "Mr. Dyson, no such fabric as you are looking for exists") to turn up the right product for the job — in this case, a 26-ounce per square yard double-woven nylon fabric, used by the pulp-mill industry in dust-control systems engineered exactly like the bag on a Hoover vacuum cleaner, but on a vastly larger scale. Abrasion of all previous materials had been the problem, the engineers told me, and in creating this nearly $\frac{1}{16}$-inch-thick, two-ply nylon fabric (with a tensile strength of over 1,200 pounds per inch) they had inadvertently created the toughest skin any baidarka on earth had ever worn.

To begin the covering of the baidarka, the frame is turned upside down, a boat length of cloth is centered along the keel, and a loose basting seam is run along both gunwales to hold the cloth in place.

Ann E. Yow

The deck seam *(above)* is sewn with two needles operating at once, leapfrogging each other along the seam. The temporary lacing seam was left overlapped ¾ inch or so along the deck. As the finished seam approaches, the temporary seam, lacing and all, is cut through with the hot knife to the aluminum surface below. (Watch out when passing over the deck-stringer lashings, when an aluminum backing strip must be placed under the seam.) This leaves an even butt joint that is sewn up using the two needles in a crisscross fashion, the stitches spaced one centimeter apart, and composed of single strands of twine. The thick fabric, unshrunk and uncoated, sews easily.

Bare fingers are all that is required to do the job, with hemostats to hold things in place along the way. No great tension is called for; the heat-shrinking applied later will pull everything tight (or too tight, as I would later find out in the case of this first attempt). A curved carpet-layer's needle is used. *Ann E. Yow*

With the baidarka turned right side up, the skin is trimmed to approximate size along the ridge of the deck and around the hatchways. A temporary, overlapped seam is first basted the entire length of the boat. This takes very little time and keeps everything in place as the final seams are sewn. All cuts in the fabric are made with a "hot knife," consisting of a soldering gun with a sharpened tip. The cloth's edges are thus prevented from fraying by being melted as they are cut, and the finished seams can be sewn directly without the need to hem the raw edges of the cloth.

Ann E. Yow

Stitching of the seam *(right)* along the deck is nearly complete. Having started amidships and proceeded alternately fore and aft, here I am nearing the bow. The raw fabric is sixty-eight inches in width, just wide enough to envelop the entire baidarka in one piece — with the exception of a narrow triangle to be spliced in along the ridge of the deck between stations No. 4 and No. 5. The temporary lacing along the gunwale is visible here; it will later be removed. Forward of where I am sewing can be seen the strip of surplus cloth removed in the final trimming of the overlapping skin to a butt joint. The work of sewing the skin goes quickly — much faster than the structural sewing of the frame. *Ann E. Yow*

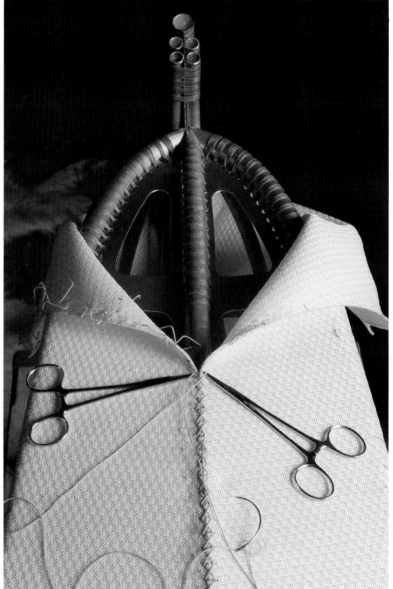

Sewing a baidarka skin is clean, leisurely work, with cooperative materials taking the vessel's shape in one's hands. It is the antithesis of the sticky, toxic, and irreversibly catalytic procedures to which I had subjected myself in building baidarkas with fiberglass skins.

At long last, I was truly building a Skin Boat — and the sterile cleanliness of nylon could not conceal the hint of sea-lion skin and sinew in the air. The surgical precision of Aleut boat-building technique was a two-way street in ancient times. Early accounts of Aleut medicine marvel at the skill displayed in sewing up frightful human wounds with a steady hand — gained, no doubt, in sewing up boats.

Ann E. Yow

With a minimum of cuts, the nylon fabric conforms readily to the complex shapes of the baidarka's bow *(above left)* and stern *(above right)*. I was surprised at the simplicity of these procedures. A piece of chalk is used to mark the surplus cloth, the cloth is cut away with the hot knife, the resulting seams are sewn up, and that, literally, is the end of it. Once the hull is coated with its hypalon/neoprene sealant, the seams will be waterproof without any further preparation. It is a prime virtue of this thick fabric that the raw seams require no additional reinforcement. A strip of 1¼-inch nylon webbing will later be laminated along the outside of the keel along its entire length, thus covering the forward seam along the baidarka's stem. Otherwise, all the seams in the boat will be left as is.

Ann E. Yow

On a warm July evening I am preparing *(left)*, to put a long splice in a length of ⅝-inch nylon rope, to serve as a cockpit coaming rim. The required tools are at hand: soldering gun, lighter, fingerless glove, vise-grips, needlenose pliers, hemostats, notebook, net-needle, and an afternoon glass of wine. The beauty of baidarka-building is that so much of it is repetitive, "mindless" work — exactly those tasks that provide precious and uncluttered time to think. One is free to daydream, become lost in thought, or even get slightly inebriated, without in any way compromising one's work. If a seam looks fumbled later, it can always be sewn again — and as to industrial safety, there is not much chance for any more serious accident than sticking a needle in one's thumb.   Ann E. Yow

The rudder, hanging prefabricated on the workshop wall *(right)* is of such obviously simple configuration that I cannot believe I struggled with this design problem for so many years.   Ann E. Yow

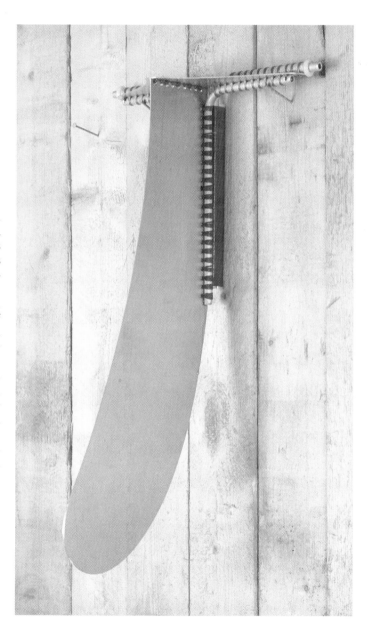

This inside view of the baidarka looks forward from station No. 6. The stations are 26 inches apart — we are seeing less than half the boat — and it is clear the vessel contains a lot of room. Not nearly so much as the *Mount Fairweather,* though: The laws of scale dictate that the 24-foot baidarka, while fully half the *Mount Fairweather*'s length, contains only one-eighth the space. Scaling in the other direction, however, we find that this 24-footer has more than twice the room of a 19-footer of similar design (about the size of a typical one-seater in Aleut times).

It is these laws of scale that favor skin-on-frame construction when it comes to longer boats. Under twenty feet it makes no great difference whether the vessel's structural rigidity derives from an internal framework, as seen here, or from a rigidly molded shell, as in conventional fiberglass boats. But as size increases, the weight of fiberglass (or polyaramid, or graphite fiber, though with these lighter materials some additional advantage may be gained) required to meet structural demands through single-shell construction becomes prohibitive, and we are unlikely to see such single-shelled unframed vessels approach the twenty-five to thirty-foot lengths of Russian times. Unless, as would seem the next logical step, commercial kayak builders start going to foam-cored, compound skins — allowing those third-power variables in the equations to work to their advantage rather than their demise.

Ann E. Yow

Unfortunately, this is the last glimpse we will have through this baidarka's skin. The elastomeric coating that will soon seal the skin of this baidarka is opaque, in contrast to the seal-oil coatings of the past that rendered an already translucent epidermis nearly transparent through a waxed-paper sort of effect.

I seriously considered (and made numerous experiments, that deserve full-scale trial on a boat) using an oil/wax formulation to seal the nylon skin. The coatings were perfectly waterproof, and would have produced exquisitely beautiful results. But sunlight is the enemy of all polymers, those of the waterproof coating as well as the nylon fibers underneath. I wished to avoid the traditional baidarka's need to have its skin re-oiled every few weeks, and rebuilt or replaced every year.

Ann E. Yow

Whatever coating *(left)* is used for the baidarka's skin, resistance to sunlight, moisture, and abrasion are essential, with elasticity and adhesion to the nylon substrate of equal importance in making a choice. Of all available elastomers, that long-proven workhorse known as neoprene (chloroprene) seems the most suited to the job, with hypalon (chloro-sulfonated polyethylene) a useful if less elastic adjunct for the inner and outer coats. The most readily available form in which we find these synthetic rubbers formulated for brush-coating use is in domestic and industrial sun-deck coatings. For this use a neoprene base coat is selected for its high adhesion and elasticity, with a hypalon topcoat for abrasion resistance, ultraviolet stability, and a choice of pastel colors to match the deck chairs and the pool.

The first step in this process is the application of a couple of thinned coats of hypalon solution, which penetrate through the skin, saturating the inside nylon surface — something the more viscous neoprene will not readily achieve. The hypalon is white, and this prevents the inside of the baidarka from becoming an uneven, ugly battleship gray, as it would if the subsequent layers of neoprene were able to soak through. The solvents for these rubber solutions are volatile, aromatic xylenes — thus the absolute necessity of maximum ventilation (one of three exhaust fans is visible here) and fresh activated-charcoal cartridges in the respirator that is always worn when applying the coating.   Ann E. Yow

The next coat *(above)*, over the entire hull and deck, is a high-solids neoprene solution — a thick, gray, syrupy liquid applied with a brush. The coating takes some care to apply smoothly to sloping surfaces, but since it reduces in thickness by almost fifty percent as it cures, unevenness that stands out while it is wet is less discernable once the coating has cured.

With the boat entirely covered with neoprene — an extra coat being given for good measure and surface smoothness to the hull — the whole skin is painted again, this time with two coats of hypalon, unthinned. All told, it took about two gallons each of hypalon and neoprene solution to cover this boat, the surface area being approximately 105 square feet.

Ann E. Yow

Convergent evolution, rather than tradition, has finally led me to a paddle design very close to that of the Aleuts. After years of feathered designs *(above)* I have now unfeathered the blades, as was settled upon by baidarka builders perhaps thousands of years ago. Aleut paddles were entirely of wood: "always of California *chaga* [cedar, or redwood] as the lightest wood," says Veniaminov. In the most recent design (under construction, *left)*, there is still some wood, and wood-carving: yellow cedar (from a drift-log) is being formed into the paddle's central rib. The shaft is aluminum tubing, and the blade is aluminum sheet. These paddles are long — between nine and nine-and-a-half feet, as opposed to about seven feet in the case of the Aleuts — reflecting a wider, lengthier boat, and the span of this paddler's arms. Ann E. Yow

On August 29, 1984 *(right)*, the first of these 7.37-meter baidarkas was launched. I had settled on designing a 24-footer before converting it to metric — almost exactly 737 centimeters — and, yes, I chose 737 because that was the Boeing Aircraft Company's most successful model of plane. Almost every piece of the baidarka, after all, has been shaped to some degree by Boeing's discarded tools.

For the same reason the Boeing 737 was a successful airplane, I believe that the 737 baidarka will be a successful boat: Both excel in moving people around. Before the Boeing 737 airplane, there was no such thing as a short-haul commercial jet; and before the 7.37-meter baidarka, there was no kayak or baidarka suitable for two people to paddle in, set sail from, sleep in, and generally live out of for extended periods without being unreasonably cramped. But here the similarity ends. You can build your own baidarka; only Boeing could build you the plane. Ann E. Yow

On the beach at Burnett Bay *(left)*, Queen Charlotte Sound, the completed baidarka displays most of its standard cruising equipment on deck: mast, sail, paddles, and a bilge pump mounted aft. I cannot enumerate all the advantages of a soft-skinned baidarka such as this, and surely have not even discovered all of them yet. One most obvious advantage is silence: Things do not clatter on the baidarka's decks, and the hull slips along quietly in comparison with a fiberglass boat. It lands against rocks with a dull, rubbery thud rather than a crunch. Abrasion resistance of soft nylon and neoprene against rocks is much, much greater than that of hard fiberglass, as paradoxical as that may seem. Next is the sense of touch: The paddler's hands and knees feel a skinlike surface against his own skin, and there is noticeably less claustrophobia than is sensed when going below in a hard-shelled boat. Of course, I believe that soft-skinned baidarkas gain an advantage in terms of speed, but we will have to conduct controlled experiments before giving an objective statement on that.

George B. Dyson

After experimenting with several other ideas, I returned to a fan-shaped sail *(above)*. Only this time the two halves of the sail are raised separately from a short, central yellow-cedar mast. The total sail area is twenty-four square feet, ample power for this easily driven hull. Few other vessels would get very far with one square foot of sail per foot of length. The "wings" of the sail are attached with a soft nylon hinge (scraps of the vessel's skin) to a sort of "shoulder blade" fitting secured to the mast just above the deck. There are absolutely no moving metal parts. The ribs in the sail are split cedar battens. There wasn't enough wind on this occasion to put a full belly into the sail. Ann E. Yow

In the golden haze of a Belcarra Park twilight, Paul Caffyn and I are taking the new baidarka around a measured course — and coming up with an average speed of better than six knots, or about seven miles per hour. The one-hatch, 21-foot baidarka I am working on now promises to be an even more efficient boat.

Paul has paddled his own one-man kayak, alone, around Australia — ten thousand miles in 364 days. And in the Northern hemisphere, in the wake of our Aleut predecessors, the capabilities of the baidarka for long voyages have hardly begun to be re-explored. The past tells us what was once possible, and it is all still possible today.

Ann E. Yow

Plans

In introducing the following plans for a baidarka, I can hardly do better than to quote Joshua Slocum in his appendix to the 1900 edition of his *Sailing Alone Around the World,* where he presented the public with the lines and sail-plan of the *Spray.* "To young men contemplating a voyage," wrote Slocum, "I would say go."

Table of Offsets
measurements in centimeters to center of longitudinals

vertical measurement from **baseline**
horizontal measurement from **centerline**

Station	0	1A	1	2	3	4	5	6	7	8	9	10	11	12	13	14	15	
V	28.85	32.8	33.8	34.7	35.9	36.8	37.3	37.3	36.5	35.6	34.4	33.0	32.85	32.7	32.55	32.35		DECK
IV	30.5	29.7	28.7	27.6	26.75	26.4	26.4	26.7	27.5	28.6	30.0	31.6	31.8	32.0	32.2	32.35		GUNWALE
	16.4	18.8	23.8	29.5	33.8	35.8	35.5	33.4	29.8	24.6	18.2	11.3	10.4	9.1	6.8			
III		21.8	19.15	16.95	15.45	14.7	14.7	15.4	16.8	19.05	21.95	25.9	26.6	27.4	28.7	32.35		STRINGER
		12.75	19.4	24.8	28.7	30.4	30.4	28.5	25.1	20.35	14.7	7.9	7.2	6.3	4.75			
II	15.15	13.3	10.25	7.8	6.0	5.15	5.2	5.95	7.6	10.3	14.05	19.2	19.95	20.9	22.35	26.3		STRINGER
	0.65	6.2	13.65	19.0	22.5	24.0	24.0	22.4	19.2	14.75	9.6	4.25	3.6	2.9	2.0			
I	10.0	8.3	6.1	4.1	2.8	2.05	2.15	2.85	4.35	6.95	10.55	16.0	16.75	17.7	19.25	22.95		STRINGER
	0.65	3.1	7.0	10.1	11.6	12.3	11.7	10.8	9.25	7.05	4.7	2.3	2.0	1.7	1.3			
0	5.4	4.15	2.5	1.3	0.5	0.0	0.0	0.7	2.0	4.5	8.25	13.6	14.4	15.3	16.75	19.9		KEEL
Distance from stern	0.0	36.3	102.8	169.2	235.7	302.1	368.6	435.1	501.5	567.9	634.4	700.9	708.2	715.5	722.9	730.2	737.5	

The plans that follow illustrate the construction methods used to build one recent example of a vessel whose design is constantly being improved. For the reader who has decided to go ahead and build a boat, the use of current, full-size blueprints is advised. For information on an updated series of designs for baidarkas, contact Dyson, Baidarka & Company, 435 West Holly St., Bellingham, WA 98225.

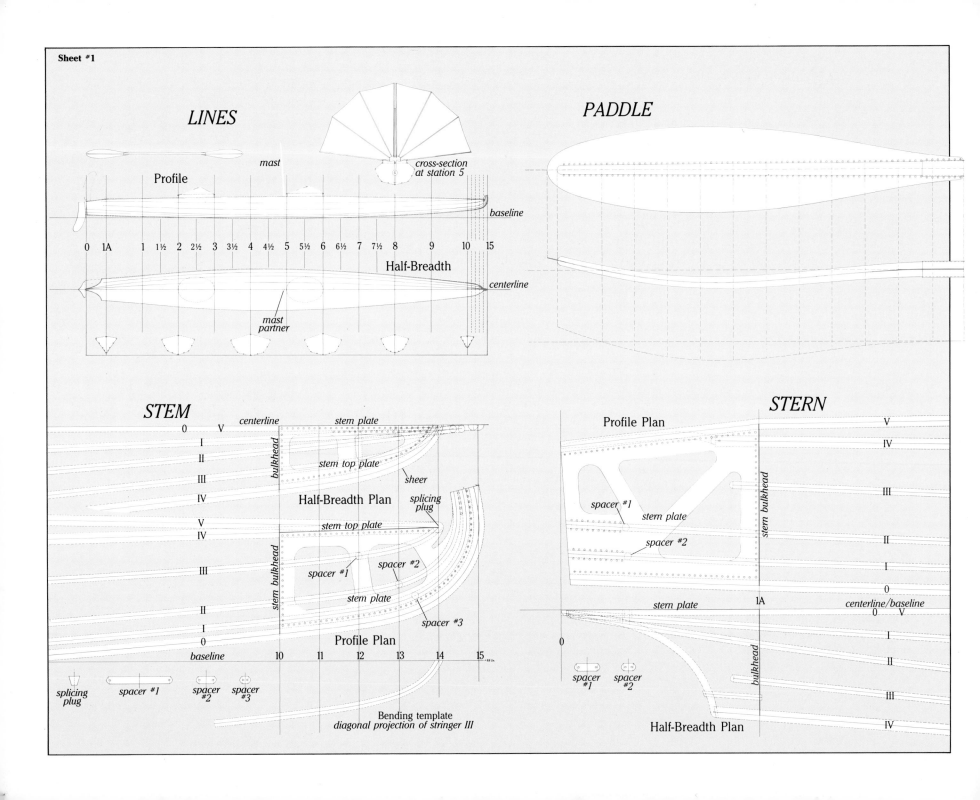

LINES

PADDLE

mast

Profile

cross-section at station 5

baseline

0 1A 1 1½ 2 2½ 3 3½ 4 4½ 5 5½ 6 6½ 7 7½ 8 9 10 15

Half-Breadth

centerline

mast partner

STEM

STERN

centerline *stem plate*

Profile Plan

V

IV

V

bulkhead

I

stern bulkhead

II

III

stem top plate

sheer

III

Half-Breadth Plan

splicing plug

IV

spacer #1

stern plate

V

stem top plate

IV

spacer #2

II

stern bulkhead

III

spacer #1

spacer #2

I

II

stem bulkhead

spacer #1

stem plate

0

I

spacer #3

centerline/baseline

0

1A

0 V

0

baseline 10 11 12 13 14 15

Profile Plan

I

splicing plug

spacer #1

spacer #2

spacer #3

spacer #1 *spacer #2*

bulkhead

II

Bending template
diagonal projection of stringer III

Half-Breadth Plan

III

IV

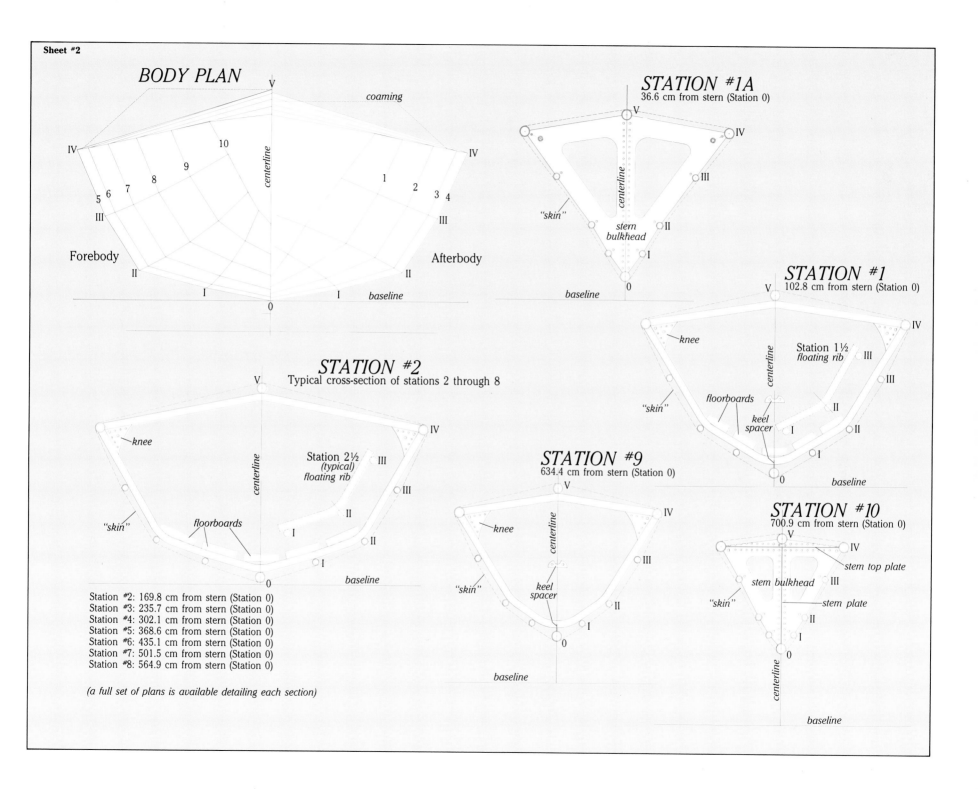

BODY PLAN

coaming

Forebody

Afterbody

baseline

STATION #1A
36.6 cm from stern (Station 0)

"skin"

stern bulkhead

baseline

STATION #1
102.8 cm from stern (Station 0)

knee

Station 1½ floating rib

"skin"

floorboards

keel spacer

baseline

STATION #2
Typical cross-section of stations 2 through 8

knee

Station 2½ (typical) floating rib

"skin"

floorboards

baseline

Station #2: 169.8 cm from stern (Station 0)
Station #3: 235.7 cm from stern (Station 0)
Station #4: 302.1 cm from stern (Station 0)
Station #5: 368.6 cm from stern (Station 0)
Station #6: 435.1 cm from stern (Station 0)
Station #7: 501.5 cm from stern (Station 0)
Station #8: 564.9 cm from stern (Station 0)

(a full set of plans is available detailing each section)

STATION #9
634.4 cm from stern (Station 0)

knee

"skin"

keel spacer

baseline

STATION #10
700.9 cm from stern (Station 0)

stem top plate

stem bulkhead

stem plate

"skin"

baseline

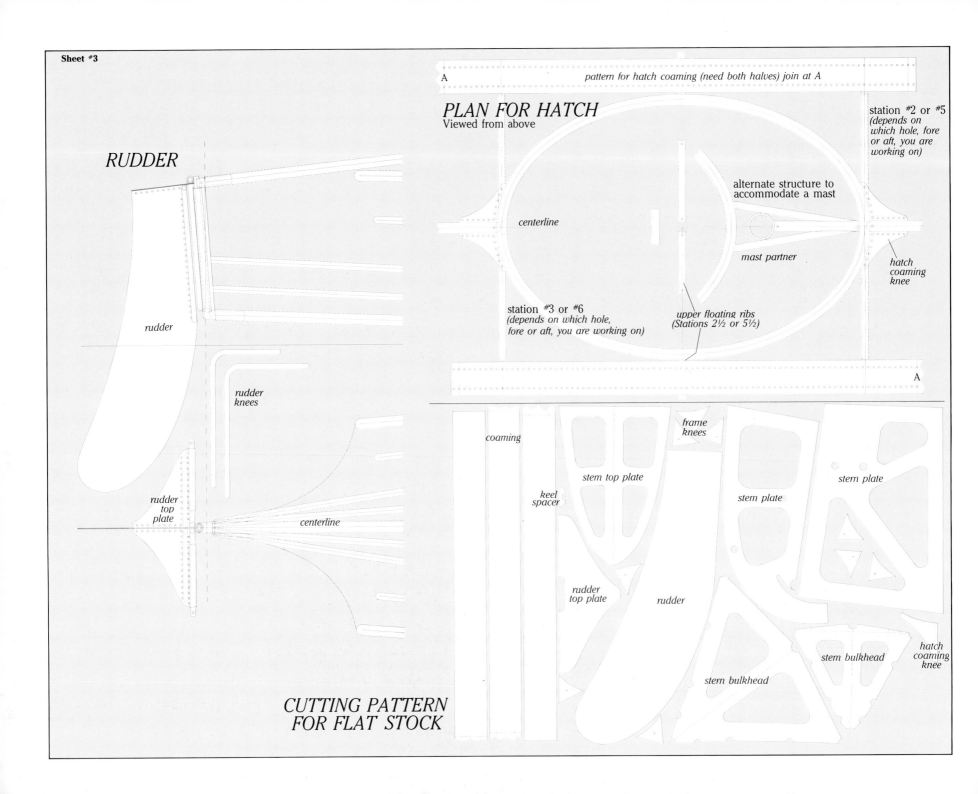

Sheet #3

RUDDER

rudder

rudder
knees

rudder
top
plate

centerline

CUTTING PATTERN
FOR FLAT STOCK

A   pattern for hatch coaming (need both halves) join at A

PLAN FOR HATCH
Viewed from above

station #2 or #5
(depends on
which hole, fore
or aft, you are
working on)

alternate structure to
accommodate a mast

centerline

mast partner

hatch
coaming
knee

station #3 or #6
(depends on which hole,
fore or aft, you are working on)

upper floating ribs
(Stations 2½ or 5½)

A

coaming

frame
knees

stem top plate

keel
spacer

stem plate

stern plate

rudder
top plate

rudder

stem bulkhead

stern bulkhead

hatch
coaming
knee

In Conclusion

Here, then, we conclude this account of the baidarka; there remain only the following notes and references to refer you to the original sources of information. But the written history, however fascinating, tells only half the tale. The story goes back far beyond our written records, and will continue to unfold in the future. We are talking about legends: both those of times gone by, that our own experience now brings back to life, and the legends yet to be told.

I leave you with a legend that has survived intact from long before the written history of the baidarka. This is the story of an escape, the triumph of two Atkan prisoners of war who were being held captive on Amukta Island and saw a severe winter gale as their one chance to regain their freedom. Unarmed and outnumbered, they made it to their baidarkas and put out to sea, where the fearsome weather was their only protection against pursuit. Cedor L. Snigaroff, born in 1890, told of these events to the Norwegian linguist Knut Bergsland at Atka Village in 1952, in the same words his father had used:

. . . and they saw that a host of warriors started out after them as they took off in the direction of the strait, heading west, with the wind behind them.

At first, as he was passing the shore towards the strait, trying his best to catch up with his partner, who was going on the high waves like a feather blown by the wind, he was deathly afraid of being overtaken from behind, but when he got to the rough sea in the strait, his partner no longer was ahead and he himself was in front. While he had not caught up to his partner along the shore, the situation was reversed when he got into the strait, and he worried about his partner that he might be overtaken, for when his own baidarka started to go, it just hopped along the waves, he said.

So he went on, and when he got into the strait, they did not see anymore the warriors who had come after him, they said. Indeed, they were no sea animals, those warriors who came after him, and the cousins did not think that they made it back safely, at least not all of them, they used to say. The agitated sea was as if covered with smoke . . .

By daybreak the two paddlers had reached Amlia Island in safety, having crossed some ninety-two miles of open ocean during the night. And during those long hours of storm-borne darkness, with eyes narrowed against the spray and paddles clenched in untiring hands, it was the now-forgotten legends of their own forefathers, I am sure, that kept the two paddlers afloat, giving them the strength to carry on until dawn brought their homeland into sight.

So, when you set off in your own baidarka, carry the legends and history with you, as you would carry a spare paddle, a compass, a lifejacket, some dry matches, and a pump. The legends will survive only through being used and retold, and you should add to them if you can. The magic of history is that we are adding to it all the time.

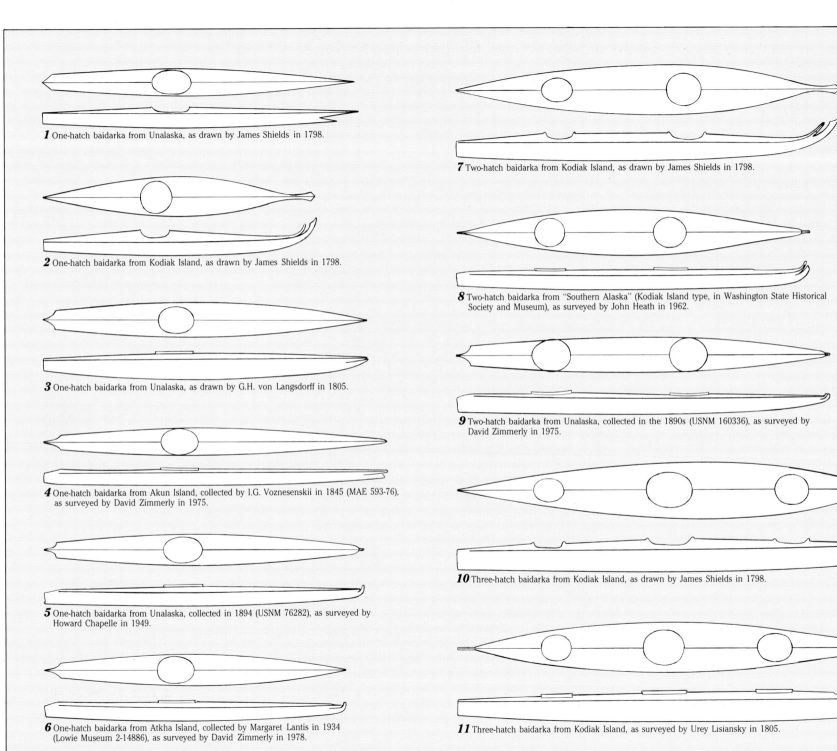

1 One-hatch baidarka from Unalaska, as drawn by James Shields in 1798.

2 One-hatch baidarka from Kodiak Island, as drawn by James Shields in 1798.

3 One-hatch baidarka from Unalaska, as drawn by G.H. von Langsdorff in 1805.

4 One-hatch baidarka from Akun Island, collected by I.G. Voznesenskii in 1845 (MAE 593-76), as surveyed by David Zimmerly in 1975.

5 One-hatch baidarka from Unalaska, collected in 1894 (USNM 76282), as surveyed by Howard Chapelle in 1949.

6 One-hatch baidarka from Atkha Island, collected by Margaret Lantis in 1934 (Lowie Museum 2-14886), as surveyed by David Zimmerly in 1978.

7 Two-hatch baidarka from Kodiak Island, as drawn by James Shields in 1798.

8 Two-hatch baidarka from "Southern Alaska" (Kodiak Island type, in Washington State Historical Society and Museum), as surveyed by John Heath in 1962.

9 Two-hatch baidarka from Unalaska, collected in the 1890s (USNM 160336), as surveyed by David Zimmerly in 1975.

10 Three-hatch baidarka from Kodiak Island, as drawn by James Shields in 1798.

11 Three-hatch baidarka from Kodiak Island, as surveyed by Urey Lisiansky in 1805.

Baidarkas of the North Pacific, 1798-1986: An evolutionary sketch

Scale in feet

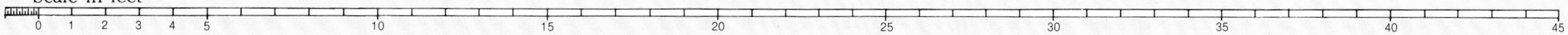

0 1 2 3 4 5 10 15 20 25 30 35 40 45

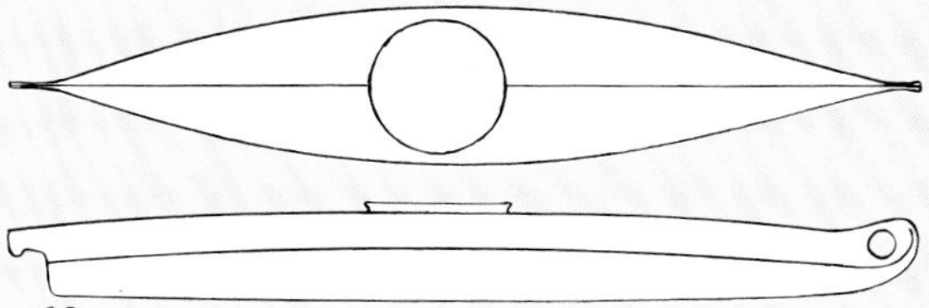

12 One-hatch kayak from Nunivak Island, collected in 1889 (USNM 160345), as surveyed by Howard Chapelle in 1946 and replicated by George Dyson in 1970.

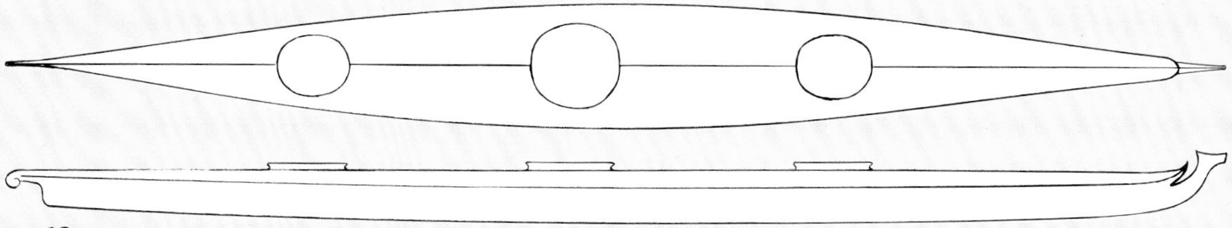

13 Three-hatch baidarka designed and built by George Dyson in 1972.

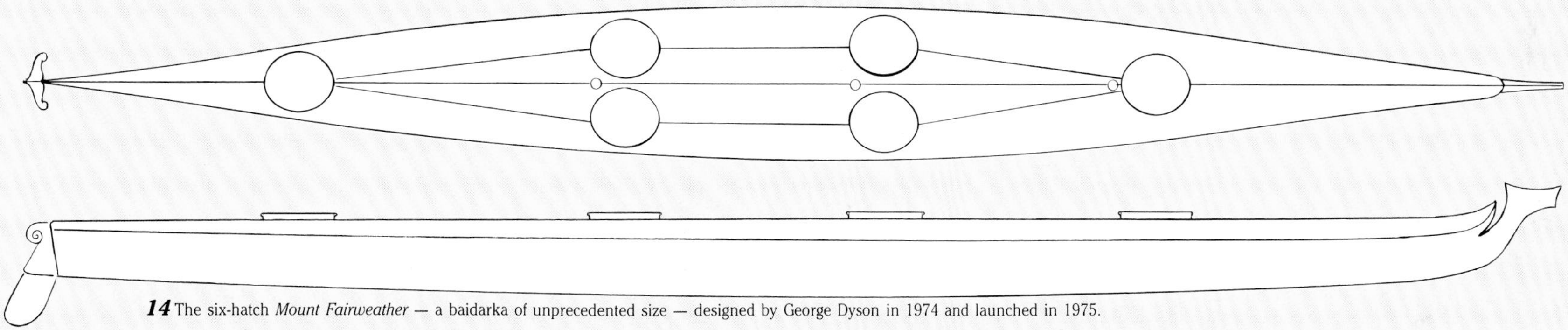

14 The six-hatch *Mount Fairweather* — a baidarka of unprecedented size — designed by George Dyson in 1974 and launched in 1975.

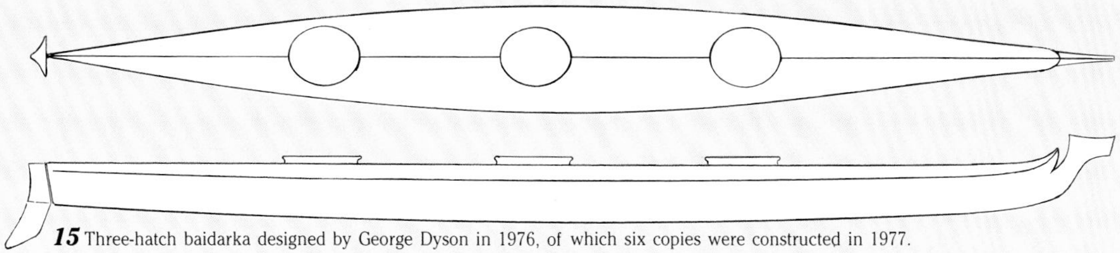

15 Three-hatch baidarka designed by George Dyson in 1976, of which six copies were constructed in 1977.

About their own origins the Koniagas have the oddest of ideas: some say that a baidarka with the first people in it fell from the sky . . .

—Gavriil Davydov, 1810

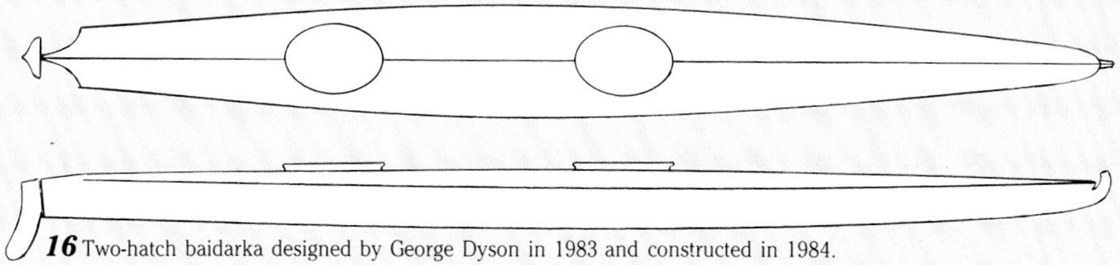

16 Two-hatch baidarka designed by George Dyson in 1983 and constructed in 1984.

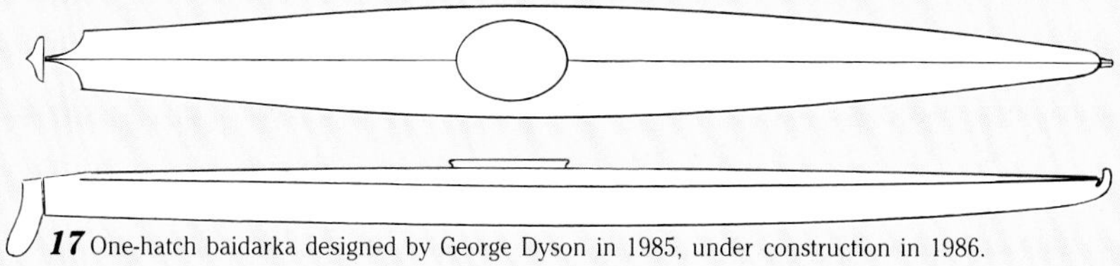

17 One-hatch baidarka designed by George Dyson in 1985, under construction in 1986.

Glossary

ALIASKA (also *Aliaksa, Alashka, Alaschka, Aliakskha,* etc.). Originally a general term used by Aleut and Kodiak Natives to refer to the Alaska Peninsula and the American mainland beyond; in Russian-American times usually referred to the Alaska Peninsula in particular. Became Alaska of present usage after the Russian-American possessions were acquired by the U.S.

ARSHIN. Russian unit of measurement. One arshin = approximately 28 inches = 71.1 centimeters.

BAIDAR. Russian term applied to different kinds of small boat or canoe; usually refers to either a baidarka or a baidara, though sometimes used in reference to Native dugout craft (which could be quite large).

BAIDARA. Russian term, originating on the Dnieper River of the Ukraine, introduced in Alaska to describe the Natives' large (anywhere from twenty-five to sixty feet in length), open skin-covered boats. The boats had been a central feature of communal village life and intertribal trade. These large vessels were soon appropriated by the Russians, who began using them both for local transportation and freight, and, on a number of occasions we know about, for voyages between Asia and America along the Aleutian Chain.

BAIDARKA (also *bydarka, bidarka, bidarky, baidarky, baydarka, baydarky;* pl. *baidarki, baidarkas,* etc.) A term introduced by the Russians to describe the Aleut skin boat with a deck; a kayak (in Aleut *iqjaX* or *uluXtaX*) with one, two, or three hatches.

   Three broad distinctions can be used to distinguish the baidarka from other kayaks in use throughout the northern world: 1) The baidarka was associated with areas of Russian influence and sea-otter hunting — i.e., the Aleutians, the Alaska Peninsula, Kodiak Island, Prince William Sound, the Gulf of Alaska coast, and the shoreline farther south, wherever the Russians went; 2) Baidarkas were the only form of kayak commonly built with three hatchways, though there is some dispute as to whether this was a Russian invention or not; 3) Almost all baidarkas had forked, bifurcated bows, whereas most other kayaks did not.

BAIDARSHCHIK. Originally, the head or chief of a baidara crew; later used to identify any head or manager of a Russian-American Company outpost; sometimes (in later years) erroneously used in reference to the owner/operator of a baidarka.

BARABARA (also *barabora, borabora*). Originally a Kamchadal term for a small semi-subterranean structure for storage or temporary summer use; in Alaska came to be applied generally to the dwellings of the Aleuts.

CALENDAR, JULIAN. In the nineteenth century, the old-style (Julian) calendar, as used in Russia and Russia America, was twelve days behind the new style (Gregorian), and therefore twelve days must be added to most Russian accounts to match the system of dates now in use.

CHUGACH. The Natives of Prince William Sound (Chugach Bay), who were of Eskimo extraction (termed Pacific Eskimo) and therefore culturally distinct from both the Tlingit and the Aleut, though geographically in between.

CREOLE. A person of mixed Russian-Alaskan parentage. In official terms, designating civil status in the Russian-American colonies equivalent to that of a townsman in metropolitan Russia, inherited in the male line and with both duties and privileges attached. Though subject to ten to fifteen years obligatory service in the Russian-American Company, the Creoles were granted preferential education and other benefits in return, so that toward the later years in the colonies, most mid-level management and professional positions in Alaska were occupied by Creoles. Though resented by many Russians who were themselves of lower class, this preferential treatment of the native-born was a deliberate colonial policy that resulted in an unusually stable ruling class: allied equally both to the Natives and to the Crown.

ELL. An obsolete (and ambiguous) measurement, usually of cloth, ranging from twenty-one to forty-five inches, depending on which standard was being used.

EVRASHKA. Ground squirrel (Aleutian ground squirrel; *Citellus parryii ablusus*).

FOX ISLANDS. Sometimes applied to the Aleutian Islands as a whole, but more particularly, in Russian usage, to the easternmost group of islands, i.e., Unimak, Unalaska, Umnak, and immediate smaller neighbors.

GALIOT. Generally, a broad, full-bodied, coastal cargo vessel, typically with one or two short, heavy masts and displaying a trademark bowsprit sail. In the Russian-American trade, the capacity of these primitive vessels was sometimes beyond belief. Sailing from Okhotsk to Kodiak in 1794, the 63-foot-long *Tri Ierarkha [Three Hierarchs]* carried, according to Tikhmenev (1978, p. 36) "126 passengers, including ten clergymen, two prikashchiks, and sixty-two promyshlenniks, along with fowl, cattle, seed grain, agricultural tools, and provisions, so that in addition to the crew and 120 barrels of fresh water she was laden with 13,000 puds [480,000 lbs]."

HIEROMONK. A monk in the Russian Orthodox Church who was also a priest.

IUKOLA (also *yukola*). Fish, usually salmon, that has been split, dried, and stored for winter or travel use — the staple food of the baidarka expeditions in Russian-American times.

KAD'IAK. Island or archipelago in the Gulf of Alaska, also spelled *Kadiak, Kadyak, Cadiack,* and now *Kodiak.*

KAMLEIKA (also *kamleia* or *kamlei*). A waterproof, hooded, knee-length outer garment, with drawstrings at face and wrists, usually made of sea-mammal intestines (occasionally from bear intestines, fish skins, or the membrane from the sea-lion's throat). Worn in bad weather ashore, and essential for travel at sea; in cold weather, worn over an undergarment of bird-skins or furs.

KAYAK. A small, decked, skin-covered canoe, and, more particularly, as the origins of the word seem to indicate, a hunting craft. The same word, for the one-seater at least, was used by all the different builders of these craft — demonstrating either a common ancestry or significant contact between skin-boat builders throughout the world: *qajaq* of the Arctic and Greenland Eskimos; *iqjax, ikakh,* or *ikyak* of the Aleuts; and, at the southern extreme of the vessel's range, *qayak^(ɯ)* of the Tlingit on the Gulf of Alaska coast.

KOLOSH (also *Koliuzh, Kaluschian,* etc.). The Russian name for the Tlingit Indians of Southeast Alaska and Yakutat. Possibly derived from the verb *kolot,* "to pierce," since the Tlingit women were characterized by pierced lower lips, in which they wore *kaluzhka,* or labrets.

KONIAG (or *Koniaga, Konyag,* etc.). The Native inhabitants of the Kodiak Island group, originally quite distinct from the Aleuts. Under Russian influence the distinction began to be lost and the Koniag people came to be included in the general term "Aleuts."

LAVTAK (or *laftak,* sometimes *lakhtakh*). The dressed skins of sea mammals, particularly those used for the covering of baidaras and baidarkas, i.e., sea-lion skins, split walrus hide, or fur-seal or hair-seal skins.

NEAR ISLANDS. The westernmost group of islands in the Aleutian Chain, hence near Russia, i.e., Attu, Agattu, and Semichi Islands.

NORFOLK SOUND. Sitka Sound, in Southeast Alaska.

NOVO ARKHANGEL'SK (New Archangel). The capital of Russian America, now Sitka, on Baranof Island.

NUCHEK. Harbor, village, settlement, and trading center on Hinchinbrook Island, Prince William Sound, founded by the Russians in 1793. Also called Constantine Harbor, Port Konstantine, and Port Etches.

PARTOVSHCHIK. A Native member of a (usually sea-otter) hunting party.

PAVLOVSK (Harbor). St. Paul Harbor, on Kodiak Island; now the harbor and town of Kodiak.

PEREDOVSHCHIK. The foreman of a hunting party or baidarka expedition.

PORT MULGRAVE. Yakutat.

PROMYSHLENNIK. Originally a Siberian fur-trapper, fur-hunter, or trader. In Alaska the word came to mean any Russian adventurer engaged in the sea-otter trade, particularly one who actively supervised the hunt.

PUD. 1 pud = 36.11 pounds = 16.38 kilograms.

RUBLE. One silver ruble, or 100 kopeks, in the early 1800s was about equal to one half-dollar U.S., with a paper value worth substantially less: 68 kopeks in 1794, 25 kopeks in 1810, and 20 kopeks in 1815.

SAINT PETERSBURG. The capital of Russia, founded in 1703 by Peter the Great on the Neva River near the Gulf of Finland; name changed to Petrograd in 1914. Replaced as the capital by Moscow in 1918, and then again renamed, as Leningrad, in 1924.

SAZHEN. 1 sazhen = 7 feet = 2.1 meters.

SEA-DOG. A seal. In particular, *Phoca vitulina,* or harbor seal.

SEA-HORSE. Walrus.

SHITIK (pl. *shitiki*). In Siberia, a crude "sewn-plank" wooden boat with a deck. The seams were fastened with willow wands or leather thongs — no metal at all was used. Usually had leather rigging, stone anchors, and animal-skin sails. Originally developed for river use, but some of the earliest Russian voyages toward America were made with this type of boat.

TLINGIT. A large, extensive, and at times powerfully allied group of distinct yet related Native tribes, of Athapaskan extraction. Inhabited the "panhandle" coast of Alaska, ranging from Yakutat in the north to Prince of Wales Island in the south.

TOYON (or *toyen, toen, toion,* etc.). Of Yakut origin, meaning tribal elder or hereditary chief; in Russian America applied specifically to those Native elders appointed or recognized by the Russian-American Company as the spokesmen and leaders of their island, village, or other Native group. Rank was usually inherited by brother, son, son-in-law or nephew, if an eligible candidate was at hand.

UMIAK. Eskimo word for a large, open skin boat; in Russian, a baidara.

UNALASKA (also *Unalashka, Oonalashka, Ounalachka,* etc.). The largest and most important of the Eastern Aleutian Islands, and the site of an early Russian settlement consolidating a number of earlier villages of the Aleuts. Often used in referring to the main settlement, properly called Iliuliuk, in Captain's Bay.

VERSHOK. 1 vershok = 1.75 inches = 4.4 centimeters.

VERST. 1 verst = ⅔ mile = 1.068 kilometers (1 verst = 500 sazhen = 1500 arshins).

YURT. In Siberia, a dome-shaped above-ground dwelling, usually covered with skins; in Alaska sometimes applied to the underground habitations of the Aleuts.

Footnotes

Part I: A CHAIN OF EVENTS

1. Ivan Veniaminov (St. Petersburg, 1840), quoted here as translated by Ivan Petroff in *Report on the Population, Industries, and Resources of Alaska* (Washington, 1884), 147. Also translated by Lydia Black in *Notes on the Islands of the Unalashka District*, ed. Richard A. Pierce (Kingston: The Limestone Press, 1984), 297-298.

2. Eli L. Huggins, 1874, as compiled in *Kodiak and Afognak Life*, edited by Richard A. Pierce (Kingston: The Limestone Press, 1981), 4.

3. These instructions, drawn up by Peter the Great just before his death and given to Bering by Empress Catherine, were as follows (from *The Report of Fleet-Captain Bering . . .*, translated by F.A. Golder in *Bering's Voyages*, 1:9-10): I. Build in Kamchatka or in some other place in that region one or two decked boats. II. Sail on these boats along the shore which bears northerly and which (since its limits are unknown) seems to be a part of America. III. Determine where it joins with America, go to some settlement under European jurisdiction; if you meet a European ship learn from it the name of the coast and put it down in writing, make a landing to obtain more detailed information, draw up a chart and come back.

4. Michael Gvozdev, manuscript journal from the archives of the Ministry of Marine, Petrograd, as excerpted and translated by F.A. Golder in *Russian Expansion on the Pacific . . .* (Cleveland, 1914), 162.

5. Georg Wilhelm Steller, manuscript journal as translated by F.A. Golder in *Bering's Voyages . . .* (New York, 1922-1925), 2:90.

6. Ibid., 2:95-96.

7. Ibid., 2:90.

8. Stepan P. Krasheninnikov, *Opisanie . . .* (St. Petersburg, 1755), as translated by E.A.P. Crownhart-Vaughn, *Explorations of Kamchatka* (Portland: Oregon Historical Society, 1972), 72.

9. Steller (trans. Golder), *Bering's Voyages*, 2:95.

10. Clarence L. Andrews, in *The Story of Sitka* (Seattle, 1922, page 9) relates "a dim tradition among the Sitkans of men being lured ashore in the long ago . . . Chief Annahootz . . . dressed himself in the skin of a bear and played along the beach . . . the Russians in the excitement of the chase plunged into the woods in pursuit and there the savage warriors killed them to a man . . ."

11. Alexei Chirikov, in the *Journal of the St. Paul*, entry for September 9, 1741, from the manuscript copy in the Archives of the Ministry of Marine, Petrograd, as translated by Frank A. Golder in *Bering's Voyages* (New York, 1922-1925), 1:303.

12. Ibid., 1:304.

13. William Coxe, *Account of the Russian Discoveries between Asia and America* (London, 1780; 3d edition, 1787), 20-21.

14. Ibid., 9.

15. Ibid., 178.

16. Ibid., 87-88.

17. Hieromonk Father Gedeon, *Ethnographic Notes*, compiled at Kad'iak 1804 to 1807, and first published at Moscow in 1894; here quoted as translated by Colin Bearne in *The Russian Orthodox Religious Mission in America, 1794-1837*, ed. Richard A. Pierce (Kingston: The Limestone Press, 1978), 126.

18. Ibid., 132.

19. William Coxe, *Account . . .* (1787), 129.

20. Heinrich Johan Holmberg, *Ethnographische Skizzen . . . (Ethnographic Notes . . .)*, (Helsingfors, 1856), p 412; here quoted from an unpublished translation by Richard A. Pierce, 1974.

21. Coxe, 129-130.

22. Charles Clerke, in the journal of the *Discovery*, entry for May 13, 1778 at Hinchinbrook Island, Prince William Sound; from J.C. Beaglehole, *Journals of Captain Cook* (Cambridge: The Hakluyt Society, 1967), 3:334.

23. David Samwell, journal, entry for May 18, 1778; from Beaglehole, *Journals*, 3:1113.

24. James Cook, journal, entry for October 23, 1778; from Beaglehole, *Journals*, 3:462-463.

25. Ibid., 463.

26. Charles Clerke, journal; from Beaglehole, *Journals*, 3:1338.

27. John Ledyard, *Journal of Captain Cook's Last Voyage . . .* (Hartford, 1783), 90-91.

28. James King, journal, entry for October 7, 1778; from Beaglehole, *Journals*, 3:1445.

29. James Cook, journal, entry for October 8, 1778; from Beaglehole, *Journals*, 3:449.

30. James Burney, *A Chronological History of North-Eastern Voyages of Discovery . . .* (London, 1819), 252.

31. David Samwell, journal, entry for October 7, 1778; from Beaglehole, *Journals*, 3:1138.

32. John Ledyard, *Journal . . .* (1783), 93.

33. Ibid., 96.

34. Ibid.

35. James Burney, *Chronological History . . .* (1819), 253.

36. James Cook, journal for October 14, 1778 (in Beaglehole, *Journals*, 3:450).

37. James Cook, journal for October 15, 1778 (in Beaglehole, *Journals*, 3:450).

38. James Cook, journal for October 19, 1778 (Ibid., 3:457).

39. Thomas Edgar, journal for October 16, 1778, at Samganoodha (Ibid., 3:1357).

40. F.A. Golder, *Bering's Voyages*, 1:235.

41. *Documents on the History of the Russian American Company*, ed. Richard A. Pierce (Kingston: The Limestone Press, 1976), 66. It was further claimed, by Shelikhov, in the *Personnel book of the Three Saints*, under "overcharges of the employee's account" and "immoral and harmful actions against the Company and others" that Izmailov "took 1,008 rubles of vodka . . ." and "stole 600 r. of spirits" (Richard A. Pierce, ed., *A Voyage to America*, Kingston, 1981, page 117).

42. Grigorii I. Shelikhov, letter to Baranov from Okhotsk, August 9, 1794, in Petr A. Tikhmenev, *Istoricheskoe . . .* (St. Petersburg, 1861-1863), vol. 2 (appendix of documents); as translated by Dmitri Krenov, *A History of the Russian American Company, vol. 2, Documents*, Richard A. Pierce, ed. (Kingston: The Limestone Press, 1979), 52-53.

43. James Cook, journal for October 18, 1778 (in Beaglehole, *Journals*, 3:452).

44. Ibid.

45. James King, journal for October 15, 1778 (Ibid., 3:1446).

46. Charles Clerke, journal for October 1778 (Ibid., 3:1335).

47. Comments Lydia Black: "Stepan Cherepanov and [Fedor] Kul'kov independently reported in the 1750s that on Attu and other Near Islands single, two, and three hatch baidarkas were used." (letter, 23/8/84).'In *Atka: An Ethnohistory of the Western Aleutians* (Kingston, The Limestone Press, 1984) Professor Black elaborates further: "Elsewhere, apparently, three-hatch kayaks were not used in pre-contact times. It is widely assumed, quite erroneously in my opinion, that the three-hatch baidarkas were invented by the Russians to accommodate passengers. If Cherepanov's account is considered on its merits, it is much more likely that the three-hatch baidarkas were encountered by the Russians in the Near Islands and carried eastward from there." (page 57) The relevant passage from Cherepanov's statement, made on August 3, 1762 in the chancery in the Port of Okhotsk, and witnessed by Fedor Kul'kov, is as follows: "They [the inhabitants of Agattu Island] hunt sea otters with slender arrows about an arshin and a half [3½ feet] long; sharp bone points, toothed on both sides, about a quarter [arshin?] in length [i.e., seven inches], are inserted on the tips. They are thrown from boards [*doshchechki*]. When they have wounded a sea otter, they give chase in small skin baidarkas (containing two persons each, sometimes three, sometimes one) until the creature is exhausted . . ." (Translated by Jack McIntosh from "Skazka totemskogo kuptsa Stepana Cherepanova ob ego prebyvanii na Aleutskikh ostrovakh v 1759-1762 gg." [The Story of the Tot'ma Merchant Stepan Cherepanov of his Stay in the Aleutians, 1759-1762], in A.I. Andreev, *Russkie otkrytiia v Tikhom okeane i Severnoi Amerike v XVIII veke. Sbornik Dokumentov.* [Russian Discoveries in the Pacific Ocean and North America in the Eighteenth Century. Collection of Documents.] Moscow/Leningrad, 1948, pp. 116-117.)

48. James Cook, journal for October 23, 1778 (in Beaglehole, *Journals*, 3:462).

49. Frederica de Laguna, *Under Mount Saint Elias* (Washington, 1972), 581.

50. Ivan Veniaminov, *Notes* . . . (St. Petersburg, 1840), as translated by Lydia Black (Kingston, 1984), 208.

51. David Samwell, journal for October 15, 1778 (in Beaglehole, *Journals of Captain Cook*, 1967, 3:1140).

52. Gavriil I. Davydov (St. Petersburg, 1810-1812), in *Two Voyages to Russian America*, translated by Colin Bearne and edited by Richard Pierce (Kingston, 1977), p. 159.

53. Don Francisco Antonio Maurelle, as extracted and translated in La Pérouse, *Voyage Around the World* (London, 1799), 1:251-252.

54. John R. Swanton, in *Tlingit Myths and Texts*, Smithsonian Institution, Bureau of American Ethnology Bulletin 39 (Washington, D.C., 1909), 349-350.

55. Tomás de Suria, Journal, mss., 1791, as translated and edited by Henry R. Wagner, "Journal of Tomás de Suria of his voyage with Malaspina," *Pacific Historical Review*, vol. 5, no. 3 (1936), pp. 248 and 259.

56. There is another possibility, of course: that the Vancouver Island Natives had acquired the baidarkas themselves, through the same trade routes that copper, dentalium, and slaves followed up and down the coast. "I doubt that the artist added them from Suria's Yakutat sketches," answered Professor Lydia Black in response to my inquiry on this matter. "Phil Drucker always maintained that Nootka had connection with Alaska. I am of the same opinion. If the kayaks can be documented there, we will be making a giant step forward." (July 9, 1985.)

57. Views of the Aleutian Islands appear as engravings in Sarycev's *Atlas* . . . (St. Petersburg, 1802).

58. Martin Sauer, *An Account of a Geographical and Astronomical Expedition* . . . (London, 1802), 157.

59. Carl Heinrich Merck, *Journals* . . . (manuscript 1788-1792), as translated by Fritz Jaensch, *Siberia and Northwestern America* . . ., ed. Richard A. Pierce, (Kingston: The Limestone Press, 1980), 172.

60. Carl Heinrich Merck, journal entry for June 21, 1790, as translated by Fritz Jaensch, Ibid., 90.

61. Gavriil A. Sarycev, *Account of a Voyage of Discovery* . . . (London, 1806-1807), 2:73.

62. Carl Heinrich Merck, journal for June 21-July 4, 1791, at Unalaska, as translated by Fritz Jaensch (Kingston, 1980), 172.

63. Sarycev, *Voyage* . . . (London, 1806-1807), 2:73.

64. Captain Joseph Billings, journals 1789-1791, as compiled by Z.D. Titova in *Ethnograficheskie materialy Severo-Vostochnoi Geograficheskoi Ekspeditsii. 1785-1795* (Magadan, 1978) and here quoted as re-translated by Fritz Jaensch as an excerpted appendix to *Siberia and Northwestern America 1788-1792* (Kingston, 1980), ed. Richard A. Pierce, 203-204.

65. "About two fathoms long," says Steller (note 6, above); "about twelve feet long," says Cook (note 24, above); "about fifteen feet long," says Chirikov (note 11, above); "six to seven arshins [14 to 16 feet]," says Veniaminov (1840, 1:224; 1984, 273); "14 feet 6 inches," says Lisiansky (1814, 212); all this refers to one-hatch boats. It is apparent that the vessels were becoming slightly longer during the period 1750-1850; museum specimens collected towards the end of the Russian period (such as that collected by Voznesenskii in 1845, MAE No. 593-76, 5.63 m in length; see Liapunova, 1964, and David Zimmerly's plans thereof) reached 19 feet in length, with 18 feet being common for one-hatch craft — and up to 30 feet for the three-man boats.

66. Rumors have persisted that Shelikhov, 47 years old and otherwise in perfect health, had in fact been poisoned by his wife (see *A Voyage to America.* ed. Richard A. Pierce, 1981, pp 30-31 and 138-145). A close family friend would later write: "He suffered a great pain in his stomach, and had such an inflammation that in an instant, to alleviate the fire, he swallowed a whole plateful of ice" (Ibid., 30). Natal'ia Shelikhov, perhaps grieving over her loss — or calculating what she had gained — had a monument erected in her husband's memory, inscribed with a florid epitaph concluding with the cost of the monument itself: 11,760 rubles, a substantial sum.

67. Quoted here as translated by Colin Bearne in *The Russian Orthodox Religious Mission in America*, ed. Richard A. Pierce (1978), 5.

68. K.T. Khlebnikov (St. Petersburg, 1835), as translated by Colin Bearne, *Baranov*, ed. Richard A. Pierce (Kingston: The Limestone Press, 1973), 2-3.

69. Ibid., 5.

70. Baranov, letter to Shelikhov from Kad'iak, May 20, 1795, first published in Tikhmenev's *Istoricheskoe* (Vol. 2, St. Petersburg, 1863) and here translated by Dmitri Krenov in *A History . . . vol. 2: Documents*, ed. Richard A. Pierce (Kingston, 1979), 60.

71. Baranov, letter to Delarov, as translated (most likely by Ivan Petroff) in H.H. Bancroft's *History of Alaska* (San Francisco, 1886), 386.

72. *Report, Company employees Egor Purtov and Demid Kuliakov, to Baranov, from Paul's Harbor, August 9, 1794*, first published in Tikhmenev's *Appendix of Documents* (St. Petersburg, 1863) and translated by Dmitri Krenov, ed. Richard A. Pierce (Kingston, 1979), 46.

73. George Vancouver, *A Voyage of Discovery* . . . (London, 1798), 3:150.

74. Egor Purtov, *Report* (1794), in Tikhmenev, *Documents* (1979), 49.

75. Ibid., 50.

76. Ibid., 49.

77. Ibid., 51.

78. Ibid. Could this "three-hatch baidarka" have been a model, perhaps? Exactly such a model exists in the collections of the British Museum, attributed — erroneously, I suspect — to Cook's visit to Prince William Sound in 1778.

79. George Vancouver, *Voyage* . . . (London, 1798). 3:232.

80. Hieromonk Father Gedeon, *Notes 1804-1807* (Moscow, 1894), as translated by Colin Bearne (Kingston, 1978), 137-138.

81. Kyrill T. Khlebnikov, *Zapiski* . . . (St. Petersburg, 1861), translated and edited by Basil Dmytryshyn and E.A.P. Crownhart-Vaughn as *Colonial Russian America: Kyrill T. Khlebnikov's Reports, 1817-1832* (Portland: Oregon Historical Society, 1976,) 1.

82. Gavriil Ivanovich Davydov, *Puteshestvie v Ameriku* . . . (St. Petersburg, 1810-1812), as translated by Colin Bearne, *Two Voyages to Russian America, 1802-1807*, ed. Richard A. Pierce (Kingston, The Limestone Press, 1977), 194.

83. Hieromonk Father Gedeon, *Notes 1804-1807* (Moscow, 1894), transl. Colin Bearne, ed. Richard A. Pierce (1978), 138.

84. G.I. Davydov (St. Petersburg, 1810-1812), trans. Colin Bearne, edited by Richard A. Pierce (1977), 178.

85. Ibid., 202-203.

86. Ibid., 164.

87. Ibid., 203.

88. Ibid.

89. Ibid., 127. (Journal for July 19, 1803).

90. Ibid., 114.

91. Ibid., 115.

92. Ibid., 117.

93. Ibid., 121.

94. Ibid., 122.

95. Ibid., 133-134.

96. G.H. von Langsdorff, *Voyages* . . . (London, 1814) 2:301. The tragedy was immortalized by Vice-Admiral A.S. Shishkov (who posthumously completed the publication of Davydov's Alaskan notes) in the following words: "O strange Fate! O mortal man!
That which neither steppes nor desert could take
Nor steep mountainside nor fearful ravine
Nor savage beasts nor the fierce enemy himself,
Was taken by one careless step." (Translated by Colin Bearne in Davydov's *Two Voyages to Russian America* . . ., 1977, 21.)

97. See David W. Zimmerly in *Sea Kayaker* 1:4 (Spring 1985) page 8 for details of this vessel as studied in 1975.

98. Urey Lisiansky, *Voyage* . . . (London, 1814), 212.

99. John D'Wolf, *A Voyage to the North Pacific* . . . (Cambridge, Mass., 1861), 72.

100. G.H. von Langsdorff, *Voyages and Travels* . . . (London, 1814), 2:41-42.

101. Ibid., 43.

102. Khlebnikov, *Baranov* . . . (St. Petersburg, 1835), as translated by Colin Bearne (Kingston, 1973), 57.

103. Khlebnikov, *Zapiski* . . . *(Notes* . . *.)* (St. Petersburg, 1861), in appendix no. 8, as translated by Basil Dmytryshyn and E.A.P. Crownhart-Vaughn (Portland, 1976), 145.

104. See Berkh, 1823 (1974, 93, 98-106); Khlebnikov, 1861 (1976, 34, 136-141); also Fedorova, 1971 (1974, 189) whose figures (transposed by mistake with those for fur-seals) are based on those of Tikhmenev (1861; 1978, p 153, 207, 360).

105. Lisiansky, *Voyage* . . . (London, 1814), 203-204.

106. Anonymous, in *The Russian Orthodox Religious Mission in America* (Moscow, 1894), translation by Colin Bearne (1978), 11. This observation closely follows Veniaminov's (1984, 163): "By the time a Russian sees a baidarka, an Aleut already recognizes the faces of the paddlers."

107. G.H. von Langsdorff, *Voyages and Travels* . . . (London, 1814), 2:39.

108. Veniaminov, *Notes* . . . (1840 2:134), as translated by Lydia Black (1984), 224.

109. Hieromonk Father Gedeon (Moscow, 1894), as translated by Colin Bearne (1978), 142.

110. Ibid., 141.

111. Ferdinand P. Wrangell, *Russian America; Statistical and Ethnographic Information* (St. Petersburg, 1839), as translated by Mary Sadouski, ed. Richard A. Pierce (Kingston: Limestone Press, 1980), 27.

112. See Robert F. Heizer, *Aconite Poison Whaling in Asia and America: an Aleutian Transfer to the New World.* Smithsonian Institution, Bureau of American Ethnology Bulletin no. 133; Anthropological Papers no. 24. Washington, D.C., 1943, pages 415-468.

113. Aleš Hrdlička, *The Aleutian and Commander Islands and their Inhabitants* (Philadelphia, 1945), 612.

114. G.H. Von Langsdorff, *Voyages* . . . (London, 1814), 2:37-38.

115. G.I. Davydov, as translated by Colin Bearne, 1977, page 152.

116. G.H. von Langsdorff, *Voyages* (London, 1814).

117. Captain Edward Belcher, in *H.M.S. Sulphur on the Northwest and California Coasts, 1837 and 1839*, edited by Richard A. Pierce (Kingston: Limestone Press, 1979), 22-23.

118. Veniaminov, *Notes* . . . (St. Petersburg, 1840), 219-221, quoted here from an anonymous translation in Human Relations Area Files, Aleut Division; see also translation by Lydia Black (1984), 270-271.

119. Ibid., 221-222; 271-272.

120. Ibid., 221-223; 271-272. A dismantled baidarka, collected at Akutan in the 1920s and preserved at the Burke Museum at the University of Washington in Seattle, exhibits these finely crafted bone parts exactly as described in Veniaminov's notes. All the wooden components of the framework have been fitted with ivory bearing surfaces where they adjoin; the keelson scarfs are fitted with interlocking ivory ball-and-socket joints; and even the composite bow and stern blocks, when taken apart, exhibit ivory bearings within. (Joe Lubischer, of Port Townsend, Washington, is preparing a study of these parts.) It is my conjecture that these baidarkas probably had their moving parts lubricated with grease.

121. Ibid., 223-224; 272-273.

122. Ibid., 224; 273.

123. Ibid., 225; 274.

124. Ibid., 225-226; 274.

125. Ibid., 227-228; 275.

126. Veniaminov, *Characteristics of the Aleuts of the Fox Islands* (manuscript, 1834), first published in F.P. Wrangell's *Statistical and Ethnographic Information* . . . (St. Petersburg, 1839), and here translated by Mary Sadouski, edited by Richard A. Pierce (Kingston, 1980), 96.

127. Veniaminov, *Notes* . . . (1840), 258, as translated by Aleš Hrdlička (1945), 15.

128. Ibid., 303; 471. See also translation by Lydia Black (1984), 150.

129. John Muir, *The Cruise of the Corwin* (Boston, 1917), 67. This was June 15, 1881, at Plover Bay.

130. Feodor Lütke, *Voyage autour du Monde* . . . (Paris, 1835-1836), 275, given here in my own translation.

131. Ibid., 235.

132. Ibid., 223.

133. Ibid., 325.

134. Alexander Baranov, letter of instructions to Lieutenant L.A. Podushkin on his departure for Hawaii, February 15, 1816. From a translation in the Bancroft Library, included by Richard A. Pierce in *Russia's Hawaiian Adventure* (Berkeley: University of California Press, 1965), 51.

135. Dr. G.A. Schaeffer, in his journal of his stay in the Sandwich (Hawaiian) Islands, entry for June 21, 1816. From a mss. transcription (made by Alphonse Pinart in St. Petersburg in 1874) in the Bancroft Library, translated by G.V. Lantzeff. Pierce, Ibid., 176-177.

136. Adele Ogden, *The California Sea Otter Trade, 1784-1848* (Berkeley, 1941), 59.

137. Among those captured was the hunter Tarakanov, whose purported journal of his imprisonment and torture at the hands of the Spanish Fathers, transcribed and translated by Ivan Petroff (Bancroft manuscript collections) is, according to Richard A. Pierce, who has examined it closely, in all probability a fake. Petroff seems to have had an axe to grind with the church, and against the Russian Orthodox fathers he exercised a fraud that was sharper yet: Petroff's "find" of the journal of Father Juvenal (a priest who did indeed disappear on a mission to the mainland from Kodiak in 1796), and its prominent inclusion in Bancroft's *History of Alaska*, was certainly a plant. Petroff's legend of Father Juvenal gained wide acceptance and readership over the years. "In the middle of the night I awoke to find myself in the arms of a woman whose fiery embraces excited me to such an extent that I fell a victim to lust, and a grievous sin was committed before I could extricate myself," supposedly wrote the priest on September 25, the day before his lurid death. See Bancroft (1886), 365-374.

138. G.H. Von Langsdorff, *Voyages and Travels* . . . (London, 1814), 2:201-202.

139. F.P. Wrangell (St. Petersburg, 1839), as translated by Mary Sadouski, edited by Richard A. Pierce (1980), 20.

140. Ibid., 19.

141. Alexander Baranov, letter to Larionov on Unalaska, March 22, 1801. From Tikhmenev's *Appendix of Documents* (St. Petersburg, 1863), no. 31, as translated by Dmitri Krenov, and edited by Richard A. Pierce (Kingston: Limestone Press, 1979), 127.

142. Hieromonk Father Gedeon, letter to Metropolitan Amvrosii, June 2, 1805 (Moscow, 1894), as translated by Colin Bearne, edited by Richard A. Pierce (1978), 58.
143. Ivan Petroff, *Report on the Population, Industries, and Resources of Alaska* (Washington, 1884), 24.
144. Iakov Netsvetov, journal for August 1, 1830, translated by Lydia Black in *The Atkha Years . . .*, edited by Richard A. Pierce (Kingston: Limestone Press, 1980), 49.
145. K.T. Khlebnikov, *Baranov . . .* (St. Petersburg, 1835), translation by Colin Bearne (1973), 25.
146. G.H. Von Langsdorff, *Voyages and Travels . . .* (London, 1814), 2:82.
147. K.T. Khlebnikov, *Baranov . . .* (St. Petersburg, 1835), translation by Colin Bearne (1973), 43.
148. Urey Lisiansky, *Voyage . . .* (London, 1814), 153.
149. K.T. Khlebnikov, in *Baranov . . .* (St. Petersburg, 1835), as translated by Colin Bearne, and edited by Richard Pierce (1973), 48.
150. Khlebnikov (1835), translation by Colin Bearne (1973), 65.
151. Eduard Blaschke, "Some observations on handling baidarkas and on the Aleuts of the Fox Islands," published in *Morskoi Sbornik* (Naval Anthology) Volume 1, St. Petersburg, 1848. Here quoted as translated by Dr. Jack McIntosh from a manuscript transcription (Alphonse Pinart's?) in the Bancroft Library. See *Sea Kayaker*, volume 1 no. 3 (Winter 1984).
152. Ibid.
153. Ibid.
154. Ibid.
155. Ibid.
156. Ibid.
157. Ibid.
158. Ibid.
159. L.A. Zagoskin, 1843, in *Lieutenant Zagoskin's Travels in Russian America, 1842-1844* (Moscow, 1956), as edited by Henry N. Michael (Toronto: Arctic Institute/University of Toronto, 1967), 263.
160. Ibid., 264
161. Ibid., 263
162. P.N. Golovin (St. Petersburg, 1862), as translated by Basil Dmytryshyn and edited by E.A.P. Crownhart-Vaughn, *Captain P.N. Golovin's Last Report . . .* (Portland: Oregon Historical Society, 1979), 49.
163. Ibid., 77.
164. Ibid., 78.
165. Ibid.
166. Agnes C. Laut, *Vikings of the Pacific* (New York, 1915), 69-70.

167. John Muir, *The Cruise of the Corwin* (1917), 13.
168. Captain J.C. Glidden, *A Trip to Alaska,* manuscript journal, Bancroft Collection, 1883, pp. 2-4.
169. Ibid., 5.
170. Eli L. Huggins, in *Kodiak and Afognak Life,* edited by Richard A. Pierce (1981), 4.
171. Ibid., 24.
172. Ibid., 4. See also Lydia T. Black in *The Atkha Years* (1980), 298.
173. Ibid., 25-26.
174. Alphonse Pinart, manuscript diary, entry for September 14, 1871, in the Bancroft Library manuscript collection, George B. Dyson transcription.
175. Much of this material is at the Bancroft Library, Berkeley, California, which kindly provided the microfilm copy I have quoted from. Pinart used four different languages in his Alaskan diaries: French, English, Russian, and Aleut.
176. Ivan Petroff, *Report . . .* (1884), 20.
177. Veniaminov, *Notes . . .* (1840), 222, as anonymously translated in Human Relations Area Files, Aleut Division; see also Lydia Black translation (1984), 272.
178. Ivan Petroff, *Report . . .* (1884), 154.
179. Waldemar Jochelson, *History, Anthropology, and Ethnology of the Aleut* (Washington, 1933), 57.
180. Veniaminov, in *Characteristics of the Aleuts . . .* (manuiscript 1834; first published St. Petersburg 1839), as translated by Mary Sadouski in F.P. Wrangell's *Statistical and Ethnographical Information . . .* (1980), 100.
181. Henry Swanson, *The Unknown Islands,* in *Cuttlefish #6,* published by the Unalaska High Shool, 1982.
182. Ibid.
183. Ibid.
184. Bill Tcheripanoff, in *Cuttlefish #1,* published by the Unalaska High School, 1977.
185. Larry Matfay, as told to Dennis Evans, in *The Cama-i Book* (New York: Doubleday, 1983), edited by Ann Vick, pp. 6-7.
186. Ibid., 7.
187. Frederica de Laguna, letter of July 7, 1981.
188. Kaj Birket-Smith, *The Chugach Eskimo* (Copenhagen, 1953), 47.
189. Ibid.
190. Ibid., 48.
191. Ibid.
192. Frederica de Laguna, letter of July 7, 1981.
193. Kaj Birket-Smith, *The Chugach Eskimo* (1953), 32.
194. Ibid., 47-48.
195. Jöelle Robert-Lamblin, *Le Kayak Aléoute . . .,* in *Objets et Mondes: La Revue du Musée* de L'Homme 20:1

(Spring 1980) page 12. Translation by the Canadian Dept. of State for the National Museum of Man, Ottawa.
196. G.I. Davydov (St. Petersburg 1810-1812), translation by Colin Bearne, edited by Richard A. Pierce (1977), 177.

***Part II*: FRAME OF MIND/Inside Passage**

1. Ivan Veniaminov, *Notes . . .* (St. Petersburg, 1840) vol 2, p. 226, quoted here from an anonymous translation in the Human Relations Area Files, Aleut Division (M-5); see also translation by Lydia Black (Kingston, Ontario: The Limestone Press, 1984), 274.
2. From the anonymous (attributed variously to Jose Espinosa y Tello, Fernandez de Navarrette, or D.A. Galiano) *Relacion del viage hecho por las goletas Sutil y Mexicana . . .* (Madrid, 1802), here quoted as translated by Cecil Jane as *A Spanish Voyage to Vancouver and the Northwest Coast . . .* (London, 1930), 57.
3. K.T. Khlebnikov (St. Petersburg, 1835) as translated by Colin Bearne in *Baranov: Chief Manager of the Russian Colonies in America* (Kingston, Ontario: The Limestone Press, 1973), 44.
4. Alexander Baranov, as quoted by his assistant and biographer Kyril T. Khlebnikov in *Zhizneopisanie Aleksandr Andeevicha Baranova . . .* (St. Petersburg, 1835), as translated by Colin Bearne (1973), 44-45.
5. Ivan Petroff (1882, page 575) given here as quoted by Kaj Birket-Smith and Frederica de Laguna in *The Eyak Indians of the Copper River Delta, Alaska* (Copenhagen, 1938), 344-345. Birket-Smith notes that this "curious statement . . . must be understood in the light of [Petroff's] erroneous belief that the Eyak were Eskimo."
6. Henry Wood Elliott, in *Our Arctic Province* (New York, 1886), 72.
7. Frederica De Laguna, in *Under Mount Saint Elias . . .* (Washington, 1972), 91.

***Part II*: FRAME OF MIND/A Necessary Monster**

1. Albert Einstein, in his travel diary, entry for December 10, 1931 (while crossing the Atlantic by ship on his way to the United States), as translated and edited by Helen Dukas and Banesh Hoffman in *Albert Einstein: The Human Side.* (Princeton University Press, 1979), 23.

***Part II*: FRAME OF MIND/6061-T6**

1. Urey Lisiansky, in *A Voyage Round the World . . .* (London, 1814), 154. (This was on September 28, 1804.)

Part II: **FRAME OF MIND/The Path of Least Resistance**

1. James Shields, in a report to Alexander Baranov, quoted in M.D. Teben'kov's *Hydrographic Notes* . . . (St. Petersburg, 1852), page 7, as translated by Richard Pierce (Kingston, Ontario: The Limestone Press, 1981), 28.
2. Fleet Captain-Lieutenant L.A. Hagemeister, in a letter of instructions dated June 19, 1818 (original in the U.S.

National Archives, Correspondence of Governors General of the Russian American Company, Communications sent, Vol. 1, folio 93), here quoted as translated by Richard Pierce in *The Russian-American Company: Correspondence* . . . (Kingston, Ontario: The Limestone Press, 1984), 117.
3. Captain James Colnett, mss. Journal of the *Prince of Wales*, 16 October, 1786 to 7 November, 1788, in the Public Record Office, London (Adm. 55/146), given here

as quoted by Frederica de Laguna in *Under Mount Saint Elias* . . . (Washington, 1972), 131.
4. La Pérouse, *A Voyage Round the World* . . . (London, 1799), vol. 1, 390.

Part III: **IN ALLIANCE WITH THE PAST**

1. Fridtjof Nansen, *Farthest North* (London, 1898), vol. 2, page 86. (Journal for June 6, 1895, at 82° 17.8′ N.)

Index

About the Author

George Dyson, born in Ithaca, New York, in 1953, has been building kayaks since the age of twelve. Settling in British Columbia in 1970, Dyson supported himself along the fringes of the working waterfront, voyaging periodically to Alaska, and becoming a dual citizen of Canada and the United States. In 1984 he founded the Baidarka Historical Society (P.O. Box 5454, Bellingham, WA 98227-5454) established to "further the knowledge of the Aleut baidarka and its role in Russian–American history, and to encourage, by the way of its renaissance, the continued evolution of the skin boat."

Since the original publication of *Baidarka* in 1986, understanding of the evolution of the Aleut kayak has deepened, with conjecture that its origins may reach as far back as 9,000 years. Propelled by sea kayaking's growing popularity and recognition of the ingenuity reflected in the Aleut approach to design, the craft's future continues to unfold.

Dyson is married to photojournalist Ann E. Yow, who took many of the pictures in this book. With their daughter, Lauren, they now live in Bellingham, Washington, where Dyson has established workshop facilities in a converted tavern on the shore of Puget Sound. In addition to researching and writing another book, Dyson is presently working to develop a series of baidarka kits intended, in his words, "to allow other twelve-year-olds—in age or spirit—to continue where I leave off."